JACOB,

   This might be a boring read for your first book, but give it a shot and maybe you'll learn something. Tell your MOM & DAD TO Move back to Houston.

5/5/02

Interdomain
Multicast Routing

Interdomain Multicast Routing

Practical Juniper Networks and Cisco Systems Solutions

Brian M. Edwards

Leonard A. Giuliano

Brian R. Wright

ADDISON–WESLEY

Boston • San Francisco • New York • Toronto • Montreal
London • Munich • Paris • Madrid
Capetown • Sydney • Tokyo • Singapore • Mexico City

Many of the designations used by manufacturers and sellers to distinguish their products are claimed as trademarks. Where those designations appear in this book, and Addison-Wesley, Inc. was aware of a trademark claim, the designations have been printed with initial capital letters or in all capitals.

The authors and publisher have taken care in the preparation of this book, but they make no expressed or implied warranty of any kind and assume no responsibility for errors or omissions. No liability is assumed for incidental or consequential damages in connection with or arising out of the use of the information or programs contained herein.

The publisher offers discounts on this book when ordered in quantity for special sales. For more information, please contact:

Pearson Education Corporate Sales Division
201 W. 103rd Street
Indianapolis, IN 46290
(800) 428-5331
corpsales@pearsoned.com

Visit A–W on the Web: www.aw.com/cseng/

Library of Congress Cataloging-in-Publication Data

Edwards, Brian M.
    Interdomain mulitcast routing : practical Juniper Networks and Cisco Systems solutions / Brian M. Edwards, Leonard A. Giuliano, Brian R. Wright.
        p.   cm.
    Includes bibliographical references and index.
    ISBN 0-201-74612-3
    1. Routers (Computer networks)   I. Giuliano, Leonard A.   II. Wright, Brian R.   III. Title.

TK5105.543 .E38 2002
004.6—dc21

2002018254

ISBN 0-201-74612-3
Text printed on recycled paper
1 2 3 4 5 6 7 8 9 10—MA—0605040302
First printing, April 2002

In loving memory
of Sue Madding.

"Don't anthropomorphize computers—they hate it."

—Author unknown

Contents

Foreword

It is with great pleasure that I introduce Brian Edwards, Leonard Giuliano, and Brian Wright's book *Interdomain Multicast Routing*. I expect the publication of this text will improve the networking community's understanding of the promise of multicast.

In thinking about multicast, I'm drawn to two topics that the authors discuss in the introductory chapter: the question of multicast's *killer application* and the complexity of multicast (reverse path forwarding, packet replication, the many routing protocols in the control plane, the unique requirements of multicast with respect to scaling and network management, etc.).

One reaction to the *killer application* question is the observation that the ability to deliver the same content to many users in an efficient way is an important capability of a multi-service network. In other words, using a specific example, IP needs scalable multicast in order for it to subsume the delivery of services such as broadcast television. The point isn't that the broadcast television infrastructure needs to be replaced with an IP network—that's just an example—but instead the point is that scalable multicast allows a whole new set of applications and services to leverage IP networks. To make the same statement negatively, if IP networks don't support scalable multicast then a set of applications and services will be precluded from being able to leverage IP networks. The Internet community has an honorable trait of solving hard problems, even if some questions remain unanswered. The work done with multicast over the last fifteen years (!) is one manifestation of that trait.

The more interesting reaction to these topics, in my opinion, is a reaction to them as an intertwined pair. Some could argue that in the absence of a *killer application*, tackling a problem as complex as multicast isn't well advised. I see this argument as very shortsighted exactly because of multicast's complexity. Multicast presents an opportunity for learning about the science of networking far more than if we conservatively stay in our *comfort zone.* A recent example of this phenomenon in networking is MPLS. In the case of MPLS, the *killer application* started as fast packet forwarding but then morphed to IP VPNs, then traffic engineering, then "layer 2" VPNs and, most recently, the generalization of the MPLS signaling suite to non-packet-switching technologies (optical switching, TDM switching, and others). Work on MPLS continued, in spite of some *killer applications* withering away and/or becoming less trendy than newer ones, and that work taught the networking community extremely valuable lessons such as the distinction between the control plane and data plane and the advantage of having a suite of signaling protocols that can be leveraged for many applications. In the case of multicast, I believe our community of protocol designers, system vendors and, most importantly, network operators has already benefited—we have had to think very creatively about the interaction between unicast and multicast routing, the impact of various multicast routing approaches to dynamics in the control and data planes, how to design, implement and deploy multicast in highly scalable ways, how to engineer and operate services that require more than simple point-to-point connections, and so forth. Independent of multicast itself, we gain a richer intuition about networking in general and become better at designing all kinds of protocols, implementing all kinds of networking systems and deploying all kinds of network infrastructures. The fact that networking is still young enough for us to learn such lessons is one of the reasons why it is such an exciting industry!

So I invite you to read the following text with a curious and open mind. You will certainly walk away from the experience with a greater understanding of networking in general, which will better arm you for the future. And perhaps in being particularly curious and particularly open minded, you might come up with the World Wide Web for multicast!

— John W. Stewart, III
   JUNOS Product Line Manager, Juniper Networks
   San Francisco
   January 2002

Preface

Interdomain Multicast Routing is a book on the timely technology of multicasting and is written, mainly, for network engineers responsible for configuring and maintaining that capability within their networks. It is a practical reference guide that includes Cisco Systems *and* Juniper Networks technology. The authors' goals are to explain the rationale and benefits of multicast routing on the Internet, to include the two leading vendors of routers and routing technology and note how they differ when applying interdomain multicast routing (IMR), and to explain the underpinnings of interdomain multicasting in simple, clear language. For a preview of the topics within this book, the following chapter listings detail the topic matter.

Chapter 1, "Interdomain Multicast Fundamentals," begins with a definition of multicast transmisson of data in contrast to other means of data delivery, within and outside the Internet, and then provides an introductory explanation of some of the issues affecting successful routing of multicast traffic on the Internet. Those seeking to understand the enormous potential for multicast may wish to tune in directly to this section.

Chapter 2, "IMR Overview," is a general description of how to generate and receive multicast traffic, including a description of methods for routers to detect sources and receivers of multicast traffic. The discussion then proceeds from multicast single-domain routing using PIM-SM (Protocol Independent Multicast-Sparse Mode) to interdomain multicast routing using MSDP (Multicast Source Discovery Protocol).

Chapter 3, "Multicast Routing Protocols," examines the two primary types of multicast routing protocols, describing the main features and examples of each.

Chapter 4, "Protocol Independent Multicast-Sparse Mode (PIM-SM)," lays out PIM-SM, the predominant multicast routing protocol for interdomain routing. Since PIM-SM is commonly used in the initial sequence of activities that gets multicast up and running within a single domain, the procedure dominates the scope of this chapter. PIM messages for both version 1 and version 2 of the protocol are covered, as is the use of anycast rendezvous point (RP) to improve load balancing and redundancy. Ample diagrams and corresponding examples describe distribution tree construction and teardown for various topologies, and the chapter ends with a discussion of multicast scoping.

Chapter 5, "Multicast Source Discovery Protocol (MSDP)," demonstrates how to use MSDP to connect multiple PIM-SM domains and subdomains. MSDP is an any source multicast (ASM) mechanism for giving Internet multicast routing its "interdomain" reach. This chapter contains a number of illustrations of the rules that determine the reverse path forwarding (RPF) peer, a critical component in MSDP. Recognizing the paucity of clear information about MSDP peer-RPF rules, which are quite complex, the authors have provided detailed rule descriptions, as well as diagrams and realistic examples. The intent is for Chapter 5 to become the most definitive guide available on the subject (MSDP peer-RPF rules). The chapter concludes with sections on mesh groups, susceptibility to operational problems, and a discussion of the prospects for the widely used MSDP *vis a vis* the upcoming version of Border Gateway Multicast Protocol (BGMP).

Chapter 6, "Source-Specific Multicast (SSM)," is a critical component of the book. SSM, a recent addition to the ever-changing multicast routing landscape, holds the greatest amount of promise for deployment, considering that many believe the most dominant commercial use of Internet multicast will likely conform to a one-to-many model. This chapter explains the rationale for development of this SSM service model versus ASM and how SSM can serve as a basis for learning the more complex world of ASM.

Chapter 7, "Multiprotocol Extensions for BGP (MBGP)," and Chapter 8, "Multi-topology Routing in Intermediate System to Intermediate System (M-ISIS)," focus on how to create two separate virtual topologies, one for unicast and one for multicast. MBGP and M-ISIS can be used side-by-side to build a dedicated multicast RPF table, just as BGP and ISIS have traditionally coexisted in unicast intra-AS and inter-AS environments.

The remaining chapters of *Interdomain Multicast Routing* cover critical hands-on, real-world examples and tools. Chapter 9, "Configuring and Verifying Multicast Routing on Juniper Networks Routers," and Chapter 10, "Configuring and Verifying Multicast Routing on Cisco Systems Routers," provide practical methods and guidelines for actually configuring and verifying multicast routing on Juniper Networks and Cisco Systems routers.

Chapter 11, "Case Study: Service Provider Native Deployment," provides a representative case study for native deployment of IMR by an Internet service provider; Juniper Networks and Cisco Systems router configurations for all router roles in this example network are also set forth.

Chapter 12, "Management Tools for Multicast Networks," discusses management tools for multicast networks, chiefly Simple Network Management Protocol (SNMP) and the mtrace facility for IP multicast.

Chapter 13, "Other Related Topics," covers topics such as the development of BGMP incorporating Multicast Address Set Claim (MASC) protocol mapping, bidirectional PIM, and use of real-time transport protocol (RTP) for host-to-host transport over IP networks. RTP is suited to real-time applications such as video and audio streaming.

The Appendixes list packet formats for Internet Group Management Protocol (IGMP), PIM, and MSDP.

Finally, because any new world of knowledge comes to be mastered only by intelligent use and definition of its key concepts, we spent a considerable amount of time gathering and refining pertinent terminology; we hope the Glossary clarifies key abbreviations, acronyms, and definitions and even serves to stimulate dialog leading to more exact rendering of terms in future iterations of the book.

ACKNOWLEDGMENTS

The authors have been blessed with many excellent reviewers, ensuring our approach and description were accurate and unbiased. Among the many, those who spent considerable time reading our manuscripts are Ravi Prakash, Matthew Naugle, Dave Thaler, John N. Stewart, Bill Fenner, Brian Haberman, Matthew Davy, Greg Shepherd, Marshall Eubanks, Jill Gemmill, Jennifer Joy, Liming Wei, Naiming Shen, John Brassil, Walter Weiss, Tom Pusateri, Paras Trivedi, Hannes Gredler, Amir Tabdili, William Lemons, Supratik Bhattacharyya, Aviva Garrett, Patrick Ames, Hallie Giuliano, and Margaret Searing.

Further, the authors would like to thank Karen Gettman and Emily Frey of Addison-Wesley for helping to guide us through the intricacies of turning manuscripts into printed works. We would also like to pause and acknowledge the support and assistance of Juniper Networks for allowing us to work on this project and to occasionally use corporate resources.

Finally, the authors, individually, would like to thank the following friends, family, peers, and coworkers for their fortitude and inspiration:

Brian Edwards wants to thank the following people because each has provided a tremendous amount of support and guidance throughout his life and professional career: Christine Hatchett, Mabry and Linda Edwards, John Madding, Sr., Ronald Smallwood, and Chip Leonard.

Leonard A. Giuliano first thanks his loving wife, Hallie, along with his parents and sisters for their endless support and encouragement. Over the years, he has had the pleasure to work with and learn a great deal from the following individuals: Amir Tabdili, Gary Barnhart, Rob Rockell, James Milne, Dale Morey,

James Zahniser, Timothy Flynn, Tom Pusateri, Greg Shepherd, Mujahid Khan, Jeff Loughridge, Paras Trivedi, Peter Lothberg, Supratik Bhattacharyya, and Christophe Diot. Finally, he would like to thank the following individuals for challenging and encouraging him to learn more: Patricia Kendall, Ralph Lane, Bill Lemons, Daemon Morrell, Stephen Miller, Marty Schulman, and Kaydon Stanzione.

Brian Wright especially salutes his coauthors for their practical contributions to the development of IMR, as well as their idea that a hands-on book on the subject would be worthwhile. Thanks to the aforementioned first-rate talent at Juniper Networks and Addison-Wesley. And he would like to mention, in particular, the following individuals among many who, through the seasons or from time to time, inspired or helped him to develop personally and/or professionally: Truman and Phyllis Wright, Rose Wright, Trese Hercher, James Cline, James Castner, Charles Nelson, Al Suggs, Kathy Kennelly, Serita Lockhart, Sam Mills, Cathy Keller, Mary Jo David, Pat Markey, Jordan Mergist, Glen Gibbons, Charlie Christal, Teena Thompson, Michael Boughner, Nora Kryza, Paul Swantek, Stephen Brancaleone, Kimberly Hall, and Brenda Ackerman.

— Brian Edwards, Leonard Giuliano, Brian Wright
    January 2002

Interd🮐main Multicast Fundamentals

This chapter introduces and describes the fundamental concepts of multicast. Subsequent chapters build upon these concepts, illustrating how they are specifically used in the protocols and technologies that enable the operation of interdomain multicast. This chapter also defines terms and conventions that will be used throughout the book.

1.1 WHAT IS MULTICAST?

The three main methods of data delivery are **unicast**, **broadcast**, and **multicast**. These methods are summarized as follows:

- **Unicast:** Data is delivered to one specific recipient, providing one-to-one delivery.
- **Broadcast:** Data is delivered to all hosts, providing one-to-all delivery.
- **Multicast:** Data is delivered to all hosts that have expressed interest. This method provides one-to-many delivery.

The Internet was built primarily on the unicast model for data delivery (see Figure 1-1). However, unicast does not efficiently support certain types of traffic.

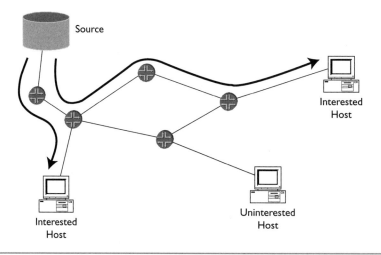

Figure 1-1 Unicast delivery

Multicast, originally defined in RFC 1112 by Steve Deering, provides an efficient method for delivering traffic that can be characterized as "one-to-many" or "many-to-many."

Radio and television are examples of traffic that fit the one-to-many model. With unicast, a radio station would have to set up a separate session with each interested listener. A duplicate stream of packets would be contained in each session. The processing load and the amount of bandwidth consumed by the transmitting server increase linearly as more people tune in to the station. This might work fine with a handful of listeners; however, with hundreds or thousands of listeners, this method would be extremely inefficient. With unicast, the source bears the burden of duplication.

Using broadcast (see Figure 1-2), the radio station would transmit only a single stream of packets, whether destined for one listener or for one million listeners. The network would replicate this stream and deliver it to every listener. Unfortunately, people who had not even tuned in to the station would be delivered this traffic. This method becomes very inefficient when many uninterested listeners exist. Links that connect to uninterested end hosts must carry unwanted traffic,

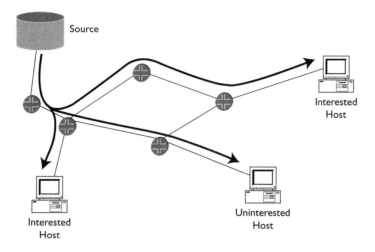

Source

Interested
Host

Interested
Host

Uninterested
Host

Figure 1-2 Broadcast delivery

wasting valuable network resources. With broadcast, the network carries the burden of delivering the traffic to every end host.

Multicast, on the other hand, provides the best of both worlds without introducing the disadvantages of each (see Figure 1-3). Multicast enables the radio station to transmit a single stream that finds its way to every *interested* listener. As in the case of broadcast, the processing load and the amount of bandwidth consumed by the transmitting host remain constant, regardless of audience size. The network is responsible for replicating the data and delivering it only to listeners who have tuned in to the station. Links that connect to uninterested listeners do not carry the traffic. This method provides the most efficient use of resources because traffic flows only through links that connect to end hosts that want to receive the data.

To deliver data only to interested parties, **routers** in the network build a **distribution tree**. Each subnetwork that contains at least one interested listener is a *leaf* on the tree. When a new listener tunes in, a new branch is built, *joining* the leaf to the tree. When a listener tunes out, its branch is *pruned* off the tree. Where the tree branches, routers replicate the data and send a single flow down each branch. Thus no link ever carries a duplicate flow of packets.

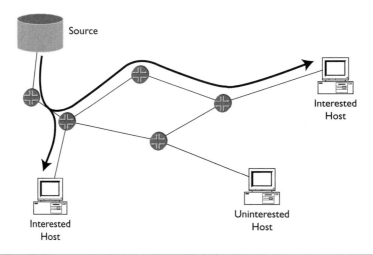

Figure 1-3 Multicast delivery

With multicast, the source is not burdened because it must transmit only a single stream of data, and the network is not burdened because it must deliver traffic only to end hosts that have requested it. However, in the zero-sum world of networking, where nothing is free, the burden of multicast falls on network engineers who must design and manage the mechanisms that make it work!

1.2 INTERNETWORKING BASICS

To facilitate the reader's understanding, this section covers some of the notation and conventions used in the book and thus indicates the level of the typical reader's internetworking knowledge anticipated by the authors.

Throughout the book we use the slash notation for bit mask when describing **IP** address ranges. The slash notation indicates how many bits of the address remain constant throughout the range of addresses. For example, 10.0.0.0/8 indicates a range of IP addresses all with the first 8 bits equal to 10. The range is from address 10.0.0.0 to 10.255.255.255.

We also make reference to **classful** networks. The class A, B, and C networks constitute all unicast IP addresses as follows:

- **Class A networks:** Describe the range of networks from 1.0.0.0/8 through 126.0.0.0/8.
- **Class B networks:** Describe the range of networks from 128.0.0.0/16 through 191.255.0.0/16.
- **Class C networks:** Describe the range of networks from 192.0.0.0/24 through 223.255.255.0/24.

Originally, networks were assigned to organizations along classful boundaries. That meant class A networks were assigned in /8 blocks, class B in /16 blocks, and class C in /24 blocks. Classful allocation was inefficient because organizations that required slightly more than 254 addresses could be assigned an entire class B. **Classless interdomain routing (CIDR)** enabled the assignment and routing of addresses outside of classful boundaries. An organization that needed enough addresses for 500 hosts could be assigned one /23, instead of an entire class B network.

All **multicast addresses** fall in the class D range of the **IPv4** address space. The class D range is 224.0.0.0 through 239.255.255.255. Multicast addresses do not have a **mask** length associated with them for **forwarding** purposes. Each address is treated independently so the mask used for forwarding is always assumed to be /32. We use shorter mask lengths on multicast addresses in some parts of the book for reasons other than forwarding. These masks generally are used to describe ranges of multicast addresses. For example, the address range reserved for **Source-Specific Multicast (SSM)** is 232.0.0.0/8.

We refer throughout the book to unicast and **multicast routing protocols**. **Unicast routing protocols** are used by routers to exchange routing information and build routing tables. Unicast IP routing protocols are further categorized into **interior gateway protocols (IGPs)** and **exterior gateway protocols (EGPs)**.

IGPs provide routing within an administrative **domain** known as an **autonomous system (AS)**. EGPs provide routing between ASs. **Routing Information**

Protocol (RIP), **Open Shortest Path First (OSPF)**, and **Intermediate System to Intermediate System (IS-IS)** are examples of IGPs, while **Border Gateway Protocol (BGP)** is an example of an EGP. Multicast routing protocols are used by routers to set up multicast forwarding **state** and to exchange this information with other multicast routers. Examples of multicast IP routing protocols are **Distance Vector Multicast Routing Protocol (DVMRP)**, **Protocol Independent Multicast–Dense Mode (PIM-DM)**, and **Protocol Independent Multicast–Sparse Mode (PIM-SM)**.

The terms **control packets** and **data packets** are used to differentiate the types of packets being routed through the network. Control packets include any packets sent for the purpose of exchanging information between routers about how to deliver data packets through the network. Control packets are typically protocol traffic that network devices use to communicate with one another to make such things as routing possible.

Data packets use the network to communicate data between hosts; they do not influence the way the network forwards traffic. Letters delivered via postal mail are analogous to data packets. Information exchanged between post offices to describe what ZIP codes mean is analogous to control packets. In the IP world, all packets sent for an **FTP** session between hosts are considered data packets, while a BGP **Update message** is an example of a control packet.

1.3 MULTICAST BASICS

A multicast address is also called a multicast **group address**. A group member is a host that expresses interest in receiving packets sent to a specific group address. A group member is also sometimes called a **receiver** or **listener**. A multicast *source* is a host that sends packets with the destination IP address set to a multicast group. A multicast source does not have to be a member of the group; sourcing and listening are mutually exclusive.

Because there can be multiple receivers, the path that multicast packets take may have several branches. A multicast data path is known as a *distribution tree*. Data flow through the multicast distribution trees is sometimes referenced in terms of **upstream** and **downstream**. Downstream is in the direction toward the receivers. Upstream is in the direction toward the source. A downstream interface is also known as an *outgoing* or *outbound* interface; likewise, an upstream interface is also known as an *incoming* or *inbound* interface.

Routers keep track of the incoming and outgoing interfaces for each group, which is known as *multicast forwarding state*. The **incoming interface** for a group is sometimes referred to as the **IIF**. The **outgoing interface list** for a group is sometimes referred to as the **OIL** or **olist**. The OIL can contain 0 to N interfaces, where N is the total number of logical interfaces on the router.

Multicast forwarding state in a router is typically kept in terms of "**(S,G)**" and "**(*,G)**" state, which usually are pronounced "ess comma gee" and "star comma gee," respectively. In (S,G), the "S" refers to the unicast IP address of the source. The IP header of the multicast data packet contains S as the packet's source address. The "G" represents the specific multicast group IP address of concern. The IP header of the multicast data packet contains G as the packet's destination address. So for a host whose IP address is 10.1.1.1 acting as a source for the multicast group 224.1.1.1, (S,G) state would read (10.1.1.1,224.1.1.1).

In (*,G) notation, the asterisk (*) is a wild card used to denote the state that applies to any source sending to group G. A multicast group can have more than one source. If two hosts are both acting as sources for the group 224.1.1.2, (*,224.1.1.2) could be used to represent the state a router could contain to forward traffic from both sources to the group. The significance of (S,G) and (*,G) state will become more apparent when we discuss shortest path and **shared trees** in Chapters 2 and 3.

1.3.1 REVERSE PATH FORWARDING

Multicast routing involves a significant paradigm change from standard unicast routing. In general, routers make unicast routing decisions based on the destination address of the packet. When a unicast packet arrives, the router looks up the destination address of the packet in its **routing table**. The routing table tells the router out from which interface to forward packets for each destination network. Unicast packets are then routed from source to destination.

In multicast, routers set up forwarding state in the opposite direction of unicast, from receiver to the root of the distribution tree. Routers perform a **reverse path forwarding (RPF)** check to determine the interface that is topologically closest to the root of the tree (see Figure 1-4). RPF is a central concept in multicast routing. In an RPF check, the router looks in a routing table to determine its *RPF interface*, which is the interface topologically closest to the root. The RPF interface is the incoming interface for the group.

In a **shortest path tree (SPT)**, the root of the distribution tree is the source. If a router learns that an interested listener for a group is on one of its directly connected interfaces, it tries to join the tree for that group. In Figure 1-5, this router somehow knows the IP address of the source of this group. To build an SPT, it executes an RPF check by scanning its routing table for the source address. The RPF check tells the router which interface is closest to the source. The router now knows that multicast packets from this source to this group should flow into the router through this RPF interface.

The router sends a **Join message** out the RPF interface to inform the next router upstream it wants to receive packets for this group from this source. This message is an (S,G) Join message. The router receiving the (S,G) Join message adds the interface on which it was received to the OIL for the group and performs an RPF check on the source. This upstream router sends an (S,G) Join message out its RPF interface for the source informing its upstream router that it wants to join the group.

Each upstream router repeats this process of propagating Joins out the RPF interface until this new branch of the tree either a) reaches the router directly connected to the source or b) reaches a router that already has multicast forwarding state for this source-group pair. In this way, a new branch of the tree is created from receiver to source. Once this branch is created and each of the routers has

1. Server A sends data packets to a specific multicast group, but at this point, router B does not know of any hosts interested in receiving them, so router B discards them.

2. Host A announces to router A its interest in receiving from server A multicast data packets that are destined for the specific multicast group.

3. Router A does an RPF lookup for server A's address revealing that router B is the RPF neighbor for server A's address. Router A requests that router B forward the data packets for the multicast group.

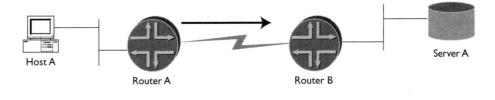

4. Now both routers know the correct interfaces out of which to forward the data packets. The data packets are delivered successfully from server A to host A.

Figure 1-4 Reverse path forwarding (RPF)

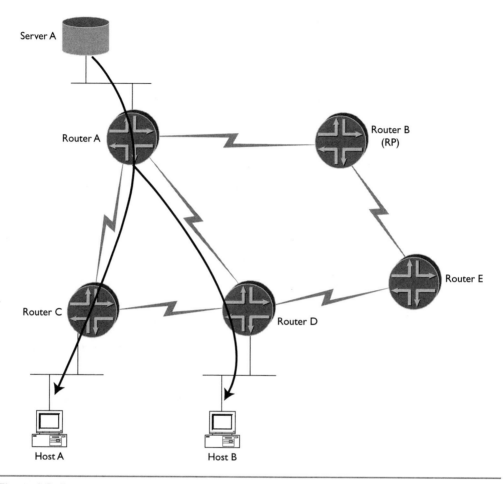

Figure 1-5 Shortest path tree (SPT)

forwarding state for the source-group pair, multicast packets can flow down the tree from source to receiver.

In a shared tree, the root of the distribution tree is a router somewhere in the core of a network. In PIM-SM, this core router is called a **rendezvous point (RP)**. If a router learns that an interested listener for a group is on one of its directly connected interfaces, it tries to join the tree for that group. In Figure 1-6, this router

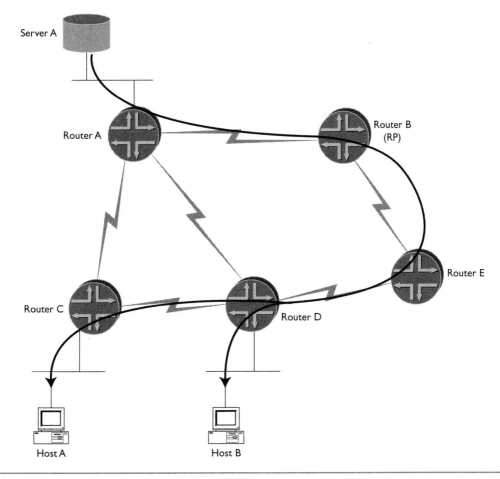

Figure 1-6 Rendezvous point tree (RPT)

does not know the address of the source of this group. However, it does know that another router in the network is aware of the source. The router that somehow knows the sources for all multicast groups is the RP (we will find out just how it knows this in Chapters 2 and 3).

The router with the directly connected listener, or the last-hop router, performs an RPF check for the IP address of the RP. This RPF check yields the RPF interface for the RP, and a (*,G) Join is sent out from this interface toward the RP. Notice that this is a (*,G) Join instead of an (S,G) Join because the last-hop router does not know the source. It needs to know only a) that the RP should know the source and b) how to get to the RP. By sending the (*,G) Join toward the RP, the last-hop router is telling the upstream router it is interested in receiving multicast packets for the group via the shared tree, or **rendezvous point tree (RPT)** as it called in PIM-SM.

The router receiving the (*,G) Join message adds the interface on which it was received to the OIL for the group and performs an RPF check on the RP. This upstream router sends a (*,G) Join message out its RPF interface for the RP, informing its upstream router that it wants to join the group. Each upstream router repeats this process of propagating Joins out of the RPF interface until this new branch of the tree either a) reaches the RP or b) reaches a router that already has multicast forwarding state for the group along the RPT. In this way, a new branch of the tree is created from receiver to RP.

To forward multicast packets down the RPT, the RP itself must be receiving the multicast packets. To receive this traffic, the RP can execute an RPF for the source and send an (S,G) Join toward the source. By joining the SPT, the RP is able to transmit packets down the RPT. Multicast packets now flow from the source to the RP via the SPT and then from RP to the receiver down the RPT.

Further details of SPT, RPT, and PIM-SM operation are examined in greater depth in subsequent chapters. For now, it is most important to understand the concept of reverse path forwarding.

1.3.2 POPULATING THE RPF TABLE

The routing table used for RPF checks can be the same routing table used to forward unicast data packets, or it can be a separate routing table dedicated to multicast RPF. In either case, this RPF table contains only unicast routes. It does not contain multicast group addresses because RPF checks are performed only on unicast addresses (either the source or the RP).

If the same routing table used to forward unicast data packets is used for RPF, it is populated by the traditional unicast routing protocols (RIP, OSPF, IS-IS, BGP, and so on). If a dedicated multicast RPF table is used, it must be populated by some other means. Some multicast routing protocols (for example, DVMRP) include mechanisms for populating a dedicated RPF table. Others (for example, PIM-SM and PIM-DM) rely on other protocols to set up this table.

Some traditional routing protocols (such as BGP and IS-IS) now have extensions that can be used to differentiate between different sets of routing information (for example, **Multiprotocol Extensions to Border Gateway Protocol— MBGP—**and **Multitopology Routing in IS-IS—M-ISIS**). Routes can be tagged as multicast RPF routes and thus distinguished from unicast routes. The advantage of having a dedicated RPF table is that a network administrator can set up separate paths and policies for unicast and multicast traffic. Chapters 7 and 8 examine in detail MBGP and M-ISIS, respectively.

1.4   INTERDOMAIN MULTICAST ROUTING

For years multicast has enjoyed niche success in many financial and enterprise networks. Financial institutions have applications, such as stock tickers, that require sharing the same data across the network. Using unicast for these applications is inefficient and not cost effective. Likewise, some enterprise networks serve companies with applications ideally suited to multicast delivery—for example, a central headquarters that must feed hundreds of branch sites with price lists and product information. Transferring these identical files to all sites individually with unicast simply is not efficient.

In the past, enterprise networks have frequently looked much different than the networks managed by **Internet service providers (ISPs)**. This difference existed because these networks had to meet a set of radically different requirements. Enterprise networks connect the offices of a single company, which often involves transporting primarily a single type of data (for example, file transfer). Transporting only a single type of data enables the network to be built in a way that optimizes delivery of that type of traffic. Also, few, if any, of the routers in an enterprise network connect to routers controlled by another entity.

ISP networks couldn't be more different. ISPs can have up to thousands of different customers, each a separate administrative entity. The data can include an unclassifiable mix of voice, video, e-mail, Web, and so on. Providing ubiquitous support for these various traffic types across the interdomain world of the Internet has always set ISPs apart from enterprises in the way they are designed and operated.

Unicast and multicast routing on enterprise and financial networks has often involved deploying protocols and architectures that best meet the needs of the companies they connect. These protocols and architectures often do not address the scalability and interdomain requirements of ISPs. However, recent trends have shown that the networking needs of enterprises have evolved to more closely resemble those of ISPs. Accordingly, many enterprise networks today are beginning to use the same principles and philosophies found in the engineering of ISPs' networks, albeit on a smaller scale.

The focus of this book is to describe the technologies and challenges faced by ISPs when deploying and operating multicast across the Internet. The first reason for this focus is neglect. Most networking books concentrate on enterprise networks rather than the unique demands of service provider networks. Second, ISP networks generally possess the superset of requirements that are found on other types of networks. For example, financial networks typically need to support many-to-many applications. Other enterprise networks may need to support only one-to-many applications. Because ISPs may be delivering service to both types of networks, they must be equipped to handle *both* types of applications. Additionally, ISP networks have scalability demands that are rarely found on any other types of networks.

While ISPs continue to have unique requirements for scalability and interdomain stability, most of the same multicast technologies found in ISP networks can be applied for use on other networks. By adopting these ISP philosophies, financial and enterprise networks are capable of ubiquitously supporting all types of multicast traffic. This flexibility enables a network to be prepared if traffic types change in the future.

The scope of this book is confined to the protocols and technologies currently used in the production networks of service providers. In order to provide a pragmatic examination of the challenges faced by ISPs today, little to no mention is made of protocols that have not been implemented by routing vendors or deployed by service providers at the time of writing. Accordingly, IPv6 is outside the scope of this book.

1.5   WHERE IS MULTICAST?

The **Multicast Backbone**, or **MBone**, refers to the networks on the Internet that are enabled for multicast. The original MBone was built in the early 1990s as a network of multicast-enabled routers that were connected by **tunnels**. These routers were frequently UNIX servers running multicast routing software developed before router vendors had stable implementations of multicast software.

Tunnels allowed these early multicast-enabled "islands" to appear to be virtually connected to one another. Multicast packets were encapsulated within unicast packets and sent in the tunnel. Routers that were not multicast-enabled simply saw the unicast IP packet and routed it toward the tunnel destination. When the unicast packet reached the tunnel destination, the router decapsulated the unicast header to find the multicast packet within. If that packet had to be forwarded to another tunneled router, it was once again encapsulated and sent out another tunnel.

As router vendors implemented more stable multicast routing code, ISPs began to replace tunnels with *native* multicast routing in the late 1990s. Native multicast routing means routers forward raw multicast packets without encapsulating the multicast data within unicast packets. Most of the world's largest ISPs are multicast-enabled in at least some portion of their production networks today.

Multicast Internet Exchanges (MIXs) were built to connect multicast-enabled ISPs. MIXs are usually found in **network access points (NAPs)** where ISPs publicly peer with one another. A MIX enables ISPs to exchange multicast traffic on separate equipment from what is used for unicast peering. SprintNAP, in Pennsauken, New Jersey, and the NASA Ames Research Center **Federal Internet Exchange (FIX**-West), in Mountain View, California, contain two of the most popular MIXs used for public multicast peering.

Most people think of the old tunneled network of UNIX boxes when they hear the word "MBone," but it technically refers to any network that is multicast-enabled. Unanimous agreement has not been reached on a catchy word or phrase to colloquially refer to the native multicast-enabled portion of the Internet.

1.6 MULTICAST ON THE **LAN**

Throughout this book we focus primarily on the protocols that enable multicast packets to be forwarded within and between different domains. However, to provide a complete picture, we should examine what occurs on the link, or **local area network (LAN)**, on which group members reside.

1.6.1 IGMP

When a host wants to become a multicast receiver, it must inform the routers on its LAN. The **Internet Group Management Protocol (IGMP)** is used to communicate group membership information between hosts and routers on a LAN.

To join a multicast group that is not already being forwarded on its LAN, a host sends an IGMP Report to a well-known multicast group. All IGMP-enabled routers on that LAN are listening to this group. Upon hearing a host's IGMP Report for a multicast group, G, one of the routers on the LAN uses a multicast routing protocol to join that group. In the case of PIM-SM, this router sends a (*,G) Join toward the RP for the specified group.

IGMP versions 1 and 2 allow a host to specify only the group address that it is interested in receiving. IGMP version 3 allows a host to express interest in only specified sources of a group, triggering an (S,G) Join by a PIM-SM router on the LAN. This is a key component of Source-Specific Multicast, which we examine in section 1.7.

A host must support IGMP in order to receive multicast packets. The version of IGMP supported is a function of the host's operating system. For example, unless otherwise modified, PCs running Windows 95 support IGMPv1. Likewise, PCs running Windows 98 or 2000 support IGMPv2, while IGMPv3 is available in Windows XP.

1.6.2 IGMP PROXYING

When a host reports interest in a multicast group from a source outside its LAN, it is the responsibility of a router on the LAN to join that group using a multicast routing protocol like PIM-SM. However, some routers do not support any multicast routing protocols. Low-end routers and legacy equipment such as dialup **remote access servers (RAS)** are examples of routing devices that sometimes do not support any multicast routing protocols.

Nearly all routing devices support IGMP. A common technique used in routers that do not support any multicast routing protocols is **IGMP proxying**. A router that hears an IGMP Report from a host simply relays that IGMP message to an upstream router that does support a multicast routing protocol. IGMP messages simply "hop over" a local router and reach a router that is capable of joining the group via a protocol like PIM-SM. IGMP proxying lowers the bar that low-end routing devices need to meet in order to deliver multicast.

1.6.3 LAYER 3 TO LAYER 2 MAPPING

The layers of the **OSI** reference model that we are most concerned with in this book are the data link, or layer 2, and the network, or layer 3. Here we focus on Ethernet, by far the most common layer 2 LAN technology. All layer 3 packets, in this case IP, are encapsulated with an Ethernet header and trailer and transmitted onto a LAN as an Ethernet frame.

All devices on the Ethernet have a unique 48-bit **Media Access Control (MAC) address**. To speak to one another, devices on the LAN keep a table that maps unicast IP addresses to MAC addresses. When packets are encapsulated in frames, the destination MAC address in the frame header is set to the MAC address corresponding to the IP address in the header of the IP packet.

IP multicast packets are destined to class D group addresses, which do not correspond with a single end host. Likewise, the MAC address used for multicast packets cannot be the address of a single station on the LAN. A special range of MAC addresses must be used for multicast.

The high order four bits of the first octets of class D addresses are always the same. Thus 28 bits may be varied in a multicast IP address. To provide a 1:1 mapping between MAC addresses and multicast IP addresses, the MAC address range must allow up to 28 bits to be varied.

The MAC address range that is assigned for multicast is only 24 bits long. One other bit in the address range is reserved, so that leaves only 23 bits of a MAC address to map to 28 bits of an IP address. As legend has it, Steve Deering, the father of multicast and a graduate student at the time, had only enough funding to purchase a 24-bit block of MAC addresses from IEEE. Because of this, every multicast MAC address corresponds to 32 different IP addresses.

As we see in Figure 1-7, the first 24 bits of a MAC address corresponding to an IPv4 multicast address is always 01-00-5E (in hexadecimal). The remaining 24 bits can vary from 00-00-00 to 7F-FF-FF (the first bit is always 0). The low-order 23 bits of the multicast IP address map to the MAC address. So an IP address of 224.1.1.1 maps to 01-00-5E-01-01-01. With 32:1 oversubscription, 224.129.1.1, 225.1.1.1, and 29 other IP addresses also correspond to this MAC address.

Collisions caused by oversubscription are handled by the IP stack of the receiving host. That is, a host interested in receiving 224.1.1.1 also receives Ethernet frames containing packets for 225.1.1.1 if they are on the LAN. After decapsulating the

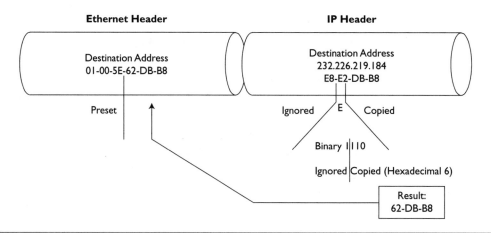

Figure 1-7 Layer 3 to layer 2 address mapping

Ethernet frame and discovering the IP address of the unwanted packet, the host discards the packet.

1.6.4 LAYER 2 SWITCHES

Ethernet switches have replaced hubs as the most popular way to connect hosts on a LAN because they inexpensively create a separate collision domain on each port. That is, while hubs transmit all traffic out all ports, switches transmit traffic only out a port that is destined for the station connected to that port. Frames destined for MAC addresses that a switch does not know the owner of are broadcast out all switch ports. Multicast packets fit in this category and, accordingly, are broadcast out all ports by a switch.

Flooding multicast packets out all switch ports wastes valuable network resources. Also, hosts that receive this unwanted traffic must use processing cycles to examine packets that they will eventually discard. **IGMP snooping** is one way to eliminate this inefficiency. Switches that support IGMP snooping can usurp responsibilities not usually associated with switches. An IGMP snooping switch looks at IGMP messages to determine which hosts are actually interested in receiving multicast traffic. Multicast packets are forwarded only out ports that connect to a host that is an interested listener of a specified group.

Cisco Group Management Protocol (CGMP) is a proprietary mechanism that provides the same functionality as IGMP snooping. CGMP enables Cisco System routers and switches to communicate with one another to determine which hosts are interested in each multicast group. CGMP works only in an environment of Cisco routers and Cisco switches. No other router or switch vendors are known to provide implementations of CGMP.

In switched environments that connect hosts to routers, IGMP snooping and CGMP generally provide a sufficient solution for eliminating broadcast traffic. However, not all switched environments involve IGMP. Switches are commonly used to connect routers together across multiaccess interfaces, forming transit LANs.

When only routers are connected together on a transit LAN, multicast routing protocols, not IGMP, are involved in controlling transit multicast traffic. The switch does not look at the multicast routing protocol packets, so there is no way to see which port connects to a router that has joined a group. There has been some discussion of "PIM snooping," but it would be very difficult to implement because PIM is far more complex than IGMP.

The only way to prevent multicast traffic from being flooded out all switched ports in this environment is to change the logical topology with **virtual LANs (VLANs)**. VLANs can be used to create a point-to-point logical interface, or *subinterface*, between every router connected to the switch. By changing the logical topology from broadcast to point-to-point, multicast traffic is sent only to routers interested in receiving it. However, using VLANs to create this kind of logical topology can force routers to perform more replication out these logical interfaces and consume more bandwidth over the physical interface than the logical interfaces use. Additionally, creating all of these VLANs can be a significant administrative and operational burden.

1.7 ASM VERSUS SSM

The original vision for multicast in RFC 1112 supported both one-to-many and many-to-many communication models and has come to be known as **Any-Source Multicast (ASM)**. Radio and television, as we have already discussed, are obvious examples of the one-to-many model. Applications such as online gaming and videoconferencing, in which some or all of the participants become sources, are examples of the many-to-many model. To support the many-to-many model, the network is responsible for source discovery. When a host expresses interest in a group, the network must determine all of the sources of that group and deliver them to the receiving host.

The mechanisms that provide this control plane of source discovery contribute the majority of the complexity surrounding interdomain multicast. However, applications that are believed to possess the greatest potential for commercial viability on the Internet use the one-to-many model. Since the bulk of the complexity is providing the least important functionality, the "ratio of annoyance" is disproportionately high in ASM.

It recently has been suggested that by abandoning the many-to-many model, multicast could deliver more "bang for the buck" on the Internet. By focusing on the one-to-many model, the most appealing of multicast applications could be supported while vastly reducing the amount of complexity required. Source-Specific Multicast (SSM) is a **service model** that supports multicast delivery from only one specified source to its receivers.

By sacrificing functionality that many may consider less important on the Internet, the network no longer needs to provide the control plane for source discovery. This control plane is now the responsibility of receivers. Typically, the application layer (via a mouse click, for example) informs the receiver who the source is. When the receiver informs its directly connected router that it is interested in joining a group, it specifies the source as well as the group. This last-hop router is then able to join the SPT directly, instead of having to join the RPT.

SSM eliminates the need for RPTs, RPs, and **Multicast Source Discovery Protocol (MSDP)**, radically simplifying the mechanisms needed to deliver multicast. Best of all, this service model is realized through a subset of functionality already present in existing protocols. Very little needs to be added.

It is important to note that ASM and SSM are service models, not protocols. Different protocols are implemented and configured to deliver the service model. For example, SSM is a service model that is realized through a subset of functionality of PIM-SM and IGMPv3. The first five chapters of this book examine interdomain multicast generally from an ASM point of view because ASM is much more interesting from a protocol perspective. With a clear understanding of ASM, the operation and benefits of SSM become apparent. Chapter 6 describes SSM in detail.

1.8 ADDRESSING ISSUES

The addresses available for multicast usage range from 224.0.0.0 to 239.255.255.255. This plentiful, but finite, range is controlled by the **Internet Assigned Numbers Authority (IANA)**. Certain subranges within the class D range of addresses are reserved for specific uses:

- **224.0.0.0/24:** The link-local multicast range
- **224.2.0.0/16:** The **Session Announcement Protocol (SAP)/Session Description Protocol (SDP)** range

- **232.0.0.0/8:** The SSM range
- **233.0.0.0/8:** The AS-encoded, statically assigned **GLOP** range (RFC 3180)
- **239.0.0.0/8:** The administratively scoped multicast range (RFC 2365)

For a complete list of IANA assigned multicast addresses, refer to the *http://www.iana.org/assignments/multicast-addresses* Web site.

If class D addresses had been assigned in the same manner unicast addresses were allocated, this address space would have been exhausted long ago. In general, IANA allocates static multicast addresses only used for protocol control. Examples of this type of address include

- **224.0.0.1:** All systems on this subnet
- **224.0.0.2:** All routers on this subnet
- **224.0.0.5:** OSPF routers
- **224.0.0.6:** OSPF **designated routers (DRs)**
- **224.0.0.12:** DHCP server/relay agent

To protect against address exhaustion, a simple dynamic address allocation mechanism is used in the SAP/SDP block. Applications such as **Session Directory Tool (SDR)** that use this mechanism randomly select an unused address in this range. This dynamic allocation mechanism for global multicast addresses is somewhat analogous functionally to DHCP, which dynamically assigns unicast addresses on a LAN.

Unfortunately, some applications require the use of static multicast addresses. GLOP, described in RFC 3180, provides static multicast ranges for organizations that already have reserved an AS number. In GLOP, an AS number is used to derive a /24 block within the 233/8 range. The static multicast range is created in the following form:

```
233.[first byte of AS number].[second byte of AS number].0/24
```

For example, AS 12345 is automatically allocated 233.48.57.0/24. Here is an easy way to compute this:

1. Convert the AS number to hexadecimal: 12345 = 0x3039.
2. Convert the first byte back to decimal: 0x30 = 48.
3. Convert the second byte back to decimal: 0x39 = 57.

Thus any organization with an AS number is automatically assigned a /24 of multicast addresses. GLOP is not an acronym or abbreviation; for some odd reason it was selected as the name for this clever mechanism.

Addresses in the 239/8 range are defined as administratively scoped. Packets destined for these addresses should not be forwarded outside an administratively defined boundary (typically a domain border), which is somewhat analogous to unicast private address space, such as 10/8. Scoping is discussed in further detail in Chapter 4.

Addresses in the 232/8 range are reserved for SSM. A wonderful byproduct of SSM is that the group address no longer needs to be globally unique. The source-group tuple, or *channel,* provides all the required uniqueness because the receiver is specifying interest in only one source for the group.

Multicast addressing allocation had long been a headache for multicast engineers. The recent addition of of SSM finally provided the long-sought *coup de grace* in this struggle. It is now generally agreed that between SSM, GLOP, administrative scoping, and SAP/SDP, current multicast address allocation schemes are sufficient for the Internet until IPv6 becomes prevalent. In IPv6, the number of multicast and unicast addresses available is practically infinite.

1.9 APPLICATIONS

The most widely used application on the old MBone was SDR. By launching SDR, a host listens to the well-known SAP group, 224.2.127.254. Any source host that wants to advertise a session (usually audio and/or video) describes its session in SDP messages. These SDP messages contain the address of the source, type of session, contact information for the source, and so on and are transmitted on the SAP multicast group.

Thus every host running SDR learns about every session on the Internet by receiving these SDP messages on the SAP group. By clicking one of the sessions listed in the SDR window, applications such as VIC (video conferencing tool) or VAT (visual audio tool) are launched to display the video or audio. An interesting feature of many of the applications launched by SDR is that by joining a session, you also become a source for that session. Because every receiver is also a source, each participant can see the others, which makes these applications ideal for collaboration and videoconferencing (and unscalable for sessions with lots of participants!).

Most agree that SDR is a "neat little toy" but not really a commercially viable application. Most SDR sessions are "cube-cams" or video camera shots of ISP parking lots. Because SDR acts as a global directory service for all multicast content on the Internet, it is not expected to scale to support large numbers of sessions.

Windows Media Player (WMP) is currently a popular application for accessing multicast audio and video content. WMP has excellent scaling potential for the Internet because, unlike many SDR-launched applications, receivers do not become sources to the group they join. Also, WMP has the capability to attempt to join a multicast session first, failing over to a unicast session if unsuccessful, which is ideal for content providers seeking the efficiency of multicast and the availability of unicast. Cisco System's **IP/TV** is another promising application for delivering multicast multimedia content. IP/TV supports multicast content only.

Juniper Networks and Cisco System routers can be configured to listen to the SAP group and keep a cache of SDR sessions. Joining the SAP group is useful in troubleshooting. It is a quick and easy way to determine whether the router has multicast connectivity with the rest of the Internet.

1.10 MULTICAST PERFORMANCE IN ROUTERS

When deploying multicast, it is important to consider whether the routers in a network are well suited to support multicast. Just as some cars provide speed at a cost of safety, some routers provide unicast performance at a cost of multicast. As high-end routers are built to scale to terabits and beyond, router designers sometimes compromise multicast performance to optimize unicast forwarding. The two most important considerations when evaluating a router for multicast are state and forwarding performance.

A router must keep forwarding state for every multicast group that flows through it. Pragmatically, this means (S,G) and (*,G) state for PIM-SM. It is important to know how many state entries a router can support without running out of memory. MSDP-speaking routers typically keep a cache of Source-Active messages. Likewise, knowing the maximum number of Source-Active entries a router can hold in memory is crucial.

The obvious next question is "how many entries should a router support?" Like many questions in life, there is no good answer. Past traffic trends for multicast are not necessarily a reliable forecast for the future. Traffic trends for the Internet in general are rarely linear. Growth graphs of Internet traffic frequently resemble step functions, where stable, flat lines suddenly yield to drastic upward surges that level off and repeat the cycle.

The best policy is to select a router that can hold far more state than even the most optimistic projections require and monitor memory consumption. When state in a router begins to approach maximum supportable levels, take appropriate action (upgrade software or hardware, redesign, apply rate limits or filters, update your resume, and so on). With the exception of the Ramen **worm** attacks (see Chapter 5), state has not been much of a problem yet. Of course, as with mutual funds, past performance does not ensure future success.

Forwarding performance is characterized by **throughput** and **fanout**. Throughput describes the maximum amount of multicast traffic a router can forward (in packets per second or bits per second). Fanout describes the maximum number of outgoing interface for which a router can replicate traffic for a single group. As port densities in routers increase, maximum supported fanout becomes a critical factor. Also, it should be understood how increasing fanout levels affects throughput. As is the case with state, it is important to be aware of the performance limits, even if the exact amount of multicast traffic on the network is not known.

Forwarding performance is primarily a function of hardware. The switching architecture a router uses to forward packets is usually the most important factor in determining the forwarding performance of a hardware platform. *Shared memory* switching architectures typically provide the best forwarding performance for multicast. A shared memory router stores all packets in a single shared bank of memory.

Juniper Networks' M-series routers employ a shared memory architecture that is very efficient for multicast. In this implementation, multicast packets are written into memory once and read out of the same memory location for each outgoing interface. Because multicast packets are not written across multiple memory locations, high throughput levels can be realized regardless of fanout.

Some routers are based on a *crossbar* switching architecture. The "crossbar" is a grid connecting all ports on the router. Each port shows up on both the X and Y axes of the grid, where the X axis is the inbound port and the Y axis is the outbound port. With the crossbar architecture, packets wait at the inbound port until a clear path is on the crossbar grid to the outbound port. Inbound traffic that is destined for multiple egress ports must be replicated multiple times and placed in multiple memory locations. Because of this, routers with crossbar architectures usually exhibit multicast forwarding limitations.

Router designers sometimes work around this inherent challenge by creating a separate virtual output queue dedicated to multicast and giving the queue higher priority than the unicast queues. Unfortunately, this technique can cause multicast traffic to suffer head-of-line blocking, which occurs when packets at the head of the queue are unable to be serviced, preventing the rest of the packets in the queue from being serviced as well. Such a design assumes multicasts are a small percentage of total traffic because a router incorporating this design would be inefficient under a high multicast load.

1.10.1 RP LOAD

A cursory look at PIM-SM suggests that RPs should experience high load because they provide the root of all the shared trees in their domain. However, last-hop routers usually switch to the SPT immediately (SPT switchover is described in

Chapters 2 and 3), so the shared tree is typically short-lived. One mechanism that can cause RPs to experience high load, though, is the PIM-SM register process.

As we will see in forthcoming discussions of PIM-SM (see Chapter 4), routers that learn of a new source inform the RP in their domain by encapsulating the multicast packets into unicast packets and sending them to the RP. The RP must decapsulate and process these packets. If a router sends these encapsulated packets at a very high rate, the RP can be overrun while trying to process them. To prevent this from occurring, Juniper Networks routers configured as RPs require a special interface that is used to decapsulate these packets in hardware.

1.11   DISCLAIMERS AND FINE PRINT

Throughout this book, reference is made to **RFCs** (Request for Comments) and **Internet Engineering Task Force (IETF) Internet-Drafts**. Internet-Drafts are submitted to the IETF as working documents for its working groups. If a working group decides to advance an Internet-Draft for standardization, it is submitted to the Internet Engineering Steering Group (IESG) to become an RFC. RFCs are the closest things to the official laws of the Internet. For a good description of Internet-Drafts and the various types of RFCs, visit *http://www.ietf.org/ID.html*.

It is not uncommon for protocol-defining Internet-Drafts never to reach RFC status. Likewise, vendors do not always implement protocols exactly as they are defined in the specification. Internet-Drafts that are not modified after six months are considered expired and are deleted from the IETF Web site. All RFCs and current Internet-Drafts can be found at the IETF's Web site. A good way to find an expired Internet-Draft is by searching for it by name at *http://www.google.com*. A search there will usually find it on a Web site that mirrors the IETF Internet-Drafts directory without deleting old drafts. Unless otherwise stated, all Internet-Drafts and RFCs mentioned in this book are current at the time of writing. These documents are constantly revised and tend to become obsolete very quickly.

Similarly, the implementations of Juniper Networks and Cisco System routers, the routers most commonly found in ISP networks, are described throughout this book. The descriptions and configurations are meant to assist engineers in understanding the predominant implementations found in production networks and provide a starting point for configuration. They are not the official recommendations of these vendors. It is also important to note that these vendors are constantly updating and supplementing their implementations. For officially supported configurations, it is best to contact these vendors directly.

1.12   WHY MULTICAST?

In less than a decade, the Internet has gone from a little known research tool to a dominant influence in the lives of people around the globe. It has created an age in which information can be disseminated freely and equally to everyone. The Internet has changed the way people communicate, interact, work, shop, and even think. It has forced us to reconsider many of our ideas and laws that had been taken for granted for decades.

Any person on earth with a thought to share can do so with a simple Web page, viewable to anyone with a connection onto the network. When considering the revolutionary impact their achievements have had on the way people interact, it is not ludicrous to mention names like Cerf, Berners-Lee, and Andreessen in the same breath as Gutenberg and Bell.

Nearly every aspect of communication in our lives is tied in one way or another to the Internet. Noticeably absent, however, in the amalgamation of content that is delivered prominently across the Internet is video. Video is an ideal fit for the Internet. While text and pictures do well to convey ideas, video provides the most natural, comfortable, and convenient method of human communication.

Even the least dynamic examples of video reveal infinitely more than the audio-only versions. For example, accounts of the 1960 Nixon-Kennedy debates varied widely between those who had watched on TV and those who had listened on the radio. So why then is video restricted primarily to the occasional brief clip accessible on the corner of a Web page and not a dominant provider of content for the Internet?

The answer is simple: The unicast delivery paradigm predominant in today's Internet does not scale to support the widespread use of video. Earlier attempts, such as the webcasts of the Starr Hearings and the Victoria's Secret fashion show, have failed to demonstrate otherwise.

The easiest target for video's lack of pervasiveness on the Internet has always been the limited bandwidth of the "last mile." It has often been argued that potential viewers simply do not have pipes large enough to view the content. However, with the proliferation of technologies like digital subscriber line (DSL) and cable modems, widespread residential access to video of reasonably adequate quality exists. Furthermore, for years, the number of people employed in offices with broadband Internet connectivity has been substantial. Finally, with nearly every college dorm room in the United States (and increasingly throughout the world) equipped with an Ethernet connection, client-side capacity is quickly becoming a nonissue.

The server side, on the other hand, has principally relied on unicast to deliver this content. The cost required to build an infrastructure of servers and networks capable of reaching millions of viewers is simply too great, if even possible. Compare that to the cost of delivery with multicast, where a content provider with only a server powerful enough and bandwidth sufficient to support a single stream is potentially able to reach every single user on the Internet.

Interestingly, while it has always been viewed as a bandwidth saver, the previously mentioned efficiency underscores multicast's capability as a bandwidth multiplier. With a multicast-enabled Internet, every home can be its own radio or television station with the ability to reach an arbitrarily large audience. If Napster created interesting debates on copyright laws, imagine the day when everyone on earth will be able to watch a cable television channel multicast from your very own PC.

It is worth noting that multicast need not be used solely for video. Multicast provides efficient delivery for any content that uses one-to-many or many-to-many transmission. File transfer, network management, online gaming, and stock tickers are some examples of applications ideally suited to multicast. However, multimedia, and more specifically video, is widely agreed to be the most interesting and compelling application for this delivery mechanism.

The brief history of the Internet suggests the inevitability that it someday will be a prevalent vehicle for television and radio, as all data networks converge onto a single common IP infrastructure. Accepting this, multicast provides the only scalable way to realize this vision. With such great potential for providing new services, it is logical to wonder why multicast has not been deployed ubiquitously across the Internet. In fact, to this point, the deployment has actually been somewhat slow.

The current number of multicast-enabled Internet subnets is miniscule compared to the overall Net. There is no single, simple answer why this is the case. The reasons include a collection of realities, concerns, and myths. Any discussion of multicast's benefits should also address these issues. In most cases, recent developments have been made that allay these concerns.

1.12.1 MULTICAST LACKS THE "KILLER APP"

It took Mosaic, the first modern browser, to truly harness the power of the World Wide Web, resulting in unparalleled permeation. Many have argued that multicast needs the same "killer app" to fuel an explosion of growth. However, a closer look reveals that many of today's multicast applications are more than sufficient; they just happen to work without multicast.

A common technique used by some of the most popular multimedia applications is to attempt to access the content first via multicast, then failing over to unicast, if unsuccessful. To the end user, the result is the same. The selected show looks the same, and the favorite song sounds the same, whether delivered through unicast or multicast. The true difference exists in the amount of content available. Because of unicast's inability to scale, there are fewer shows to view and fewer songs to hear.

But the applications are plenty "killer."

1.12.2 THE CONTENT VERSUS AUDIENCE CHICKEN-AND-EGG SCENARIO

An intriguing phenomenon has emerged that has been a significant hindrance to deployment. Many multimedia content providers have been slow to provide multicast content because of the limited number of capable viewers. Conversely, because of this limited amount of enticing content, there has been a perceived lack of demand from end users for multicast availability, thus resulting in a small audience.

This deadlock can be broken by multicast-enabled ISPs, partnering with content providers, to market this content to end users. This type of content provides a differentiator for these ISPs to attract more customers. To compete for these customers, more ISPs deploy multicast. Soon, multicast becomes a standard part of Internet service, expected by all end users. Eventually, ISPs that are not multicast-enabled are at a distinct, competitive disadvantage. In the meantime, content continues to increase, fueling the demand cycle.

Content providers can use the example of HDTV as inspiration. Soon after the introduction of HDTV, some TV stations began to broadcast their programming in the new format, even though very few people had the hardware that could take advantage of this technology. Despite having a miniscule audience to enjoy HDTV, these pioneering broadcasters made content available, which began to give consumers the incentive to purchase the new TV sets. Likewise, by providing an abundance of multicast content on the Internet, content providers give end users the incentive to demand access to this content from their ISPs.

1.12.3 THE "HOW DO WE CHARGE FOR IT?" SYNDROME

The first question most ISP product managers ask when considering deployment of multicast is nearly always, "How do we charge for it?" The question that should be asked, however, is "How do we make money from it?" For years ISPs have struggled with the business case for multicast. The early model was somehow to charge the users of the service. ISPs adopting this model have generally met disappointing results. While they may have found a market of enterprise and virtual private network (VPN) customers willing to pay for the service, Internet users found this model to be less than enticing.

This lack of success is predictable because it neglects to consider one of the paramount philosophies making the Internet so popular: Delivering a raw IP connection to end users, through which many services can be derived, will be far more profitable than trying to charge users for each of the services they consume.

Imagine if, in the first few years after the Web was invented, ISPs had decided to charge their customers extra fees for the **HTTP** packets that traversed their connection. It might have changed the way people used the Web. Users may not have surfed so freely from site to site. Instead, ISPs quickly discovered that if they provided a simple connection, with no stifling rules or extra charges, people used the network more. In sacrificing revenue from "toll-taking," they enjoyed explosive growth as more customers used the network for more services. Unfortunately, many ISPs view multicast along this toll-taking model.

By deploying multicast, ISPs are enabling new services to be provided. It brings traffic onto the network that wasn't previously deliverable. ISPs that have provided multicast as a free part of their basic IP service have realized little revenue directly from multicast. *But they have gained customers they would not have otherwise attracted.* Moreover, providing multicast has lured the most valuable of customers—content providers. ISPs have long known that content begets customers. Internet users recognize the value and performance benefits of being able to access sites directly connected to their ISP's network.

ISPs that have offered multicast as just another basic, value-added service, like **DNS**, have been viewed by many as leaders, but that does not mean direct revenues from multicast cannot be realized. As in the case of unicast, the higher layers should provide advanced billable multicast services, while the network layer should be responsible for simply routing packets. Following the example of the Web, providers of higher-layer services, such as content hosting and **application service providers** (ASPs), will likely find a significant market for multicast content hosting.

1.12.4 MULTICAST PROTOCOLS ARE COMPLEX AND MAY BREAK THE UNICAST NETWORK

The protocols used to deploy multicast in a scalable way on the Internet today can certainly be considered nontrivial (enough to warrant the necessity for this book!). RPF, a central concept in multicast, represents a significant change of paradigm from the traditional destination-based unicast routing.

Designers and operators of networks agree that a cost that cannot be ignored is included in deploying and maintaining multicast routing protocols, even if it involves no new hardware and simply "turning on" features already available in software. They also agree that the addition of any new protocol into a network offers the potential to introduce new bugs that can impact the stability of the network. This dilemma is faced when introducing any new technology into a network. Ultimately, the benefits provided by the new features must be weighed against the risk and cost of deployment.

Much of the complexity of multicast routing protocols has stemmed from the traditional view that multicast should provide many-to-many delivery in addition to one-to-many. To support this ASM model, the network must provide the control plane of source discovery. Recently, it has been widely agreed that the most "interesting" and commercially viable applications for multicast require only one-to-many delivery. By sacrificing functionality that may be considered somewhat less important on the Internet, much of the complexity of these protocols can be eliminated.

SSM is a service model that guarantees one-to-many delivery and can be realized with a subset of functionality from today's multicast protocols. By moving the control plane of source discovery to higher-layer protocols (like a click in a browser), the required multicast routing protocols become radically simpler. *This enables a reduction of operating and maintenance costs that cannot be overstated.*

1.12.5 CANNIBALIZATION OF UNICAST BANDWIDTH REVENUES

Throughout history, new technologies have evolved that have forced businesses to consider cannibalizing profitable incumbent technologies for new products. Generally, those who fail to embrace change get surpassed by those who do. When the automobile was first invented, imagine the dilemma faced by horse-drawn carriage makers as they pondered whether they should start building cars. Because multicast provides such efficient use of resources, some ISPs have been concerned that they will lose revenue as their customers consume less bandwidth. This view is no less shortsighted than that held by our unwise carriage-building friends.

While multicast reduces the resources required for a single session of content, it brings new content on the network. It brings more customers who will eventually demand more bandwidth for higher-quality streams. And, as mentioned earlier, multicast can be used as a traffic multiplier, consuming more bandwidth through the network as more receivers join. The lessons learned on the Internet are no different than those of previous revolutionary technical breakthroughs. History does not look favorably upon the unwillingness to sacrifice limited short-term revenues in favor of products with limitless growth potential.

1.12.6 END-TO-END CONNECTIVITY REQUIRED

For multicast to work properly, every layer 3 device on the path from source to receiver must be configured to be multicast-enabled. Pragmatically, this means every link on the Internet must be configured for PIM-SM, the de facto standard multicast routing protocol. If even one link in this path is not configured properly, multicast traffic cannot be received. This barrier can be a significant one as this path may transit many networks, each run by a different entity.

Because of this restriction, many consider multicast to be relegated to a hobbyist toy until the entire Internet is enabled. However, end-to-end multicast connectivity may not always be a requirement for applications to enjoy the benefits of multicast.

A hybrid unicast-multicast content delivery infrastructure can be built that provides the best of both worlds. A deployment of unicast-multicast "gateways" can be used to support the ubiquity of unicast with the scalability of multicast. Content can be multicast across an enabled core network to devices that can relay it to unicast-only hosts. This distributes the load that unicast must handle, relying on multicast to simply provide a back-end feeder network for the content gateways.

1.12.7 LACK OF SUCCESSFUL MODELS

Some multicast critics have suggested that no profitable services have ever been based on multicast. This observation fails to notice two communications media that have enjoyed commercial success for decades. Radio and broadcast television are based on a delivery mechanism that can be considered a special case multicast. Radio and television stations transmit data (their audio and/or video signal) across a one-hop, multiaccess network (the sky). Receivers join the group by tuning in their radio or TV to the group address (channel) of the station.

While radio and broadcast television do not use a packetized IP infrastructure (yet), the delivery mechanism used to provide content to receivers is decidedly multicast.

1.12.8 NOT READY FOR PRIME-TIME TELEVISION

After watching a 300Kbps Internet video stream on a 6-square inch section of a PC monitor, one's first inclination is definitely not to get rid of the family's 25-inch TV. While this can be considered reasonably good quality to expect on the Internet, it doesn't begin to compare to the quality and dependability that are expected from broadcast television. The bandwidth needed to approach this level of quality is orders of magnitude greater than that commonly found in most homes.

The quality and reliability of voice on the century-old **public switched telephone network (PSTN)** well exceeds that found in mobile phones. However, the functionality and limitless potential for features have enabled people to tolerate a lower voice quality in return for greater flexibility.

Likewise, the Internet has many inherent benefits that are difficult to match with broadcast communications. Despite having limited reach and no way to charge or exactly measure its audience, radio has been a viable business for the better part of a century. The Internet, with its bidirectional communication, provides the capability to log the exact behavior of every single viewer. After gazing upon an enticing advertisement, the viewer can instantly order the promoted product with the click of a mouse.

Additionally, the content that is available on television and radio is provided only by those with expensive studios and stations. On the Internet, anyone with a server and a connection can provide content accessible across the globe. Finally, multicast video on demand, generally believed to be impossible, is becoming a reality thanks to clever techniques that are being pioneered by innovative content delivery companies.

Initially, it is likely multicast video will be primarily niche content not commonly found on television, such as foreign TV channels or high school sporting events. As new technologies evolve, such as set-top boxes and hand-held devices, and as bandwidth to the home increases, the Internet will become an extremely attractive vehicle for television and radio. *Multicast provides the scalability to make this a reality.*

1.12.9 SUSCEPTIBILITY TO DoS

In the ASM service model, receivers join all sources of a group. While this functionality is ideal for applications such as online gaming, it leaves receivers open to **denial-of-service (DoS)** attacks. Any malicious user can send traffic to a multicast group, flooding all the receivers of that group, which greatly concerns content providers.

It is first worth noting that all IP traffic is susceptible to DoS, a reality in a network providing any-to-any connectivity. In fact, DoS is not even unique to the digital world. Throwing a brick through a storefront window, putting eggs in a mailbox, or parking a car in the middle of the street are only a few of an infinite number of analogs in the brick-and-mortar world. It just so happens that ASM DoS attacks are a bit easier to execute and have the potential to affect more users than their unicast counterparts. SSM, however, guarantees that the receivers will join only a single source. While DoS is not impossible with SSM, it is far more difficult to attack SSM receivers.

1.12.10 UNFRIENDLY LAST MILE TECHNOLOGIES, LESS FRIENDLY FIREWALLS

Multicast provides its benefits at the network layer. It is generally transparent to layer 2 technologies such as frame relay, ATM, and Ethernet, which means it is sometimes broadcast out all ports. Many of the high-speed last mile deployments of DSL and cable modems utilize primarily layer 2 infrastructures. Many of these architectures will be unable to realize the efficiencies supplied by multicast. Fortunately, in the world of data communications, the only constant is change. Service providers realize they must be agile enough to modify their offerings when needed to contend in this fiercely competitive landscape. As multicast becomes a standard part of the Internet, these providers will be motivated to make the necessary software or hardware upgrades to support it.

Multicast is predominantly delivered via **User Datagram Protocol (UDP)**. Those concerned with security find UDP traffic inherently scarier than its connection-oriented counterpart, **Transmission Control Protocol (TCP)**. Many firewalls and other security devices do not even support multicast. Once again, as multicast becomes ubiquitous across the Internet, makers of these devices will add support for the services their customers demand. Similarly, common practices will be developed to allay the security vulnerabilities that exist today with multicast traffic.

1.12.11 THE NEED FOR MULTICAST

In global emergency situations, multicast can play a crucial role in delivering vital communication to millions of Internet users, providing extra communications capacity at a time when heretofore conventional methods are strained to the breaking point. Indeed, nowhere has this been more precisely demonstrated than in the tragic events of September 11, 2001. In the early hours following the terrorist attacks in New York and Washington, most news Web sites were inaccessible as extraordinarily large numbers of users attempted to simultaneously access these sites.

At Northwestern University, CNN was rebroadcast as a multicast feed on the Internet and quickly gathered an audience of over 2,000 viewers. At the time, this multicast audience was believed to be the largest for a single feed in history. However, the size of this audience was infinitesimal compared to the number of users that wanted desperately to view this coverage and learn what was happening. As millions tried in vain to view pictures, video, text, anything that could have described the horrific events unfolding that day, users on multicast-enabled networks were able to watch real-time video accounts throughout the entire day.

Users on networks not enabled for multicast were forced to scramble to find radios and televisions. On September 11, 2001, multicast enabled Internet users to stay informed; in the future, multicast can be used to deliver critical information regarding public safety and security.

1.12.12 FINAL OUTLOOK

The free and open dissemination and collaboration of information provided by the Internet is among humankind's most powerful achievements. While the Internet has enjoyed unparalleled growth and has saturated nearly every element of our culture, it is poorly equipped to support multidestination traffic without multicast.

On enterprise and financial networks, multicast has enjoyed modest success for years; on the Internet, it has the capability to support content with the potential to be no less revolutionary than the World Wide Web. The reasons for its slow deployment across the Internet vary widely from validity to misunderstanding. In all cases, these obstacles are surmountable, especially given recent enhancements such as SSM. Finally, history has suggested the eventual convergence of all data networks onto a single IP infrastructure; multicast makes this forecast attainable.

IMR
Overview

Several protocols are required to enable IP multicast over multiple domains. These protocols, as well as their documentation, have been developed independently, and each has its own set of specific terms. The multiplicity of protocol development makes it challenging to create a workable, integrated multicast implementation.

The point of this chapter is to resolve the difficulty of implementation using these several protocols and to provide a working-level illustration of an interdomain multicast routing (IMR) system, end-to-end across multiple domains.

Figure 2-1 shows a simple network and serves as a reference for subsequent discussion in this chapter. The figure shows two interconnected autonomous systems (ASs) with fully functional unicast routing.

Each AS is controlled by an independent organization and has its own IGP. Based on information gained from the independent IGPs, router C and router D, in Figure 2-1, run an **External Border Gateway Protocol (EBGP)** session to exchange routing information with router E and router F, respectively.

In the remainder of this chapter, we show the step-by-step process of how to enable these two autonomous systems to route multicast traffic between them. Each step concentrates on a portion of Figure 2-1 and describes the mechanisms that must be put in place for operational multicast routing. Specifically, the focus is on enabling host B to receive multicast traffic from server A.

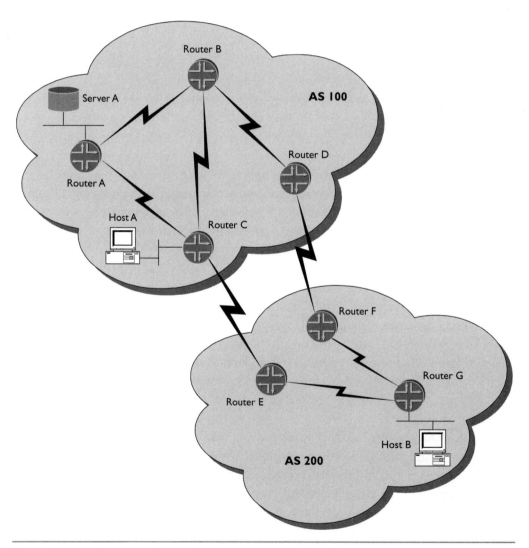

Figure 2-1 Base internetwork

2.1   RECEIVING MULTICAST TRAFFIC: IGMP FROM THE PERSPECTIVE OF THE HOST

A host must run IGMP in order to receive multicast packets. Currently, three versions of IGMP exist:

- **Version 1:** Described in RFC 1112
- **Version 2:** Described in RFC 2236
- **Version 3:** Described in draft-ietf-idmr-igmp-v3-09.txt

Hosts use IGMP to express their interest in specific multicast groups. A properly behaving host performs two tasks to join a multicast group:

- Begins listening on the layer 2 address that maps to the IP multicast group address
- Reports interest in joining a group by sending a Host Membership Report message, which triggers one of the routers on the LAN to join the group using a multicast routing protocol such as PIM-SM

To refresh state, a router on the host's LAN periodically sends IGMP Host Membership Query messages. Hosts send Report messages in response to these Query messages for each group in which they are interested.

> **Note:**   Multiple hosts on the same subnet may be interested in the same group, but it is necessary for only *one* host to respond to the IGMP Query in order for the router to forward traffic destined to the group onto the subnet.

To avoid a condition in which all hosts bombard the local network with redundant information, two strategies are used:

- When a Query message is received, a host waits a random amount of time to respond for each group in which it is interested.
- The host, in its IGMP version 1 or 2 Report message responses, sets the destination address to the group address being reported. In IGMP version 3, the

destination address of Report messages is 224.0.0.22. If a host hears a report from another host on the subnet, it suppresses the sending of its own report for that group.

The primary difference between IGMPv1 and IGMPv2 is the way they handle hosts leaving a group. In IGMPv1, when a host is no longer interested in listening to a group, it simply stops sending reports for that group. After some amount of time has passed without hearing any reports from any hosts, the router assumes all hosts on the LAN have left the group and stops forwarding traffic for that group onto the LAN. IGMPv2 introduced the concept of **explicit leave** with the addition of a Leave-Group message. This message enables hosts to report they are no longer interested in a group. The router responds to this message with a group-specific Query message to determine whether any other hosts are still interested in the group. If no other hosts respond with interest in the group, the router stops forwarding traffic onto the LAN immediately. This mechanism dramatically reduces leave latency.

IGMPv3 adds support for **exclude** and **include modes**. Exclude mode enables a host to request multicast packets for a group from all sources except those specified in the exclude list. Include mode enables a host to request multicast packets for a group from only the sources specified in the include list. Include mode enables hosts to participate in SSM, which is described in Chapter 6.

2.2 DETECTING MULTICAST RECEIVERS: IGMP FROM THE PERSPECTIVE OF THE ROUTER

IGMP Query messages are sent to the ALL-SYSTEMS multicast group (224.0.0.1) with an IP **time-to-live (TTL)** value set to 1. If more than one router exists on a subnet, the router whose Query messages contain the lowest-numbered IP source address is elected as the active **querier** for the subnet. Other routers on the subnet suppress sending of IGMP queries but still listen to and cache the information included in all IGMP messages.

On each IGMP-enabled interface, a router keeps an IGMP **group cache**, which is a simple table that keeps track of the following information:

- A list of all groups that have interested hosts
- The IP address of the host that last reported interest for each group
- The timeout value for each entry in the table

The timeout is the amount of time remaining for each group before the router determines no more members of a group exist on the interface. This timer is reset each time the router receives a Membership Report for that group on that interface. The value to which the timer is reset is called the **group membership interval (GMI)** and is calculated as follows:

GMI = (robustness variable x query interval) + query response interval

The **query interval** is the interval between general queries sent by the querier. Its default value is 125 seconds. By varying the query interval, an administrator may control the number of IGMP messages on the network; larger values cause IGMP queries to be sent less frequently.

The **query response interval** is the amount of time hosts have to respond to a IGMP Query. A 10-second default value is encoded in the Query message, which provides a time limit for the host's initial response. The host then randomly selects a response time between zero and this maximum, as described in the previous section.

The **robustness variable** defines the number of queries that can be sent without receiving a response before the cache entry times out. Increasing the robustness variable from its default of 2 safeguards against packet loss but increases the amount of time before the router detects that additional interested hosts truly do not exist.

2.3   GENERATING MULTICAST TRAFFIC

Generating multicast traffic requires no additional protocols. Server A simply starts sending traffic to a multicast group address. It is worth noting that the source can be transmitting multicast data into the network while there are no interested receivers. Nothing tells the source to "start sending." This provides in-efficiency on the source's LAN because the source can be blasting traffic that no one is interested in receiving.

There have been some preliminary discussions about adding mechanisms that would enable the network to inform a source when receivers exist. With such a mechanism, the source could wait until at least one listener is on the network before transmitting. At the time of writing, no such mechanism has been implemented or deployed.

2.4 DETECTING MULTICAST SOURCES

Routers recognize multicast packets sent by directly connected sources by examining the source and destination addresses of the packet as well as the TTL. The addresses are examined for the following conditions:

- Destination address is in the class D range and is not of link-local scope.
- Source address is part of a directly connected subnet.
- TTL is greater than 1.

Under these conditions, the router knows it is the first-hop router, or designated router (DR), for the multicast source and acts appropriately as described in the following discussion on PIM-SM operation.

2.5 ROUTING MULTICAST TRAFFIC WITHIN A DOMAIN USING PIM-SM

The first step is to get multicast routing up and running within a single domain. PIM–SM is the most commonly used multicast routing protocol for this task. We describe a *domain* in the context of PIM-SM. A PIM-SM domain is group of PIM-SM speakers interconnected with physical links and/or tunnels that agree on the same RP-to-group mapping matrix for all or a subset of the 224/4 address range.

Figure 2-1 shows two separate domains. PIM-SM domains are commonly mapped to BGP ASs, which are collections of routers controlled by the same administrative entity. However, PIM-SM domains and BGP ASs are mutually exclusive, so this need not be the case.

Multicast routing centers on the building of distribution trees. Unlike unicast routing, each router may have multiple interfaces out of which it forwards packets on behalf of a particular multicast group. Packets do not traverse the network in a straight-line path; instead, a multifingered distribution tree is rooted at one router with various branches heading toward each interested receiver.

At the core of the PIM-SM domain is a router that serves a very special role, known as the rendezvous point (RP). The RP serves as the "well-known meeting place" for multicast sources and interested listeners. PIM-SM supports the following three major phases to deliver multicast packets from a source to a receiver:

- Build the RPT that delivers packets from the RP to interested listeners
- Build the distribution tree that delivers packets from the source to the RP
- Build the SPT that delivers packets directly from the source to the interested listeners

These phases can occur for each source-receiver pair, and the distribution trees for different sources and groups may have reached different phases at any given time, depending on the existence of a source and interested listeners for that group.

The order of operation is not strict. Multicast sources can be created before receivers are created, and PIM-SM still enables delivery of multicast packets to any newly appearing receivers. Likewise, for a given multicast group, PIM-SM handles the condition in which a listener emerges after the SPT has already been built from the source to other receivers.

At this point, it is best to walk through the simplest example to explain the operation of the protocol, using a single source and a single receiver.

2.5.1 Phase 1: Building the RPT That Delivers Packets from the RP to Interested Listeners

The traffic flow of the RPT starts at the RP and flows to all hosts interested in receiving on the multicast group. The RPT is constructed in the opposite direction of traffic flow, starting at the receivers and building hop-by-hop toward the RP.

When a PIM-SM router receives an IGMP Host Membership Report from a host on a directly attached subnet, the router is responsible for initiating the creation of a branch of the RPT for the specific group of interest. This last-hop router is known as the *receiver's DR*.

The DR sends a (*,G) PIM Join[1] message to its RPF neighbor for the RP's IP address. An RPF neighbor is defined as the next-hop address in the RPF table for a specific IP address. The RPF table is the routing table used by multicast routing protocols when performing RPF checks. In PIM-SM, it is possible for the RPF table to be the same routing table used for unicast packet forwarding.

The PIM Join message is multicast hop-by-hop to the ALL-PIM-ROUTERS group (224.0.0.13) out each router's RPF interface until it reaches the RP forming the RPT. The message is sent with an IP TTL of 1, and each router along the way generates a subsequent (*,G) PIM Join message based on the information it received. Each router uses its own RPF table to determine its RPF neighbor for the RP address.

Join messages are sent to 224.0.0.13, so all routers on a multiaccess network can accept and process the packet. The address of the RPF neighbor is encoded in the message. Only the router that owns the address encoded in the packet generates its own (*,G) PIM Join toward its RPF neighbor.

2.5.1.1 Phase 1 on the Example Network AS 100 of the example network shown in Figure 2-2 is used to demonstrate the three phases of PIM-SM. The

---

1. In reality, there is no such thing as a PIM Join message. It is officially named a **Join/Prune message** because the same message can hold information for joining and pruning various distribution trees. But for clarity, we refer to Join/Prune messages as either Join or Prune, depending on the function of the message in a given instance.

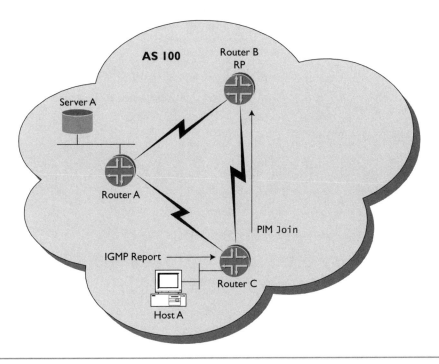

Figure 2-2 Building the RPT

first step is to choose an RP. The placement of an RP in a real network is an important decision. The RP must be accessible for PIM-SM to work. Techniques for providing RP failover and redundancy are discussed in Chapter 4. For the sake of this demonstration, router B is the RP, which makes the demonstration more interesting because the SPT and RPT for host A will be different paths.

To start phase 1, host A advertises its interest in a group (for this example, it happens to be interested in group 230.1.1.1) to router C via IGMP. This triggers router C to add its Ethernet interface to the outgoing interface list, or OIL, for the 230.1.1.1 group. Router C proceeds to forward a (*, 230.1.1.1) Join to its RPF neighbor for the RP address.

In this case, the RPF neighbor happens to be the RP itself, router B. Router B receives the Join and adds the interface on which it was received to the OIL for

230.1.1.1. Router B is the RP and therefore the root of the RPT, so there is no need to forward a (*, 230.1.1.1) Join message.

It is easy to understand the meaning of reverse path forwarding in Figure 2-2. The Join messages are forwarded in the reverse direction of the path from the RP to host A. The interface on which a Join message is received is added to the OIL for forwarding multicast data packets for this group.

At this point, no traffic is flowing because server A has yet to start sending data packets to the 230.1.1.1 group. In phase 2, the distribution tree is built to deliver packets from the source to the RP.

2.5.2 PHASE 2: BUILDING THE DISTRIBUTION TREE THAT DELIVERS PACKETS FROM THE SOURCE TO THE RP

When the RPT is built, it remains in place even if no active sources exist to generate traffic to the group. As soon as a source emerges, its traffic is delivered to the receivers. When the source starts transmitting multicast data, the PIM-SM DR directly connected to the source encapsulates the data in PIM **Register messages** and sends these PIM Register messages via unicast routing to the RP address.

The PIM-SM DR connected to the source sends a Register message each time it receives a multicast packet from the source. If an RP receives a PIM Register message for a group for which it has set up an existing RPT, it can do two things:

- Deliver the encapsulated multicast packet down the RPT to the receivers
- Send an (S,G) PIM Join message toward the source to create an SPT from the source to the RP

When the SPT is set up, the RP begins to receive duplicate multicast packets. One copy is delivered via multicast routing down the newly created distribution tree, and the other is decapsulated from the Register messages sent by the PIM-SM DR.

When the RP receives the first native, or unencapsulated, multicast packet for the source-group pair, it sends a Register-Stop message to the PIM-SM DR. When the PIM-SM DR receives the Register-Stop message, it stops sending Register messages for the source-group pair.

2.5.2.1 Phase 2 on the Example Network As illustrated in Figure 2-3, phase 2 begins when server A starts sending data packets with a destination address of 230.1.1.1. Router A recognizes these packets as being sent by a directly connected source on a LAN that router A is serving as the PIM-SM DR. Router A knows this packet is the first one received from this source for the group because it has no existing (server A, 230.1.1.1) state.

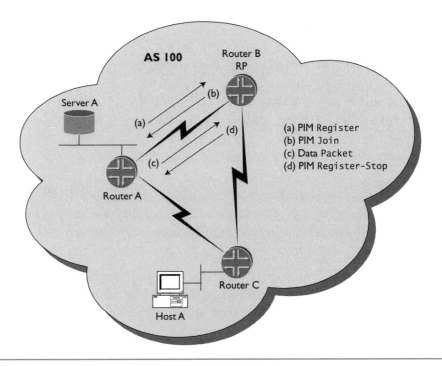

Figure 2-3 Phase 2: Source to RP interaction

Router A creates this (S,G) state, adding its Ethernet interface as the incoming interface for the source-group pair. It then unicasts a PIM Register message to the RP. The Register message has the data packet encapsulated within it. Router A sends a separate Register message to router B for every data packet from server A to 230.1.1.1 until it receives a Register-Stop message from router B.

Router B receives each Register message, decapsulates the data packet, and sends it down the RPT (which was set up in phase 1). To receive this data natively down the SPT, router B can send a Join message to its RPF neighbor for server A. In this case, router A is that RPF neighbor. Router A adds its interface toward router B to its OIL for the source-group pair.

At this point, each packet sent from server A to 230.1.1.1 is sent two times to the RP. It is both encapsulated in a Register message and sent directly out the interface in the OIL. Another way to describe this process is that the OIL has two entries:

- The point-to-point interface connecting router B
- The **virtual interface** formed by encapsulating data in Register messages

Once router B starts receiving the data packets natively, it sends a Register-Stop message to router A. When router A receives the Register-Stop, it removes the virtual interface formed by encapsulating data in Registers from its OIL and only forwards the packets natively.

When phases 1 and 2 are completed, the packets sent to 230.1.1.1 by server A are traveling to host A via the RP. The packets are delivered successfully, but the shortest path through the network is not being used. Phase 3 enables these packets to be shortcut directly from router A to router C.

2.5.3 PHASE 3: BUILDING THE SPT THAT DELIVERS PACKETS DIRECTLY FROM THE SOURCE TO THE INTERESTED LISTENERS

This phase is the final one. The disadvantage of the RPT is that the path taken via the RP to initially deliver traffic may not be the optimum path from the source to each receiver. Once a PIM-SM DR for a subnet with one or more interested listeners starts receiving multicast packets from a particular source, it can initiate the creation of the SPT by sending an (S,G) PIM Join message to its RPF neighbor for the source's IP address.

When the SPT is formed, the DR receives two copies of each packet sent by the source. One copy is received via the newly created SPT, and the other is delivered via the RPT. To stop this duplication, the DR sends a PIM **Prune message** toward the RP. This informs the RP that it is no longer necessary to forward multicast packets for this source-group pair down the RPT.

As long as the sources and receivers remain static, PIM-SM's task of setting up the optimal delivery of packets from the source to all receivers for the multicast group is finished at this point. Remember, the mechanisms discussed in this section work only if the sources and receivers are all in the same PIM-SM domain; that is, all routers between the sources and receivers agree on the same IP address for the RP of the multicast group.

2.5.3.1 Phase 3 on the Example Network Phase 3, as illustrated on the example network in Figure 2-4, starts when router C receives the initial data packet for the source-group pair (server A, 230.1.1.1). Router C knows it received this packet down the RPT and on its RPF interface for the RP. Router C can initiate the creation of the SPT by forwarding a (server A, 230.1.1.1) Join message to its RPF neighbor for server A. Its RPF neighbor for server A is router A.

Router A adds the interface connecting it to router C to its OIL for (server A, 230.1.1.1). At this point, router A forwards the data packets out both of its point-to-point interfaces. Router C receives the packets twice: once directly from router A down the SPT and once down the RPT from router B.

When router C receives the first packet down the SPT, it sends a (server A, 230.1.1.1, RPT) Prune message to its RPF neighbor for the RP. Its RPF neighbor for the RP is router B. When router B receives this Prune message, it removes its point-to-point interface connecting to router C from its OIL for (*, 230.1.1.1).

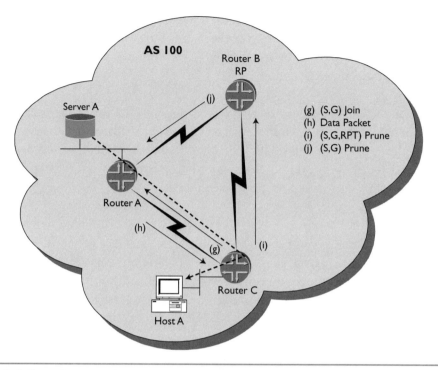

Figure 2-4 Control messages for phase 3 (The dashed line represents data flow after steps (g), (h), (i), and (j) are completed.)

Because router B now has no interfaces on this OIL, it sends a (server A, 230.1.1.1) Prune message to its RPF neighbor for server A (router A). Router A receives the Prune message and removes its interface connecting router B from its OIL for (server A, 230.1.1.1).

At the end of phase 3, data packets are delivered from server A to host A via the shortest path. It is important to realize that new hosts can report their interest in group 230.1.1.1, and these phases will take place again. The end result is a single SPT, rooted at server A with branches down the shortest path to each receiver.

At this point, the reader should have a basic understanding of multicast routing within a single PIM-SM domain. The next two sections introduce two protocols that enable the interconnection of PIM-SM domains: MSDP and MBGP.

2.6 ROUTING MULTICAST TRAFFIC ACROSS MULTIPLE DOMAINS WITH MSDP

The PIM-SM protocol in itself does not have a mechanism to enable multicast packets from a source in one PIM-SM domain to reach a receiver in another domain. The PIM-SM DR for the *source* sends its Register messages to the RP in *its* own domain, while the PIM-SM DR for the *receiver* sends Join messages toward the RP in *its* own domain.

The delivery of multicast packets from the source to the RP in the source's domain is disconnected from the RPT in the receiver's domain. Thus the following conditions are required to transit multicast traffic across multiple PIM-SM domains:

- The RP in domains that have receivers must have knowledge of the IP address of active sources.
- All routers along the path from the source to the receivers must have a route to the source's IP address in their RPF table.[2]

The first requirement is accomplished by using MSDP. MSDP provides a way to connect multiple PIM-SM domains so that RPs can exchange information on the active sources of which they are aware. Each domain relies on its own RP instead of having to share an RP with another domain.

MSDP sessions use TCP for reliable transport and can be multihop. MSDP sessions are formed between the RPs of various domains. MSDP-speaking RPs send MSDP Source-Active (SA) messages to notify the RPs in other domains of active sources. An RP constructs an **SA message** each time it receives a PIM Register message from a DR advertising a new source. SA messages include the multicast data packet encapsulated in the Register message in current implementations of MSDP.

---

2. It is possible for a receiver's DR to always remain on the RPT and never join the SPT. In this case, routers on the path between the receiver and the RP (in the receiver's domain) need to have only a route to their RP in their RPF table. This situation is not very common, though, because most DRs join the SPT immediately.

When an RP receives an SA message for a group for which interested receivers exist, the RP delivers the encapsulated data down the RPT to all the receivers in its domain. When the receiver's DR receives the multicast packets down the RPT, it joins the SPT directly to the source.

The second requirement usually is not a concern because most networks have any-to-any connectivity for unicast traffic, even for addresses in other ASs. Keep in mind the multicast RPF table need not be the same routing table used for unicast routing. In this case, the dedicated multicast RPF table must have routes for all potential multicast sources. MBGP is used to populate such an RPF table and is discussed in the next section.

2.6.1 MSDP IN THE EXAMPLE NETWORK

To show the functionality of MSDP in the example network, we continue with reference to Figure 2-5. The data packets are being delivered from server A to host A via the SPT. Now host B in AS 200 reports its interest in the 230.1.1.1 group by sending an IGMP Report message to router G.

Router G adds its Ethernet interface to the OIL for (*, 230.1.1.1). Router G has been chosen to serve as the RP for the PIM-SM domain of AS 200, so the formation of the RPT is trivial. The RPT is simply router G's Ethernet interface.

At this point, no data packets for the 230.1.1.1 group are delivered to host B because router G has no idea that server A is sending to that group. In order to get this information to router G, router B and router G are configured as MSDP peers. The problem is that router B no longer knows that server A is sending to 230.1.1.1 because it has sent a Prune message to router A for (server A, 230.1.1.1).

This is not truly a problem because router A periodically sends **Null-Register messages** (a Register message without encapsulated data) to the RP. The primary purpose of the Null-Register is to tell the RP that the source is still active without having to encapsulate any data.

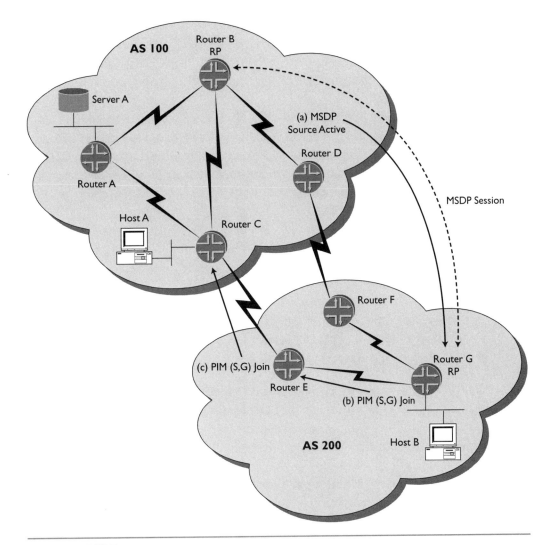

Figure 2-5 MSDP

In this case, router B has no knowledge of host B's interest in 230.1.1.1 because host B is in a different PIM-SM domain. That is to say, host B's DR sends its (*,G) Joins toward a different RP than router B. As previously noted, router G happens to be serving as both the DR and RP in this case.

Fortunately, router B forms a MSDP Source-Active message for each Register (or Null-Register) it receives and forwards it to all its MSDP peers. This is how router G discovers that server A is sending to 230.1.1.1. Router G then sends an (S,G) PIM Join message for (server A, 230.1.1.1) to its RPF neighbor for server A.

Router E is that RPF neighbor. Router E adds its interface connecting router G to its OIL for (server A, 230.1.1.1) and sends an (S,G) PIM Join toward server A. Router C receives this Join and adds its interface connecting router E to its OIL for (server A, 230.1.1.1). It is important to note that in order for this to take place, PIM-SM must be enabled on all of the interfaces connecting the two domains.

At this point, router C's OIL for (server A, 230.1.1.1) consists of two interfaces, its Ethernet interface and its point-to-point interface connecting router E. The SPT for the source-group pair successfully delivers data packets from server A to both host A and host B.

2.7 POPULATING A ROUTING TABLE DEDICATED TO RPF CHECKS WITH MBGP

The previous sections describe how the RPF mechanism uses information learned from a unicast routing table to determine the path of a multicast distribution tree. In PIM-SM it is possible for the RPF table to be populated from the same routing table used for unicast forwarding.

By taking this approach, unicast and multicast traffic follow the same path but in opposing directions. For example, a multicast packet traveling from server A to host B would traverse all the same routers and links, but in the exact opposite order, as a unicast packet traveling from host B to server A.

Some situations make such congruent routing of unicast and multicast traffic less than optimal. Figure 2-6 illustrates when it is beneficial for multicast and unicast traffic to travel separate paths.

Based on fewest AS hops, the optimal path for unicast traffic traveling from AS 100 to AS 500 is through AS 400. However, AS 400 does not support multicast

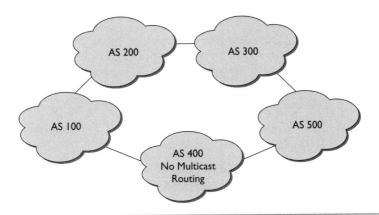

Figure 2-6 Unicast and multicast paths

routing. If the same routing table used to forward unicast traffic is used for the RPF table in all routers *and* multicast traffic must flow from AS 500 to AS 100, AS 100 is compelled to use a suboptimal path for its unicast traffic destined for AS 500. Unicast traffic from AS 100 destined for AS 500 would be forced to traverse the path across AS 200 and AS 300.

To circumvent this limitation, a table other than the one used for unicast forwarding can be used for multicast RPF. The question is how to populate such a table: How are unicast routes introduced into a separate RPF table, with next-hop information different from the table used for unicast forwarding?

One solution is to configure static routes specifically for the RPF table. Note that static routing for multicast RPF faces the same scalability limitations as static routing for unicast forwarding. That is, static routes lack dynamic failover and can be administratively burdensome because changes to topology are not automatically updated.

In real networks, it is desirable to dynamically update the entries in the RPF table. The RPF table consists of unicast routes so there is no need to invent a new routing protocol. Instead, the need is to somehow differentiate between route-control information intended for unicast forwarding and the multicast RPF table. Theoretically, this differentiation could be implemented by modifying any of the existing unicast routing protocols. However, the structure of some unicast routing protocols makes them inherently more extensible, such that adding support for multicast requires relatively few modifications to the protocol. BGP is one of the best candidates for adding such functionality.

BGP is a dynamic routing protocol that can differentiate between multiple types of routing information. This capability is designated Multiprotocol Extensions for BGP (MBGP) and is defined in RFC 2858. MBGP works identically to BGP in all respects; it simply adds functionality to BGP, such as the capability for BGP updates to tag routing information as belonging to a specific protocol or function within that protocol.

When using MBGP for updating dedicated multicast RPF tables, two sets of routes are exchanged in the MBGP updates:

- IPv4 unicast routes
- IPv4 multicast RPF routes

Each set can have duplicated **prefixes**, but the path information for the same prefix in each set can be different. Not only can multicast RPF routes have different BGP next hops (and therefore potentially different recursive next hops), but they also can have different information in any of the BGP path attributes.

From the AS 100 perspective in Figure 2-6 shown earlier, MBGP enables destinations in AS 500 to be learned through the connection to both AS 200 and AS 400. The path through AS 400 is preferred for unicast packet forwarding, with the path through AS 200 and AS 300 serving as backup. Meanwhile, path selection for multicast RPF checks are limited to the path through AS 200 and AS 300.

2.7.1 MBGP IN THE EXAMPLE NETWORK

To show the functionality of MBGP in the example network, we pick up where we left off in section 2.6. Multicast packets to group 230.1.1.1 are delivered from server A to both host A and host B via the SPT, as shown in Figure 2-7.

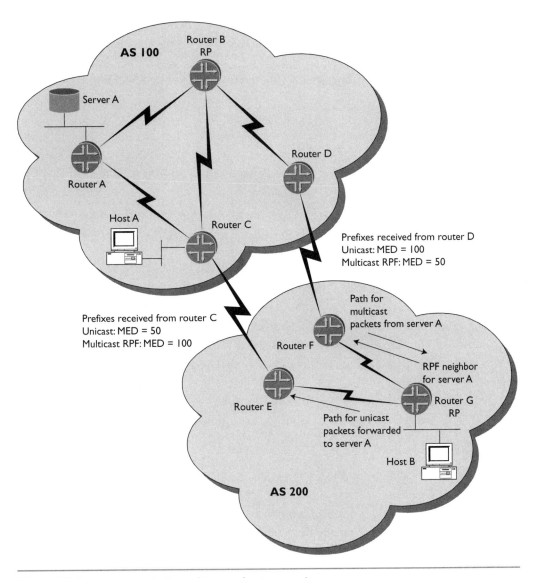

Figure 2-7 Incongruent paths for multicast and unicast routing

To make things interesting, let's pretend that our boss has mandated that the link between router C and router E not be used to carry any multicast data traffic unless the link between router D and router F fails. Additionally, unicast traffic flowing between AS 100 and AS 200 must use the router C to router E link if it is available.

The way to meet these requirements is by using MBGP. Router G's RPF neighbor for server A must change from router E to router F. This causes router G to send its PIM Join messages for (server A, 230.1.1.1) to router F rather than to router E. Therefore the SPT will be built across the router D to router F link instead of the router C to router E link.

Two steps are needed to make this scheme work:

1. Configure the routers in AS 200 to use a dedicated RPF table instead of the unicast routing table.
2. Manipulate the path attributes in the MBGP updates for the multicast RPF routes to prefer the router D to router F link.

MBGP enables separate routing policy for each address family. For instance, a BGP path attribute, such as the **multiple exit discriminator (MED)** value, could be set for all prefixes learned from both AS 100 routers. For routes learned from router C, unicast routes could be set to MED = 50, and multicast RPF routes could be set to MED = 100. For routes learned from router D, the opposite values would be used to achieve the same effect of incongruence in the opposite direction.

Figure 2-7 illustrates the use of MBGP to achieve incongruent paths for unicast and multicast routing, which is just one example of a routing policy that would give the desired effect.

We have tried to present in Chapter 2 a discussion, at a fairly high level, of the practical difficulties faced and customary solutions developed in an IMR implementation. Some key concepts and terms have also been presented, along with some important routing diagrams that can be referred to as you continue reading. Chapter 3 proceeds with a more thorough description of multicast routing protocols, in particular, making a distinction between sparse and dense protocols.

Multicast Routing Protocols

This chapter provides an overview of multicast routing protocols. For a protocol to be deemed a multicast routing protocol, it must at minimum provide the functionality of setting up multicast forwarding state and exchange information about this forwarding state with other multicast routers. By this definition PIM-DM, PIM-SM, and DVMRP are all multicast routing protocols; IGMP, MBGP, and MSDP are not.

Multicast routing protocols can generally be classified into two categories: dense and sparse. By understanding the advantages and disadvantages of each, it is clear to see why PIM-SM has become the protocol of choice for IMR. We describe the characteristics of **dense** and **sparse protocols** and briefly discuss examples of each. PIM-SM is examined in detail in Chapter 4.

3.1 DENSE PROTOCOLS

Dense protocols assume a dense distribution of receivers exists throughout the domain, which means each subnet likely has at least one interested receiver for every active group. This assumption may be valid on enterprise networks where only a few groups are active and most of the subnets contain interested listeners.

On networks where few or no prunes occur, dense protocols are actually more efficient than sparse protocols. However, on the Internet, where prunes are more prevalent, dense protocols are not well suited to interdomain deployment.

Dense protocols follow a **flood-and-prune** model. To inform the routers of multicast sources, this traffic is initially broadcast throughout the domain. Upon first receiving traffic to a dense group on its interface closest to the source, a router forwards this traffic out all of its interfaces except the interface on which it received the data. Thus the IIF initially is the RPF interface toward the source, and the OIL contains all other interfaces.

If traffic is received on the interface that is not the RPF interface toward the source, the traffic is discarded, and a Prune message is sent upstream. If a router has no interested receivers for the data (that is, its OIL becomes empty), it sends a Prune upstream. Periodic reflooding is used to refresh state.

The primary benefit of dense protocols is simplicity. The flood-and-prune mechanism enables these protocols to easily build a multicast distribution tree rooted at the source. A source-based tree guarantees the shortest and most efficient path from source to receiver. The obvious limitation is scalability; any mechanism that relies on flooding across the entire network does not scale particularly well on the Internet.

3.1.1 DVMRP

DVMRP is the multicast routing protocol first used to support the MBone. It performs the standard flood-and-prune behavior common to dense protocols. It also implements a separate routing protocol used to build the routing tables on which RPF checks are performed.

As its name suggests, DVMRP has a distance-vector routing protocol very similar to RIP. It has the same limitations found in other **distance-vector protocols**, which include slow convergence and limited **metric** (that is, hop count). Although most DVMRP deployments have been replaced by PIM-SM, DVMRP can still be found on networks with legacy equipment, such as dialup RASs. Most RASs made today support either PIM-SM or IGMP proxying.

3.1.2 PIM-DM

PIM-DM implements the same flood-and-prune mechanism mentioned previously and is quite similar to DVMRP. The primary difference between DVMRP and PIM-DM is that the latter aptly named protocol introduces the concept of protocol independence. PIM, in both dense and sparse modes of operation, can use the routing table populated by any underlying unicast routing protocol to perform RPF checks.

This ability to use any underlying unicast protocol was seen by ISPs to be a significant enhancement because they did not want to manage a separate routing protocol just for RPF (ironically, MBGP and M-ISIS were later used to do just that). PIM-DM can consult the unicast routing table, populated by OSPF, IS-IS, BGP, and so on, or it can be configured to use a multicast RPF table populated by MBGP or M-ISIS when performing RPF checks.

3.2 SPARSE PROTOCOLS

Sparse protocols make the implicit assumption that a sparse distribution of subnets with at least one interested receiver for each active group exists, which is much more consistent with what is found on the Internet. The primary difference between sparse and dense protocols is in the way the protocols handle source discovery. Where dense protocols use flooding of the actual data to inform the routers in the domain of active sources, sparse protocols designate a core node to keep track of all of the active sources in a domain. The mechanisms involved in source discovery in sparse protocols, while much more complex than those in dense, provide the scalability needed to support multicast across the Internet.

Sparse protocols follow an **explicit join** model. In this model, multicast data is forwarded only to routers that explicitly request it. In sparse protocols, the root of the distribution tree is at a core node. This core node, or rendezvous point (RP) as it is known in PIM-SM, can receive traffic from the source via the SPT. When a host wants to join a group, its directly connected router joins the distribution tree toward the RP. So traffic is received by the RP along the SPT and forwarded to interested receivers across the domain via the shared tree, or rendezvous point (RPT).

The benefit of the RPT is that it reduces the amount of state required in the non-RP routers and does not require flooding across the network to inform routers of active sources. Instead, the RP is the only router that needs to be aware of all of the active sources for a domain. All other routers simply need to know who the RP is and how to reach it.

One disadvantage of the RPT is that it introduces the potential for suboptimal routing (see Figure 3-1). Multicast data must first flow to the RP and then to the

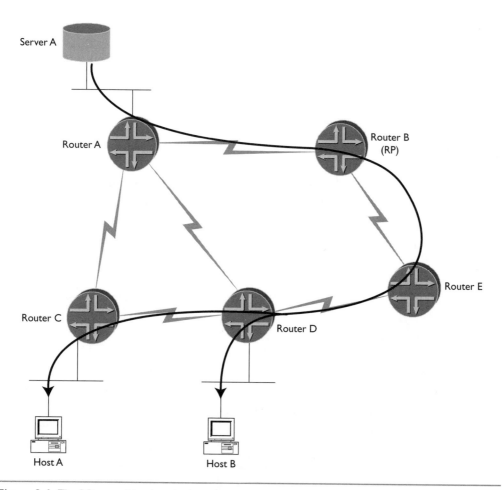

Figure 3-1 The RP tree with suboptimal routing

receivers, even if the receivers are much closer to the source. The potentially inefficient path of an RPT illustrates how the SPT always provides the most efficient
path (see Figure 3-2). To eliminate this inefficiency, PIM-SM enables the
receiver's DR to join toward the source along the SPT if traffic reaches a certain
threshold. Juniper Networks and Cisco System routers implement a threshold of
0 by default (this threshold is configurable on Cisco routers), which means once
the DR receives the first multicast packet and learns the source, it sends an (S,G)
Join toward the source. When it starts receiving data from the SPT, it then sends a

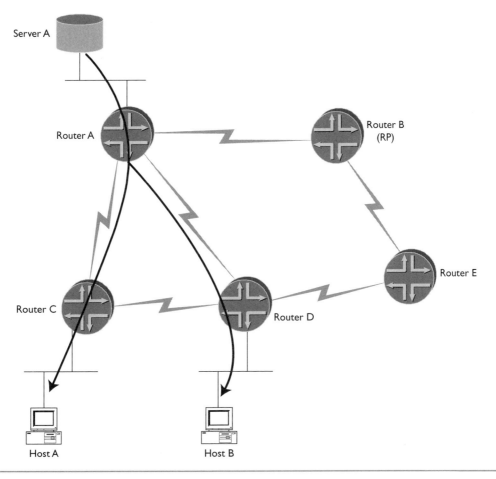

Figure 3-2 Shortest path tree (SPT)

Prune for traffic received via the RPT toward the RP. Accordingly, PIM-SM exhibits the best of both worlds by enjoying the benefits of both the RPT and the SPT without suffering their limitations.

Early multicast architects initially considered reduction of state to be a major advantage of RPTs. For example, if a group had ten active sources, ten separate (S,G) entries would have to be maintained by routers supporting SPTs. By comparison, only a single (*,G) entry is required in an RPT. It was feared that state explosion could cause routers to run out of memory. As memory became cheaper and router vendors implemented these protocols more efficiently, however, state became much less of an issue. Concerns were further allayed as predominant implementations of PIM-SM supporting the immediate switch to the SPT did not cause the feared state explosion.

PIM-SM is the only example of a sparse protocol implemented by any major router vendor. Because of its sparse operation as well as protocol independence, it is the de facto standard on the Internet today.

3.3 SPARSE-DENSE MODE

Sparse-dense mode is a mode of PIM implemented by both Juniper Networks and Cisco Systems that supports both types of operation concurrently. Sparse-dense mode enables the interface to operate in either sparse mode or dense mode on a per-group basis. Groups specified as dense groups are not mapped to an RP, and data packets destined for those groups are forwarded based on the rules of PIM-DM. Sparse groups are mapped to an RP and are forwarded based on the rules of PIM-SM.

Initially, sparse-dense mode was ideal for indecisive enterprise network designers who were not sure if they should deploy PIM-SM or PIM-DM. Today it is mainly used in networks that implement **auto-RP** for PIM-SM.

Protocol Independent Multicast–Sparse Mode (PIM-SM)

This chapter provides a detailed description of PIM-SM, the predominant multicast routing protocol for interdomain routing.

4.1 SPECIFICATIONS

The version numbers (version 1 and version 2) mostly pertain to packet format, and each version is described in several iterations of specifications. For example, version 2, sparse mode, was described in RFC 2117, which then was made obsolete by RFC 2362. The most recent specification of the PIM-SM protocol is draft-ietf-pim-sm-v2-new-04.txt. No current RFC describes PIM version 1; the Internet-Drafts that originally defined version 1 have expired.

4.2 PIM VERSIONS

The implementation of PIM by Juniper Networks and Cisco Systems enables configuration of a distinct PIM version on each interface of a router. This setting identifies the format of PIM messages sent out the interface.

4.2.1 VERSION 1

PIM version 1 messages are sent as an IGMP message (IP protocol number 2) with IGMP version set to 1 and IGMP type set to 4 (4 = router PIM messages).

The type of PIM message is distinguished by the IGMP Code field. The following are all the PIM version 1 message types:

0: Router-Query

1: Register (used in PIM-SM only)

2: Register-Stop (used in PIM-SM only)

3: Join/Prune

4: RP-Reachability (not used)

5: Assert

6: Graft (used in PIM-DM only)

7: Graft-Ack (used in PIM-DM only)

4.2.2 VERSION 2

PIM version 2 messages use IP protocol number 103. The first four bits of a version 2 message represent the version number (2). The next four bits represent the type of message. The following is a list of all PIM version 2 message types:

0: Hello

1: Register (used in PIM-SM only)

2: Register-Stop (used in PIM-SM only)

3: JoinJoin/Prune

4: Bootstrap

5: Assert

6: Graft (used in PIM-DM only)

7: Graft-Ack (used in PIM-DM only)

8: Candidate RP-Advertisement (used in PIM-SM only)

Because version 1 Router-Query messages serve the same purpose as version 2 Hellos and because version 1 RP-Reachability messages are not used, version 1 messages are a subset of version 2 messages. The added messages, Bootstrap and Candidate RP-Advertisement, are both used in the version 2 bootstrap mechanism. If the version 2 bootstrap mechanism is used, then interfaces configured as version 1 do not transmit or receive **Bootstrap messages**, which is important for two reasons:

- Accidentally setting interfaces to version 1 in a PIM domain that uses the version 2 bootstrap mechanism could prevent some routers from discovering the RP address.
- Intentionally setting an interface to version 1 at the border of a PIM domain is a technique that prevents version 2 Bootstrap messages from leaking to the neighboring PIM domain.

All routers connecting to a subnet must use the same PIM version. PIM messages received with a version other than that configured on the interface are dropped. However, some implementations recognize when version 1 packets are received on an interface and automatically switch the interface to version 1.

Configuring the PIM version alters the format of messages that are sent and limits the messages that are accepted. But configuring the version does not alter the way PIM processes those messages, which is why a router can have a mix of version 1 and version 2 interfaces.

4.3 GROUP-TO-RP MAPPING

For PIM-SM to work properly, all routers in a domain must know and agree on the active RP for each multicast group. In fact, the definition of PIM-SM domain is just that: a group of PIM-SM speakers interconnected with physical links and/ or tunnels that agree on the same RP-to-group mapping matrix for all or a subset of the 224/4 address range. There are three ways to map the RP:

- Static group-to-RP mapping
- Cisco Systems auto-RP (dynamic)
- PIM **bootstrap router (BSR)** (dynamic)

Typically, only one of these methods is used for setting the RP. The following sections describe each of these mechanisms.

4.3.1 STATIC GROUP-TO-RP MAPPING

Static RP is by far the least elaborate method. Every router in the PIM domain must be manually configured with the address of the RP for each multicast group. The major advantage to using this method is simplicity. The drawback is that it requires configuration on every router in the domain each time the address of the RP changes. Also, failover to a backup RP requires additional configuration in the event the primary RP is unreachable. Anycast RP alleviates this limitation.

4.3.2 DYNAMIC GROUP-TO-RP MAPPING: CISCO SYSTEMS AUTO-RP

Auto-RP, originally a Cisco Systems proprietary mechanism for dynamic group-to-RP mapping, is fully supported by Juniper Networks routers as well. Auto-RP relies on dense mode of operation to forward control messages to two well-known group addresses (224.0.1.39 and 224.0.1.40). Because of this reliance, all routers in an auto-RP-enabled PIM-SM domain should be configured in sparse-dense mode. With auto-RP, RPs in a domain announce themselves as such with these groups. All other routers in the domain join one or both of these dense groups and learn dynamically the address of the RPs.

Each router in a domain using auto-RP fits into one of the following roles:

- Candidate RP
- Mapping agent
- Discovery-only

Every 60 seconds, a candidate RP sends an RP-Announcement message detailing the group ranges for which it intends to serve as RP. This message is sent to 224.0.1.39 (CISCO-RP-ANNOUNCE).

The routers configured as mapping agents join the 224.0.1.39 group and listen for RP-Announcement messages. Each mapping agent uses the following criteria to determine which RPs to announce as the active RP for each group:

- When multiple RPs announce the same group prefix and mask, accept the announcement only from the RP with the highest IP address.
- Reject a group prefix if it is already covered by a less-specific prefix advertised by the same RP (for example, if RP1 announces both 227.3.3.0/24 and 227.3.0.0/16, only the less-specific 227.3.0.0/16 is accepted).
- Accept all other announcements.

Note that if one RP announces 227.3.3.0/24 and another announces 227.3.0.0/16, both of these announcements are accepted. The RP with the most specific match for a group, G, is the RP for that group.

After authoritatively selecting an RP for each group range, the mapping agents announce RP-Mapping messages to 224.0.1.40 (CISCO-RP-DISCOVERY).

Discovery-only routers join 224.0.1.40 and learn of the RP for each group range. Candidate RP routers and mapping agents also join 224.0.1.40.

Because the control messages are delivered using standard multicast routing, 224.0.1.39 and 224.0.1.40 must be forwarded using dense mode (so that they do not rely on an RP). Otherwise, a static RP must be configured for the two groups. Because this control traffic is limited and the group membership is stable, the inefficiencies of dense mode operation are not an issue. Furthermore, every router in the domain joins 224.0.1.40, so no Prunes are needed.

There is a fundamental difference between the way Juniper Networks and Cisco System routers are configured for sparse-dense mode. In Cisco routers, any ASM group that does not have an RP is automatically considered a dense group. If a Cisco router somehow loses its group-to-RP mapping, it considers all groups to be dense. Likewise, if the RP(s) in a domain becomes unreachable, all Cisco routers in that domain flood all groups according to dense mode.

Juniper Networks routers require dense mode groups to be configured explicitly. By configuring sparse-dense mode on a Juniper router, only the groups explicitly configured as such are forwarded densely, which eliminates the possibility of sparse mode groups being accidentally forwarded densely.

4.3.3 DYNAMIC GROUP-TO-RP MAPPING: PIM BOOTSTRAP

PIM bootstrap was added to PIM version 2 as a standardized way to provide dynamic group-to-RP mapping. Functionally, PIM bootstrap is very similar to auto-RP. To use PIM bootstrap as the **RP-set** mechanism, all routers in the domain must use the PIM version 2 packet formats. One or more routers must be selected to serve as candidate BSRs.

By default, a PIM router's BSR priority is set to 0. A BSR priority of 0 means that the router is not eligible to serve as BSR. In order for the bootstrap mechanism to work, at least one router in the domain must be configured with a BSR priority greater than 0.

Each candidate BSR sends Bootstrap messages out all of its interfaces. When neighboring routers receive the message, they process the packet and forward a copy of the packet out all interfaces except for the interface on which the Bootstrap message was received. PIM routers accept BSR messages received on their RPF interface only for the address of the candidate BSR that originated the message.

If a candidate BSR receives a Bootstrap message with a BSR priority larger than its own, that router stops announcing itself as a candidate BSR. Eventually, only one router in the domain—the router with the highest-configured BSR priority—will send out Bootstrap messages. These messages are sent out periodically (the default is 60 seconds).

The Bootstrap messages initially do not have any RP-set information in them unless the BSR itself is a candidate RP. The RP-set information is conveyed to the BSR by all candidate RPs in the domain. The candidate RPs periodically unicast Candidate RP-Advertisement messages to the BSR address specified in the Bootstrap messages. The Candidate RP-Advertisement messages list the group ranges for which the candidate RP is contending and for its candidate RP priority.

The BSR collects the information from all candidate RPs. It places the information for all candidate RPs into subsequent Bootstrap messages. The BSR performs the election of the active RP of each group range only for its own use. Each router in the domain is responsible for running the RP-selection hash algorithm on the candidate RP information contained in the Bootstrap messages.

The hash algorithm used to elect the active RP for group G is as follows:

1. Find all RPs with the most specific group range covering G.
2. From the subset in step 1, select all RPs with the highest priority (lowest priority value).
3. For the RPs that meet the requirements in steps 1 and 2, compute a hash value based on the group address G, the RP address, and the hash mask included in the Bootstrap messages. The RP with the highest hash value is the RP for the group.
4. In case of a tie (that is, the same group range, priority, and hash value), the RP with the highest IP address is the active RP.

The formula for computing the hash value is as follows:

$$(1103515245 * ((1103515245 * (G\&M)+12345) \text{ XOR } C(i)) + 12345) \bmod 2^{31}$$

Where $C(i)$ is the RP address, and M is a hash-mask included in Bootstrap messages. "Mod" means modulo, the mathematical functional that returns the value of the remainder when the quantity to the left of "mod" is divided by the quantity to the right of "mod." In the formula, 2^{31} is 2 to the thirty-first power.

It is wise to select two core routers in diverse locations, each to serve as both a candidate BSR and candidate RP. It is sensible to choose one of these routers to be both the primary BSR and RP.

BSR addresses some of the deficiencies of auto-RP with respect to robustness, **load balancing**, and convergence. Recall that all auto-RP mapping agents run the same selection algorithm and advertise only the elected RPs. If the mapping agents are not in synch, the routers in their domain will have inconsistent information about the RP. For this reason, BSR uses only one active router to provide this mapping functionality.

In addition, the BSR advertises all candidate RPs along with their priorities, and each router in the domain holds its own local election, which provides faster convergence and minimal disruption when an RP fails. BSR provides load balancing by distributing groups across multiple RPs using the hash function. When an RP fails, its groups are automatically distributed to the remaining available RPs.

4.4 ANYCAST RP

In PIM-SM, only one RP can be active for any single multicast group. This limitation provides a great challenge when trying to deliver load balancing and redundancy. **Anycast RP** is a clever mechanism that circumvents this limitation. **Anycast** means that multiple hosts, or in this case routers, share the same unicast IP address. This address is then advertised by a routing protocol, such as OSPF, (M-)ISIS, or (M)BGP. Packets destined for the anycast address are then delivered to the closest host with this address. If that host becomes unreachable, packets are delivered to the next closest host with the anycast address.

With anycast RP, multiple routers are configured with the same IP address, typically on their loopback interface. This shared address is used in the RP-to-group mapping, which allows multicast groups to have multiple active RPs in a PIM-SM domain. PIM-SM control messages are sent toward the shared address, and they will reach an RP with the best routing metric from the originator of the message. Register messages and (*,G) Joins are sent to the topologically closest RP.

Thus anycast RP essentially forms multiple PIM-SM subdomains within the domain, with each subdomain consisting of one of the RPs and all of the PIM-SM routers with the best routing metric for the shared address pointing toward that RP. Because the domain is broken into subdomains, it is necessary to run MSDP between the RPs to exchange information about active sources between subdomains.

The anycast RP address is typically configured as a secondary address on the loopback interface. Care should be taken to ensure that routing protocols such as OSPF, IS-IS, or BGP do not select the anycast address as the router ID. Duplicate router IDs in these protocols can cause disastrous results. For this reason, it is wise to configure a unique unicast address as the primary loopback address. This unique address is used as the router ID for routing protocols as well as the peering address for MSDP sessions.

Anycast RP enables RP tasks for a PIM-SM domain to be shared across multiple routers by localizing their responsibility to their respective subdomains. This localization provides very intelligent load balancing from a routing perspective. Anycast RP also provides redundancy around a failed RP that is as fast as the convergence of the routing protocol carrying the anycast address. If one of the anycast RPs becomes unavailable, all PIM-SM control messages that were originally destined for the failed RP are delivered to the RP with the next best routing metric. Forthcoming PIM Register and (*,G) messages will be sent to the next closest RP, and RPTs will be rooted at the next closest RP.

Anycast RP is mutually exclusive with the group-to-RP mapping mechanism, so it can be used in conjunction with static RP, auto-RP, or BSR. While auto-RP and BSR have their own methods of delivering load balancing and redundancy, most ISPs have found anycast RP provides these benefits in a much simpler and more intuitive way.

Unless the IP address of the RP changes frequently, BSR and auto-RP provide little benefit over a statically defined anycast RP. Furthermore, these dynamic mapping mechanisms introduce a great deal of complexity in a realm already replete with confusion. For example, auto-RP requires a sparse mode protocol to use a dense mode control plane. When troubleshooting, both of these topologies must be examined.

While simplicity is always a desired goal in network design, it is even more valuable when building and operating multicast networks. For this reason, it is highly recommended that anycast RP with static group-to-RP mapping be used when deploying interdomain multicast. Interestingly, most ISP engineers strongly prefer this method, while protocol designers usually insist on BSR. These differing preferences are probably due to the same reason, reflecting the opposing biases these groups frequently hold. Static anycast RP is unsophisticatedly simple; BSR is elegantly complex.

4.5 PIM REGISTER MESSAGE PROCESSING

When a PIM-SM DR receives a multicast packet sourced by a directly connected host, the DR encapsulates the packet in a Register message and sends it as a unicast packet to the RP for the group. The Register message conveys the source address, S, and group address, G. Upon receiving the Register message, the response of the RP is based on two factors:

- Whether it has an RPT set up for the group (that is, does it know of any receivers interested in the group?)
- Whether it is receiving data natively for this (S,G) pair down a distribution tree

The RP ignores the Register message and immediately sends a Register-Stop message to the DR if either of the following conditions is met:

- No RPT is set up.
- An RPT exists, but the RP is already receiving data natively from the source.

If these two conditions are not met, the RPT is set up, and the RP is not receiving packets natively yet. According to the PIM-SM specifications, the RP can decapsulate the register packets and forward them natively down the RPT. Or, optionally, the RP can join the SPT and receive packets natively from the source. For low data rate sources, not joining the SPT and decapsulating register packets may be desirable because it reduces the amount of state created. However, this strategy can lead to high join latency because the RP must wait for the DR to send register packets. Additionally, decapsulation can be a resource-intensive process for a router. Accordingly, Juniper Networks and Cisco System RPs implement this option and always join the SPT.

In this case, the RP joins the SPT by sending a (S,G) Join to its RPF neighbor for the source and waits until it receives packets natively before it sends the Register-Stop message. Meanwhile, it extracts the data packet from every PIM Register message it receives for the (S,G) pair and forwards it down the RPT natively.

Upon receiving the Register-Stop message, the DR stops sending Register messages and starts a Register-Stop timer for the (S,G) pair. The DR periodically sends a Null-Register to the RP. The Null-Register is a Register message with no encapsulated data and with the Null-Register bit set. The Null-Register message is used to probe the RP to determine whether the DR needs to start sending normal Register messages to the RP for the (S,G) pair.

The RP handles receipt of a Null-Register the same way as a normal Register message. It decides whether to send a Register-Stop back to the DR based on the rules described previously. If the RP sends a Register-Stop, the Register-Stop timer on the DR is reset before it expires, and the DR does not start encapsulating data again.

If the Register-Stop is not sent and the DR's Register-Stop timer expires, the DR starts sending normal Register messages with encapsulated data to the RP until it receives another Register-Stop. The purpose of the Null-Register is to avoid having the DR encapsulate data that is not needed by the RP.

4.6   DISTRIBUTION TREE CONSTRUCTION AND TEARDOWN

The model presented in phases 1–3 in Chapter 2 looked at the creation of PIM distribution trees in its simplest form. This section, although it does not cover all possibilities, describes how the protocol reacts in other common scenarios. PIM-SM is a very complex protocol, and covering every possible scenario could fill an entire (very boring) book. The important thing to notice in the four scenarios presented here is that PIM-SM reacts in the same way. This section should reinforce the reader's trust that PIM-SM does behave in the expected manner in the various common situations. If it seems repetitive at times, then that goal is accomplished.

4.6.1   SCENARIO 1: SOURCE COMES ONLINE FIRST, THEN A RECEIVER JOINS

This scenario, shown in Figure 4-1, essentially flips the order of phases 1 and 2 from Chapter 2 (see sections 2.5.1 and 2.5.2). When the source begins to send traffic to a group, G, the DR for its subnet encapsulates the multicast packets in

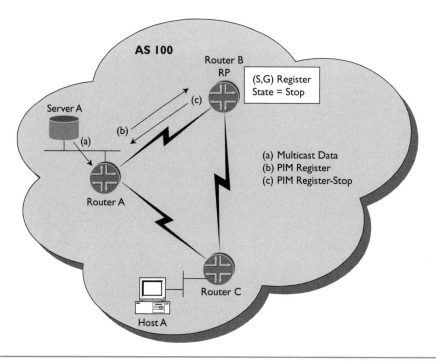

Figure 4-1 Source comes online first.

Register messages and sends them to the RP. No receivers in the domain have joined the group, so the RP's OIL for (*,G) is empty. The data packets encapsulated in the Register messages are discarded by the RP, and the RP sends a Register-Stop to the DR.

After receiving a Register-Stop message from the RP, the DR stops sending Register messages for the group and initializes its Register-Stop timer. The DR periodically sends a Null-Register message to the RP. If still no receivers have expressed interest in the group, the RP responds with a Register-Stop. The DR reinitializes its Register-Stop timer.

In Figure 4-2, we see that when a receiver wants to join the group, its DR sends a (*,G) Join toward the RP to build an RPT. Upon receiving a (*,G) Join, the RP adds the interface on which it is received to the OIL for (*,G). The RP then joins

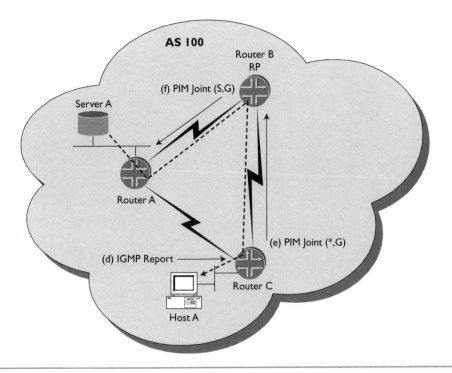

Figure 4-2 Receiver joins existing source. (The dashed line represents data flow after steps d, e, and f are completed.)

the SPT by sending an (S,G) Join toward the source. The RP is now receiving traffic natively via the SPT and distributing it down the RPT.

In Figure 4-3, the receiver's DR is now receiving the data packets via the RPT. If the multicast data exceeds a threshold, the receiver's DR can send a Join message toward the source to form the SPT. Since Cisco Systems and Juniper Networks routers have this threshold set to 0 by default, the DR joins the SPT as soon as it receives the first multicast packet via the RPT. Subsequent scenarios assume the DR's SPT switchover threshold is 0. Once the receiver's DR starts receiving packets down the SPT, it prunes the data received by this source on the RPT. It does this by sending an (S,G,RPT) Prune toward the RP. (S,G,RPT) Prune is a special message that ensures only this one source is removed from the RPT because multiple sources may be transmitted down the RPT.

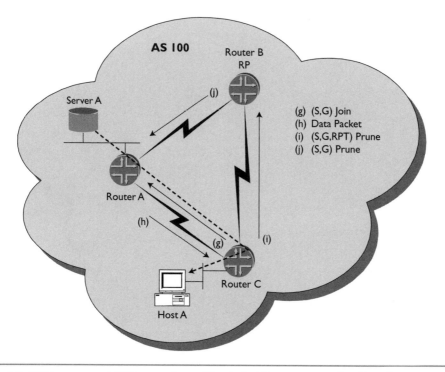

Figure 4-3 SPT is set up, and RPT is torn down. (The dashed line represents data flow after steps g, h, i, and j are completed.)

4.6.2 SCENARIO 2: SECOND RECEIVER JOINS AFTER SPT IS SET UP FOR ANOTHER RECEIVER

In this scenario, the SPT has already been constructed for a single member of group G. The receiver's DR has pruned the RPT. Assuming that the SPT and RPT do not share the same path, the RP has an empty OIL for its (*,G) state.

Now a second receiver in a different part of the network wants to join group G. The DR for this receiver sends a (*,G) Join message toward the RP creating the RPT. The RP once again adds this interface to the OIL for (*,G) and joins the SPT by sending an (S,G) Join toward the source if it has not already done so. After the second receiver's DR receives the first data packets via the RPT, it also sends an

(S,G) Join toward the source to complete its branch of the SPT. It prunes the RPT once packets are delivered via the SPT.

Throughout all these actions, the first receiver is unaffected. It continues to receive packets down its branch of the SPT. The SPT now has two branches. There is exactly one router in the network with two interfaces in its OIL for the source-group pair.

4.6.3 SCENARIO 3: RECEIVER ENDS GROUP MEMBERSHIP

In this scenario, the SPT is set up, and a receiver leaves the group. Its DR determines if it still needs to be a node on the SPT by inspecting its OIL for (S,G) state. If this list is empty, there is no need for it to be part of the SPT, and it sends a (S,G) Prune to its RPF neighbor for the source.

The router that receives this message removes the interface on which it was received from its (S,G) OIL. If this list is now empty, the router forwards an (S,G) Prune to its RPF neighbor for the source.

This process continues until a router along the SPT has a non-null OIL for (S,G) and still needs to be a node on the SPT. Otherwise, the SPT is completely pruned.

4.6.4 SCENARIO 4: CONFERENCE MODEL

In this scenario, all of the sources are also group members, which enables the application on each host to easily communicate with all other hosts joining the conference. The multicast delivery model described so far has been the lecture model, where there is a single source and multiple interested receivers.

With the conference model, each member of the conference can have a separate SPT. All the SPTs are used to deliver traffic for the same group, but each one is dedicated to a specific source. Each SPT is rooted at one of the participants in the conference and has branches to every other participant.

The SPTs are constructed in the same manner described in earlier scenarios.

4.7 DESIGNATED ROUTERS AND HELLO MESSAGES

PIM **Hello messages** are sent periodically on each interface that has PIM enabled. The primary purpose of Hello messages is to announce each router's existence on the subnet as a PIM router, so all routers can decide on a single DR for the subnet.

PIM Hello messages are sent on both multiaccess and point-to-point interfaces. Hello messages are sent to the multicast address 224.0.0.13 (ALL-PIM-ROUTERS group) with a TTL of 1. When a router first boots or is first configured for PIM, it sends out the initial Hello message and then sets its Hello timer to 30 seconds (the default).

Each time the Hello timer counts down to 0, Hello messages are sent out, and the timer is reset. If a router does not hear from a neighbor for a period of 3.5 times the Hello timer (105 seconds is the default), the neighbor is dropped (possibly causing the election of a new DR).

> **Note:** This hold-time value is actually carried in the Hello message, so routers on the same subnet can have different hold timers and not experience problems with incorrectly dropping neighbors.

The Hello messages contain the configured DR priority of the router sending the message. The router with the highest DR priority is elected DR for the subnet. If any of the routers does not support the DR priority option, the DR is the router with the highest IP address.

> **Note:** Each router on the subnet elects the DR, and the election results are never communicated to the other routers on the subnet. This is not a problem as long as each router has the same information and uses the same algorithm to determine the DR.

If the IP address of an interface is changed, the router first sends a Hello message from the old address with a hold-time of 0, which forces the other routers on the subnet to immediately purge the old address from their neighbor tables. Then a Hello message with the new address and standard hold-time is sent. Each time the neighbor table is changed, each router runs through the DR election algorithm again.

If a router loses its DR status, it no longer sends Register messages for new sources to the RP. It also stops sending (null) Registers for current sources on the subnet.

4.8   PIM ASSERT MESSAGES

PIM **Assert messages** are needed for multiaccess networks that serve as a transit for multicast traffic. Ordinarily, multiaccess networks (in the form of LANs such as Ethernet) serve as end-points of distribution trees, housing multiple hosts serving as either receivers or sources; typically only one or two routers provide access to the rest of the Internet for the hosts.

It is not uncommon, though, for a multiaccess network to connect multiple routers and no hosts. These transit LANs introduce a number of complications for setting up multicast distribution trees as compared to point-to-point links.

The PIM assert mechanism accomplishes the following tasks:

1. Recognizes when multiple routers are forwarding duplicate multicast data packets to a transit LAN
2. Holds an election to choose a single forwarder for the LAN
3. Advertises the winner of the election to all routers on the LAN
4. Overrides the RPF rules; PIM Join/Prune messages for the group are sent to the assert election winner instead of the RPF neighbor

If the assert mechanism were not available, problems could arise that involve data packets being forwarded to the LAN by two different routers. The following three situations lead to duplicate packets being forwarded to a transit LAN:

1. One router may send a (*,G) Join to its RPF neighbor for the RP, while another router on the same LAN sends an (S,G) Join to its RPF neighbor for the source. If the RPF neighbor for the RP and the source are different routers, redundant traffic will be delivered to the LAN.

2. Two routers on a LAN can have different RPF neighbors for the RP (which should be the case only when the **routing policy** is designed poorly). If both of these routers send a (*,G) Join to their respective RPF neighbor for the RP, the same multicast traffic is delivered to the LAN twice.

3. Problem 2 can also occur if two routers on the LAN have different RPF neighbors for the source and send (S,G) Joins. This situation can be common on MIXs.

Figure 4-4 illustrates a network topology that could easily lead to the occurrence of problem 1 in the preceding list.

In Figure 4-4, router A is the RPF neighbor for the source for both router C and router D. Router B is the RPF neighbor for the RP for both router C and router D. Receiver A announces its interest first, and the PIM-SM process builds an SPT from the source, through router A and router C to receiver A.

Receiver B then joins the group, and router D sends a (*,G) Join to router B. Without the PIM assert mechanism, every packet from the source would hit the LAN twice, once down the SPT and once down the RPT, until router D joined the SPT and pruned the RPT.

The fix for all three of these problems is to ensure that only one router delivers packets from a specific source to the LAN. PIM-SM does not prevent routers from sending the Joins that cause these problems. Instead, the routers delivering the duplicate packets to the LAN notice this and elect a single forwarder between them. The election rules are as follows:

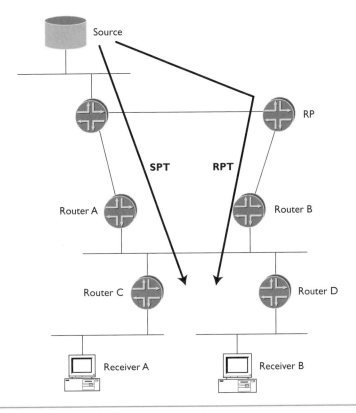

Figure 4-4 Situation that requires the PIM assert mechanism

- If only one router has (S,G) state, it is the elected forwarder.
- If more than one router has (S,G) state, the one with the best metric to the source is the elected forwarder.
- If none of the routers has (S,G) state, the one with the best metric to the RP is the elected forwarder.

The Assert messages used for this election also broadcast the assert election winner to the downstream routers. All downstream routers then send subsequent Joins to the winner of the assert election.

The Assert message is sent to the same group as the data packets. The Assert message has fields to encode the group address, source address, and metric. It also has a bit that indicates whether this router is forwarding via the SPT or the RPT.

4.9 MULTICAST SCOPING

Multicast scoping enables a network operator to configure interfaces not to receive or transmit packets for specific multicast groups. These routers are boundaries for the groups specified in the configuration. RFC 2365, "Administratively Scoped IP Multicast," is the specification for this functionality.

When a router is configured to scope group G on an interface, the router does not forward packets destined for G out the interface nor does it accept packets destined for G received on the interface. This is to say that multicast scoping is bidirectional. The router does not accept any Join messages received on the boundary interface for group G. If group G is a dense group, the router prunes the boundary interface from the OIL for group G.

Multicast scoping enables selected groups to remain within the domain without fear of the data being leaked outside the domain. Receivers within the domain will not receive data from external sources.

A router can be configured for multicast scoping on any range of group addresses on any of its interfaces. All routers on the boundary of a domain with one or more connections to routers in other PIM domains should share the same scoping configuration on their boundary interfaces. If auto-RP is enabled in a PIM-SM domain, multicast scoping should be used to block all packets destined for 224.0.1.39 and 224.0.1.40 from entering or leaving the domain. This prevents the accidental leaking of control packets to other domains.

Prior to the availability of multicast scoping, the only way to achieve the same effect was to use the TTL field in the IP header. This sloppy solution was hard to maintain because the network diameter is different from each router's perspective. The intended purpose of TTL is to eventually discard packets caught in a routing loop. Using TTL for any other reason is not good practice because it may not always produce desired results and can waste bandwidth.

RFC 2365 defines addresses within the 239/8 address range as administratively scoped. Packets destined for these addresses should not be forwarded beyond an administratively defined boundary, which is somewhat analogous to a private unicast address space, such as 10/8. Further subranges within 239/8 are defined with additional scoping classification. The 224.0.0/24 address range has link-local scope. Packets destined for these addresses should never be forwarded outside a LAN by a router.

Multicast Source Discovery Protocol (MSDP)

This chapter describes MSDP in depth. MSDP establishes a mechanism to connect multiple PIM-SM domains. With MSDP, each PIM-SM domain has its own RP and does not rely on the RP of another organization's network.

5.1 INTRODUCTION

In PIM-SM, the RP is configured to serve a range of multicast groups. The RP is responsible for knowing all of the active sources of all multicast groups in this range. There can be only one active RP for a given group. This requirement of PIM-SM presents interesting challenges when trying to support redundancy, load balancing, and interdomain connectivity. MSDP was developed to address these challenges.

Before MSDP, one technique for achieving IMR was to connect each ISP's RP on a multiaccess interface at a multicast peering exchange. This multiaccess interface was configured for PIM-DM so each RP could flood its source information to all other RPs on this interconnecting LAN.

The limitations of this hybrid PIM-SM/PIM-DM approach are obvious. First, an RP is forced to sit at the edge of the domain. Ideally, the RP is placed in a well-connected part of the core of a network to minimize suboptimal routing on the shared tree. Second, only one RP can be in each domain, and it must be located at a single interconnect point for all multicast domains in the Internet. This single interconnect limits the redundancy and scalability of each domain individually *and* collectively. Imagine what would happen if this LAN failed!

Another approach that might have been considered would create a centralized RP shared by all ISPs. Aside from the scalability issues of this idea, ISPs would not like relying on a third party for RP service. The concept of owning and managing their own RPs is important to network operators.

MSDP introduced the ability for RPs to connect to one another and to exchange information about the active sources in their respective PIM-SM domains. With this capability, each domain can have one or more RPs, enabling support for redundancy, load balancing, and interdomain connectivity.

At the time of writing, MSDP is defined in an IETF Internet-Draft (draft-ietf-msdp-spec-13.txt). The evolution of this protocol has been interesting, to say the least. The implementations of Juniper Networks and Cisco Systems are based on version 2 of the original draft. Certain items in later versions of the draft have been added to these implementations along with undocumented optimizations based on deployment experience. Other implementations have been reported to be based on later versions of the draft. By supporting various components of various versions of the specification, no implementation operates exactly the same. Despite all this, these implementations generally interoperate with one another.

The discussion in this chapter is based on the current specification but points out any major differences between the current specification and the predominant implementations. At the end of this chapter, we discuss some of the limitations of MSDP and what the future could hold for this protocol.

5.1.1 MSDP OPERATION

MSDP-speaking routers form peer relationships, similar to BGP peers, over a TCP connection. Two MSDP peers can be in the same PIM-SM domain or in two separate domains. Within a domain, MSDP enables creation of multiple RPs, facilitating redundancy and load balancing. Anycast RP is the primary example of intradomain MSDP. Between different domains, MSDP enables RPs to exchange source information from their respective domains, allowing interdomain source discovery to occur.

An RP that wants to participate in IMR must speak MSDP. However, an MSDP speaker does not necessarily have to be an RP. Non-RP routers can be configured for MSDP, which may be useful in a domain that does not support multicast sources but does support multicast transit. A non-RP MSDP speaker does not originate any source information but provides transit for source information from other domains.

When an MSDP-speaking RP receives a PIM Register message, it generates an MSDP Source-Active message for the source-group pair and forwards the message to all of its configured MSDP peers. The SA message contains the source address, the group address, and the address of the RP. Additionally, the encapsulated data in the Register message is copied by the RP into the MSDP SA.

Subsequent Register messages for the same source-group pair do not cause the creation of other SA messages, unless sufficient time has passed since the last SA was sent. More specifically, the router generates another SA only if the SA hold-down timer has expired. Each time the router sends an SA, it resets the SA hold-down timer to a default value of 30 seconds.

Upon receiving an SA message, a router checks to see if the message was received from its MSDP RPF-peer for the originator of the message. The rules used for determining the MSDP RPF-peer are different from those used for determining the PIM RPF neighbor. The rules are explained in detail in section 5.4. If the SA is received from a peer other than the RPF peer, the SA is ignored and discarded.

On the other hand, if the message was indeed received from its RPF peer, the SA is forwarded to all other MSDP peers. The process of sending SA messages to all other MSDP peers if received from the appropriate peer is known as **peer-RPF flooding**. Peer-RPF flooding guarantees the SA message will be delivered throughout the Internet but will not be unnecessarily looped back toward the originator of the message.

If the MSDP-speaking router receiving an SA happens to be an RP, additional processing of the MSDP SA message may be required. The RP determines if its domain has any interested members of the groups included in the message. If so, the RP forwards the encapsulated data packet contained within the message down the RPT for the group and sends a PIM (S,G) Join message toward its RPF neighbor for the source to join the SPT.

MSDP announces the existence of multicast sources. It does not announce the presence of multicast receivers, which is an advantage because the nature of multicast is to have fewer sources than receivers. Some PIM-SM domains do not have any multicast sources (or do not have any multicast sources that need to be announced to the rest of the Internet). MSDP provides an added advantage to these receiver-only domains because they can receive data without advertising group membership to the rest of the Internet.

Earlier drafts of MSDP did not require that every MSDP-speaking router maintain global source state. Routers were not required to maintain a cache of the information received within MSDP SA messages. If a noncaching RP receives a PIM Join message from an interested receiver in its domain, it sends an SA-Request message to an MSDP peer to request source information for that group. An SA-caching MSDP-speaker that receives an SA-Request message replies with an SA-Response message that contains the set of all SA entries it has for the requested group.

Caching SA messages reduces join latency since the RP that receives a PIM Join can quickly determine all the sources for the requested group by looking in its own SA cache without having to ask other MSDP peers. Thus receivers in this domain are delivered multicast traffic much more quickly. SA caching is also helpful when troubleshooting problems related to MSDP. Without a cache, MSDP message tracing is needed to identify the reception of each SA.

Because of these advantages, the more recent versions of the MSDP specification explicitly require SA caching. Nearly all MSDP deployments have enabled

SA caching. MSDP-speaking Juniper Networks routers implement mandatory SA caching, and this behavior cannot be disabled. On Cisco Systems routers, SA caching is a configurable option.

The disadvantage of SA caching is increased state. A caching router maintains state for every source on the Internet. This method has brought into question the ability of MSDP to scale to millions of sources and provides the potential for SA storms, which are discussed in section 5.7.

5.2 MSDP PEERING SESSIONS

The MSDP peer with the higher IP address listens for new connections on the well-known MSDP TCP port 639. The MSDP peer with the lower address repeatedly attempts to initiate a TCP session with its peer on port 639. This method prevents TCP session set-up collisions, which occur when both sides initiate a connection at approximately the same time and one session has to be dropped (as is the case with the setup of BGP peering sessions). The drawback is a possible longer set-up time for the passive (higher IP address) side of the connection.

The MSDP peer state machine has the following five possible states:

- **DISABLED:** MSDP peer is not configured.
- **INACTIVE:** MSDP peer is configured but not listening or connecting.
- **CONNECT:** Active peer attempts to initiate TCP session.
- **LISTEN:** Passive peer is configured and listening on TCP port 639.
- **ESTABLISHED:** TCP session is established.

The normal, successful state transition for the passive peer is as follows:

1. DISABLED
2. INACTIVE
3. LISTEN
4. ESTABLISHED

For the active peer (lower IP address), the normal, successful state transition is:

1. DISABLED
2. INACTIVE
3. CONNECT
4. ESTABLISHED

The active peer swaps between the INACTIVE and CONNECT states until the passive peer accepts the connection. Each time the active peer reverts from CONNECT to INACTIVE state, the active peer waits a default of 30 seconds before trying to connect again.

5.3 THE MSDP SA MESSAGE

Like IS-IS, MSDP messages use structures known as **type-length values (TLVs)**. The packet format of the MSDP SA message is as follows:

```
 0 1 2 3 4 5 6 7 8 9 0 1 2 3 4 5 6 7 8 9 0 1 2 3 4 5 6 7 8 9 0 1
+-+-+-+-+-+-+-+-+-+-+-+-+-+-+-+-+-+-+-+-+-+-+-+-+-+-+-+-+-+-+-+-+
|     Type      |            Length             |  Entry Count  |
+-+-+-+-+-+-+-+-+-+-+-+-+-+-+-+-+-+-+-+-+-+-+-+-+-+-+-+-+-+-+-+-+
|                          RP Address                           |
+-+-+-+-+-+-+-+-+-+-+-+-+-+-+-+-+-+-+-+-+-+-+-+-+-+-+-+-+-+-+-+-+
|                        Reserved               |  Sprefix Len  |
+-+-+-+-+-+-+-+-+-+-+-+-+-+-+-+-+-+-+-+-+-+-+-+-+-+-+-+-+-+-+-+-+
|                        Group Address                          |
+-+-+-+-+-+-+-+-+-+-+-+-+-+-+-+-+-+-+-+-+-+-+-+-+-+-+-+-+-+-+-+-+
|                        Source Address                         |
+-+-+-+-+-+-+-+-+-+-+-+-+-+-+-+-+-+-+-+-+-+-+-+-+-+-+-+-+-+-+-+-+
|                                                               |
|                                                               |
|                   Encapsulated Data Packet                    |
|                                                               |
|                                                               |
+-+-+-+-+-+-+-+-+-+-+-+-+-+-+-+-+-+-+-+-+-+-+-+-+-+-+-+-+-+-+-+-+
```

The first byte is the message Type code. The Length field contains the length of the MSDP SA message in octets. The length includes everything from the Type field to the end of the encapsulated data packet. Entry Count is the number of source-group pairs listed in the message. Each source-group pair is encoded with its own Reserved and Sprefix Len (source address prefix length) fields. Each source-group pair adds 12 octets to the length of the SA message.

The RP Address field indicates the address of the router that created the SA. When originating an SA message, the address selected for this field might not be the address used for the purposes of the PIM-SM RP. For example, in the case of anycast RP, the address placed in the RP Address field of the SA message should be the unique local address of the RP, not the anycast address. In some implementations, a router discards a received SA message that contains an RP address that matches one of its own addresses. To better illustrate, imagine the following scenario.

Routers A and B are anycast RPs. When a PIM-SM DR sends Register messages to router A, an SA message is created by router A and forwarded to its MSDP peers, including router B. If router A places the anycast address in the RP Address field of the SA, router B sees its own address in this received message. Believing this might be a looped or spoofed SA message, router B may discard this message.[1] If, on the other hand, router A places its own unique loopback address in the RP Address field of the SA, router B will clearly see that this message is originated by another router and will accept the message.

The Reserved field is all zeros and the Sprefix Len field is always 32 (0x20). The Group Address field encodes the group address. The Source Address field encodes the source address.

5.4 DETERMINING THE RPF PEER

The nature of MSDP is to flood SA messages to all peers except the peer from which the SA was received. Because of this behavior, it is possible for an MSDP-speaking router to receive SA messages containing duplicate information from one or more of its peers, which is normal operation of the protocol. However, if the router were to accept and flood all of these duplicate messages, it would cause

---

1. Discarding an SA message for this reason is not the behavior of all implementations.

unneeded traffic on the network. The problem would grow exponentially with complex meshes of MSDP peers. To avoid this problem, MSDP uses peer-RPF flooding to choose a peer from which to accept an SA message containing certain information.

The originating RP contained in the SA message is used to determine the RPF peer. All SA messages with the same originating RP have the same RPF peer. An SA message is accepted and forwarded to other peers only if it was received from the RPF peer; otherwise, it is ignored and silently discarded.

The rules for determining the RPF peer of a particular SA message have changed considerably throughout the revisions of the MSDP specification. As stated earlier, at the time of writing, the MSDP implementations of Juniper Networks and Cisco Systems follow version 2 of the MSDP specification (draft-ietf-msdp-spec-02.txt). This draft has now expired and is no longer available on the IETF's Web site. One easy way to find it is by searching by name for the draft at *http://www.google.com*.

The core aspects of the RPF-peer rules have remained the same throughout the various revisions of the specification. When an SA is received, the rules are evaluated in order against all MSDP peers. The only information that is considered from the SA message is the originating RP address. The source and group addresses are not involved in determining the RPF peer. The peer that matches the earliest rule is declared the RPF peer for the originating RP. SA messages are accepted and forwarded only when received from the RPF peer. The specifics of the rules have changed quite a bit, but all of these core guidelines have stayed intact.

These changes cause implementations based on varying versions of the draft to act differently. It is important to know which version of the draft your vendor supports. This information can be found in the vendor's technical publications.

5.4.1 THE CURRENT VERSIONS RPF-PEER RULES

Figure 5-1 represents a basic internetwork containing MSDP speakers. Figure 5-1 is used to discuss the RPF-peer rules. With each rule, we provide a subsequent figure, based on Figure 5-1, to illustrate the specific situation.

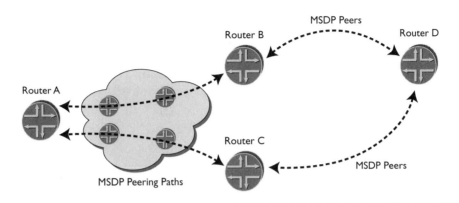

Figure 5-1 Network for explaining RPF-peer rules

All rules are examined from the perspective of router D. Router D has only two peers, which simplifies the explanation of the rules. The rules are applied to all MSDP peers that are in ESTABLISHED state at the time that the SA is received. Figure 5-1 is a generic diagram that does not include information about BGP peering sessions or other details on unicast routing that affect MSDP RPF-peer selection. These details are filled in as we discuss the rules.

The MSDP peering paths denoted in the figure are simply a chain of routers that provide MSDP connectivity from router A to router B and from router A to router C. In this discussion, we are interested only in router D's RPF-peer decision, but keep in mind that each router must make its own independent decision.

Each rule can select only one peer, if any. It is important to note the first rule that matches is the RPF peer. Because of these two facts, the RPF-peer rules select only a single peer as the RPF peer.

5.4.1.1 RPF-Peer Rule #1: If the originating RP is a peer, it is the RPF peer The first rule is simple. If router D is an MSDP peer with the originating RP, it uses the originating RP as its RPF peer. For example, if router B were the originating RP, it would be router D's RPF peer for all the SAs router B originates.

For the rest of the rules, we assume that router A is the originating RP of an SA message that router D just received from both router B and router C. Router D uses the rules described in the following sections to determine whether to accept the SA from router B or from router C.

5.4.1.2 RPF-Peer Rule #2: If the BGP next hop toward the originating RP is a peer, it is the RPF peer

If any peer is the BGP next hop of the active RPF route for router A's address, that peer is selected as the RPF peer. The BGP next-hop attribute is normally set to the address of BGP peer that advertised the route into the AS. This is not the case if the local AS uses a next-hop-self policy. If a next-hop-self policy is used, the BGP next-hop attribute is set to the address of the **Internal Border Gateway Protocol (IBGP)** peer that received the route from a neighboring AS.

To illustrate this rule, in Figure 5-2, we add more detail about the BGP topology to the original figure depicted in Figure 5-1.

Assuming that the route for router A's address is learned through router B, rule 2 is fulfilled. The only question is "by which router?" If standard BGP policy is used, router B is chosen as the RPF peer because it is the BGP next hop. However, if router C implements a next-hop-self policy, router C is chosen as the RPF peer.

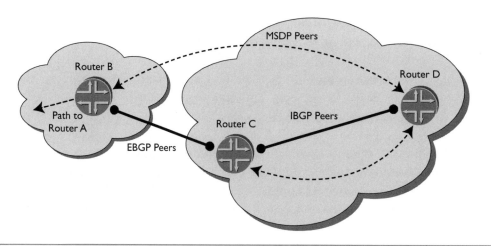

Figure 5-2 RPF-peer rule #2

5.4.1.3 RPF-Peer Rule #3: If the BGP peer that advertised the route toward the originating RP is a peer, it is the RPF peer At first glance, rule #3 looks identical to rule #2, but keep in mind that while routes learned from EBGP peers always have the BGP next hop set to the peer address, IBGP does not follow the same rules. An IBGP peer sets the next-hop attribute to be itself only if a next-hop-self policy is used. Additionally, if **route reflection** or confederations are used, it is possible to receive a route from an IBGP peer that has the next-hop attribute set to something other than that peer's address. To illustrate this rule, consider Figure 5-3, in which the MSDP session between router B and router D is removed.

This time router C does not implement a next-hop-self policy. Therefore the BGP next hop for the route to router A is router B's address and not router C's address. Because of this, rule #2 does not match any of router D's ESTABLISHED MSDP peers. Rule #3 is needed in order to accept SA messages originated by router A.

To increase your understanding of the RPF-peer rules, take a moment to sketch a diagram that shows how rule #3 could be applied in a domain where **route**

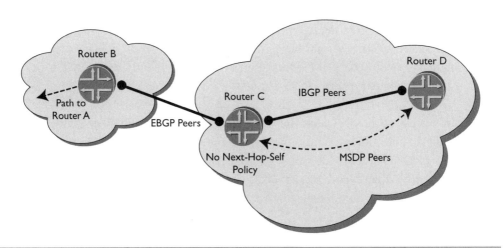

Figure 5-3 RPF-peer rule #3

reflectors are used. Once that diagram is complete, point out an MSDP peering session that could be added to make rule #2 determine the choice of the RPF peer instead of rule #3.

> **Note:** The original purpose of MSDP was to announce sources across multiple PIM-SM domains, but the protocol can also be used in the intradomain case. For example, the PIM's anycast RP mechanism relies on MSDP to announce sources between the multiple RPs in the domain. The main difference in the intradomain case is that the route to the originating RP is most likely not learned through BGP. Instead, it is learned via an IGP. If the IGP is a link-state protocol, either rule #1, static RPF peer, or **mesh groups** must be used. If the IGP is a **distance-vector protocol** (**DV protocol**), rule #3 can be used. Specifically, the RPF peer is the neighbor that advertised the route. This doesn't seem very attractive considering that the neighbors would have to be directly connected, and the primary goal of anycast RP is to provide load balancing and failover with routers in different topological locations.

5.4.1.4 RPF-Peer Rule #4: Of all the MSDP peers in the AS path toward the originating RP, the one with the highest IP address is the RPF peer

This rule is sort of a last-ditch effort to find some peer that is closer to the originating RP than the local router. In general, the design of an MSDP architecture should not rely on this rule. It is handy in a few situations, though. Looking back at Figure 5-1 and changing the underlying BGP topology, this rule is illustrated in Figure 5-4.

In this case, router B and router C are router D's only MSDP peers. Furthermore, router B and router C cannot both be in the AS path for router D's route to router A. In Figure 5-4, let's assume that the path via router B is shorter and therefore is the AS path of router D's route to router A. In this case, router B is the only peer in the AS path toward router A, so it is selected as the RPF peer.

So how does router D know in which AS router B is located? After all, MSDP does not carry AS information in any of its messages like BGP does. There are a

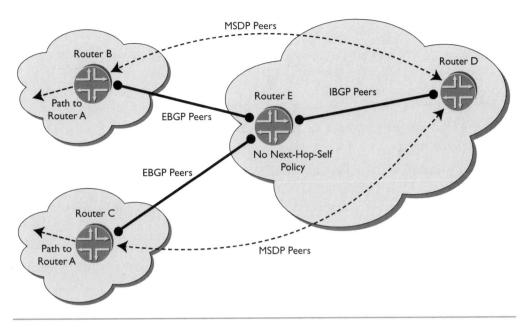

Figure 5-4 RPF-peer rule #4

few possible ways to determine in which AS each MSDP peer is located. One is to enable the user to specify the AS of each peer in the configuration file of the router. Another is to have the router check the route to the peer and extract the information from the AS path of that route. The latter strategy is dangerous because the route to the peer may change and information may get out of synch. In the event router B and router C are in the same AS, the router with the highest IP address is selected as RPF peer as a final tiebreaker.

5.4.1.5 RPF-Peer Rule #5: If a static RPF peer is configured for the originating RP, it is the RPF peer The fifth and final rule is a simple one. MSDP enables the configuration of static RPF peers. Each static RPF peer has a prefix range associated with it. That prefix range designates to which originating RPs the static RPF-peer configuration applies. If the prefix range is 0.0.0.0/0, the static RPF peer applies to all originating RP addresses and is called a *default RPF peer.*

5.4.2 RPF RULES FROM DRAFT VERSION 2

As mentioned earlier, Juniper Networks and Cisco Systems currently implement version 2 of the MSDP specification. Version 2 of the draft states the following RPF-peer forwarding rules:

1. If the originating RP is an MSDP peer of the local router, the originating RP is the RPF peer.

2. If one of the local router's MSDP peers is in the AS located first in the AS path of the MBGP route for the originating RP, that local router's MSDP peer is the RPF peer. The first AS in the AS path always borders the local router's AS.

3. If one of the local router's MSDP peers is also an IBGP peer and is advertising the active MBGP route for the originating RP's address, that local router's MSDP peer is the RPF peer.

4. If an MSDP default peer is configured, the default peer is the RPF peer.

These rules are applied in the same manner as the rules in the current draft.

5.4.3 AVOIDING PITFALLS

Three general problems related to the RPF-peer rules can occur when operating an internetwork that uses MSDP:

- **Low severity:** SA is accepted from multiple peers.
  If an SA is accepted from multiple peers, a bug is most likely in the software running on the router that determines the RPF peer. This bug is not critical because traffic can flow, but it does cause redundant exchange of information.

- **High severity:** SA is not accepted from any peers.
  This problem is most likely caused by poor network design. To troubleshoot this problem, first make sure that the SA is received by turning on protocol tracing. Take a look at the BGP attributes for the route to the originating RP. Step through the rules and determine if any of the established MSDP peers meet one of the conditions or use the router's built-in commands to test which peer should be used as the RPF peer.

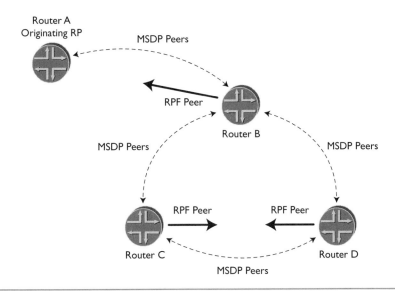

Figure 5-5 RPF-peer loop

- **High severity:** There is an RPF-peer loop (see Figure 5-5).
  This problem occurs when two or more peers are pointing to each other as RPF peers in a circular fashion. To fix this problem, you may need to create an additional MSDP peering session or modify the route information through use of BGP policy. In Figure 5-5, router C and router D are stuck in an RPF-peer loop, and neither accepts SAs originated by router A.

The principle design goal when enabling MSDP on an internetwork is to make sure that the RPF rules are satisfied for all possible originating RPs.

5.5 MESH GROUPS

An MSDP mesh group can be configured for a group of MSDP peers that are completely meshed; that is, each router in the group has an MSDP peering session with every other router in the group. The idea behind mesh groups is borrowed from IS-IS. MSDP mesh groups are able to reduce SA flooding by identifying a group of MSDP peers that are fully meshed. Using the knowledge that certain peers are fully meshed, an MSDP speaker can modify the way it behaves upon receipt of an SA message.

If an SA message is accepted from a nonmesh group peer (per the RPF-peer rules), the message is sent to all mesh group peers. If an SA message is received from a mesh group peer, the message is sent to all nonmesh group peers. If a message is received from a mesh group peer, it is not forwarded back to any other peer in the mesh group. If these fully connected peers were not configured in a mesh group, the copies of the same SA message would be flooded between these peers. Each peer might receive the same SA message from every other peer if a mesh group weren't configured.

While mesh groups were originally created to reduce SA flooding, mesh groups are used today primarily because of a side effect of RPF-peer behavior. SA messages received from mesh group peers are always accepted and are not subject to RPF-peer rules. This relaxation of the RPF rules may be desirable within a domain, for example, where SA messages exchanged between anycast RPs should always be accepted.

Because MSDP RPF-peer rules are so complicated, poorly understood, and difficult to troubleshoot, many ISPs configure anycast RPs in a mesh group to circumvent the RPF rules among these peers. All other peers not in the mesh group are subject to the RPF rules. This method creates what has been referred to as **internal MSDP (IMSDP)** peers and **external MSDP (EMSDP)** peers. The relationship between IMSDP and EMSDP resembles the relationship between IBGP and EBGP.

Mesh groups are somewhat of a necessary evil. A true protocol hack, mesh groups are often used to eliminate the need for complex MSDP/MBGP session interdependencies. However, this mechanism circumvents the entire goal of peer-RPF flooding. Furthermore, mesh groups are not supported in MSDP traceroute, which is briefly described in Chapter 12.

A router can be a member of multiple mesh groups, but this is strongly discouraged in an attempt to avoid SA looping.

5.6   MSDP POLICY

MSDP policy can be enforced using SA message filters. SA filtering can typically be performed on source address, group address, and MSDP peer address. Care should be taken before applying SA filters in transit domains because if the MSDP speakers in the domain where the filtering occurs are the RPF peer for other domains, it can cause loss of connectivity. For example, imagine the following scenario:

- A peer in domain A originates an SA for a local source and sends it to an MSDP peer in domain B.
- The peer in domain B is the RPF peer of domain C for sources in domain A.
- Domain B does not forward this SA to its peer in domain C.

In this scenario, domain C is **blackholed** from sources in domain A. For this reason, it is much better practice to influence the path of interdomain multicast traffic by using an MBGP policy to change the RPF information.

MSDP policy is most useful in preventing the leaking of SA messages that should not leave a local domain. These include SA messages containing the following:

- Sources in private address space (for example, 10/8)
- Groups that are reserved for protocol use (for example, auto-RP groups, 224.0.1.39 and 224.0.1.40)
- Administratively scoped groups (239/8)
- SSM groups (232/8)

It is good practice to apply SA filters to all MSDP sessions with peers outside a domain to prevent SA messages containing these sources or groups from leaking into or out of the domain.

5.7   SA STORMS, RAMEN, AND MSDP RATE LIMITING

Far more destructive than the delicious snack (or meal) for college students that is its namesake, the Ramen worm is a self-propagating program that caused major problems for multicast-enabled networks in early 2001. **Worms** are similar to viruses in that they are annoying or harmful and self-replicating, but they do not attach themselves to other files or programs as viruses do. The intent of Ramen was more to annoy than to harm.

Once Ramen infects a PC, it scans a range of addresses to find other vulnerable hosts to which it can attach itself. Because of sloppy coding in Ramen, multicast addresses can be scanned as well. When Ramen scans a multicast-enabled network, a Register message and an SA message are generated for every multicast address that is scanned. Ramen can scan through a /16 range of addresses in about 15 minutes, causing 65,000+ SAs to be generated. This number is compounded if multiple hosts are infected. This flood of SAs can crash routers that are not able to process all the SA messages.

No satisfactory method exists to proactively avoid such storms. Some networks have applied rate limits to MSDP traffic. However, rate limiting of control packets always provides vulnerability to denial-of-service attacks because the rate limiters cannot tell the difference between good traffic and bad traffic. For instance, imagine a rate limit is applied that allows only 200Kbps of packets to or from TCP port 639 to enter or leave an MSDP-speaking router. If a malicious attacker flooded that router with a high rate of traffic destined for TCP port 639, the allowable limit of MSDP traffic would be filled with useless data. The "good" MSDP packets from valid peers would be dropped as well, causing MSDP sessions to drop. Multicast in this domain would fail to operate properly.

IMR is still in its adolescence. When interdomain *unicast* routing was at the same point in its development, similar growing pains were experienced. MSDP SA storms are roughly analogous to the leaking of bad BGP routes, which is no longer the crippling common occurrence it once was. Over time, vendors augment their implementations, and ISPs develop best practices that reduce the likelihood of network disasters.

Accordingly, the safest current defense against SA storms is vigilance. By monitoring the size of an SA cache and being prepared to take action, such as adding temporary filters when levels become extraordinarily high, networks can become hardened to attack without adding new vulnerabilities.

5.8   OUTLOOK FOR MSDP

MSDP has been affectionately referred to as a *cocktail napkin protocol*. The protocol was created as a temporary solution for multicast routing between PIM-SM domains prior to the advent of SSM. MSDP's ability to scale can best be described as somewhere between "good enough for now" and "a disaster waiting to happen."

MSDP is not needed in SSM. In fact, MSDP is prohibited from advertising source information for SSM groups. The reduced dependence upon MSDP is actually one of the principle benefits of SSM. The arrival of SSM has delayed the necessity for the **Border Gateway Multicast Protocol (BGMP)**. BGMP is the IMR protocol expected to meet the long-term scalability needs of the Internet. BGMP is still in the early development stage, and a full discussion of it is beyond the scope of this book. It is discussed briefly in Chapter 13.

The current stance of the IETF is to use BGMP as the IMR protocol for IPv6. In the meantime, the combination of MSDP and SSM is expected to provide adequate scalability for IMR in IPv4. After all, despite its inherent weaknesses, MSDP has been successfully deployed in many production networks.

Source-Specific Multicast (SSM)

6

To this point in the book, we have generally examined multicast routing from an ASM perspective. With a clear understanding of ASM, the operation and benefits of Source-Specific Multicast (SSM) become very apparent. This chapter describes SSM and how multicast protocols are modified in order to support this service model.

6.1 INTRODUCTION

The original vision for multicast in RFC 1112 supported both one-to-many and many-to-many communication models and has come to be known as Any-Source Multicast (ASM). To support these models, an ASM network must determine all of the sources of a group and deliver all of them to interested listeners. In ASM, this function of source discovery rests squarely in the hands of the network.

We have already seen in Chapter 3 that dense protocols provide source discovery by flooding the actual data to all of the routers in a domain. While it is probably the simplest way to inform all routers of multicast sources, flooding presents significant scalability issues and inefficiently uses network resources. Sparse protocols achieve the same functionality with mechanisms that are much more scalable and efficient but present a substantial amount of added complexity. In PIM-SM, we saw how only one router in the domain (the RP) is responsible for knowing all the multicast sources, and the distribution tree is rooted around that router.

Thus it can be said that the primary shortcomings of dense protocols are inefficiency and lack of scalability, while the primary shortcoming of sparse protocols is complexity. In both cases, the mechanisms that cause these shortcomings are trying to accomplish the same goal: source discovery.

The primary beneficiary of a network-provided source discovery control plane is the many-to-many model, where sources for any given group come and go. However, applications now believed to possess the greatest potential for commercial viability across the Internet generally use the one-to-many model. Thus the primary deficiencies of the ASM do provide certain functionality; however, this functionality is now considered less important for Internet applications.

By ignoring the many-to-many model and focusing on the one-to-many model, the vast majority of "interesting" applications can be supported by mechanisms that are much simpler than those found in ASM. SSM, while supporting a subset of ASM functionality, enables this vision of desired functionality through simplicity. Moreover, SSM provides a number of added benefits as a side effect of having to support only the one-to-many model.

SSM, which is currently defined in an Internet-Draft within the IETF's SSM Working Group (draft-ietf-ssm-arch-00.txt), is a service model that supports one-to-many multicast delivery through the use of shortest path trees (SPTs). While it is theoretically possible to support this service model with any protocol that meets its requirements, SSM is generally supported through a subset of functionality in PIM-SM and IGMPv3. We focus on how these protocols specifically support SSM.

Perhaps to make up for an inherent lack of complexity, a new set of terminology is introduced in SSM that describes the same terms that we have used in ASM. When describing SSM, it is preferred to use the words **subscribe** and **unsubscribe** instead of the ASM terms *join* and *leave*. (This usage of *join* and *leave* should not be confused with the various protocol message names, such as PIM

Join messages and IGMP Leave-Group messages). The idea behind *subscribe* and *unsubscribe* is to differentiate SSM from ASM, even though the operations are identical.

The following table compares ASM and SSM terminology:

Term	Any-Source Multicast (ASM)	Source-Specific Multicast (SSM)
Address identifier	G	S,G
Address designation	group	channel
Receiver operations	join, leave	subscribe, unsubscribe
Group range	224/4 excluding 232/8	224/4[a]

a. SSM is permitted in all of 224/4 but guaranteed only in 232/8.

6.1.1 OVERVIEW OF SSM OPERATION

In SSM, source discovery is provided by some sort of out-of-band means from the perspective of the network; that is, the host is responsible for learning the source and informing the network of its interest in receiving traffic for a group from only the specified source. This source-group pair is now known as an SSM *channel*. The application layer typically provides this function. For example, when clicking on a link in a browser, the client is informed of the source *and* the group (in ASM, the receiver would be informed only of the group). The SSM receiver then uses IGMPv3 to inform the routers on its LAN of its interest in the channel. IGMPv3 has the added capability of specifying the source in report messages.

The network delivers multicast traffic from *only* the specified source. Data from all unspecified sources to the same multicast group must not be delivered to the SSM receiver. Recall from PIM-SM that the receiver's DR initially sends a (*,G) Join toward the RP because it does not know the source. Once it begins receiving multicast traffic down the shared tree, the DR is able to learn the source. The DR can then send an (S,G) Join toward the source and receive traffic down the most efficient SPT.

In SSM, the DR is able to bypass the first step because the receiver initially tells it the source. The DR simply sends an (S,G) Join toward the source and joins the SPT immediately. Notice that no RP was needed, no RPT was built, and MSDP was not used. This simplified process illustrates the drastic reduction of complexity required to deliver packets from source to receiver.

6.1.2 SSM ADDRESSES

The 232/8 range is currently reserved for SSM. While ASM behavior is not permitted in this range, SSM is not limited to this range. SSM can be run with any address in the class D range. However, 232/8 is the only range in which SSM behavior is guaranteed. For example, if a receiver sent an IGMPv3 report for 225.1.1.1 from the source 10.1.1.1, it is permissible for a DR implementation to send a (*,225.1.1.1) Join toward the RP instead of an (S,G) Join toward the source. If there were multiple sources for 225.1.1.1, the DR would transmit traffic from only 10.1.1.1 on the receiver's LAN. While the host receives traffic only from the one specified source, this scenario would not be considered pure SSM because it was delivered along the RPT.

If, on the other hand, a receiver sent an IGMPv3 report for 232.1.1.1 from the source 10.1.1.1, the DR must send a (10.1.1.1,232.1.1.1) Join toward the source. A router that performs any kind of non-SSM behavior in 232/8 is in violation of the SSM spec.

It is possible that someday the address range for SSM may change. In the unlikely event this occurs, the Juniper Networks and Cisco Systems implementations enable the SSM range to be modified through configuration. Finally, addresses in the 232.0.0/24 range are reserved and should not be used.

6.1.3 RPF IN SSM

SSM does not affect the various protocols that can be used to populate the multicast RPF table (for example, MBGP, M-ISIS, DVMRP, static routes). SSM routers still use the RPF neighbor information to forward control packets and build and/or tear down the SPT. Multicast data packets must still enter the router on the correct RPF interface for the source address in the packet. Because SSM never uses shared trees, there is no need to ever perform an RPF check on the RP (unless, of course, the RP becomes an SSM source).

6.1.4 ADVANTAGES AND DISADVANTAGES OF SSM

As we have seen thus far, the greatest benefit of SSM is simplicity. In SSM, there is no need for an RP. Thus the difficult decisions regarding BSR versus auto-RP versus static, anycast, and RP placement are not necessary to support SSM. Furthermore, eliminating the need for MSDP has brought about unanimous acclaim throughout the multicast community. Besides eliminating the need for a complex protocol, there has been widespread concern regarding MSDP's ability to scale to millions of sources.

Simplifying the mechanisms needed to deliver multicast leads to a dramatic reduction in operational costs. Engineers who manage an SSM deployment do not have to learn nearly as many features and operations as they must for an ASM implementation. Further, SSM contains fewer "moving parts." Fewer mechanisms mean fewer bugs. Thus SSM *should* provide more reliable service than ASM.

A number of additional benefits in SSM provide "icing on the cake." First, SSM solves the problem of multicast address allocation, which had long been a headache for the multicast community. In ASM, multicast groups take on global significance. An ASM receiver of 224.1.1.1 would receive the traffic sent by both 10.1.1.1 and 10.2.2.2 if they were both sending packets to this group. Thus ASM requires global coordination in allocating multicast addresses. The recent addition of GLOP to the schemes of SAP/SDP and scoping has enabled the multicast community to consider IPv4 ASM multicast allocation "good enough for now."

The most common case where current ASM address allocation schemes are inadequate occurs when a content provider requires more static group addresses than GLOP can provide. For example, an organization that has reserved only one AS number can derive only a /24 of static multicast addresses using GLOP. If that organization needs 300 static group addresses, only two options exist: Obtain another AS number (which is definitely not the reason AS numbers are assigned), or ask some other AS-possessing organization for the ability to use its GLOP-derived addresses.

In SSM, by contrast, multicast group addresses are no longer globally significant. The source-group *tuple* provides the uniqueness needed to differentiate between SSM channels. The SSM channel (10.1.1.1,232.1.1.1) is completely different from (10.2.2.2,232.1.1.1) because the sources are different. An SSM subscriber to the (10.1.1.1,232.1.1.1) channel would not receive packets for the (10.2.2.2,232.1.1.1) channel unless it explicitly subscribed to it as well.

In SSM, the group address provides only the uniqueness to differentiate different multicast streams from the same source. So if every SSM source in the world were transmitting only a single channel, all of them could theoretically use the same group address. In fact, it may seem like overkill to reserve an entire /8 of addresses for SSM when so few are actually needed. However, recall that every multicast MAC address corresponds to 32 different multicast IP addresses. This oversubscription generally has not caused many problems because the chance of two different multicast groups corresponding to the same MAC address appearing on the same LAN is relatively slim. If SSM sources all selected the same group address, the chance of MAC address collision on LANs would greatly increase. For this reason, it is recommended that SSM sources randomly select from the more than 16.7 million group addresses available in the 232/8 range.

Another major beneficial side effect of SSM is in the area of access control. ASM group members receive traffic from all sources, including the bad ones. A malicious source can easily launch a denial-of-service (DoS) attack on an ASM group by transmitting large amounts of unwanted traffic to that group. This unwanted traffic can fill up the bandwidth of the links connecting to group members and flood members with packets they must process to discard.

ASM's inherent susceptibility to this kind of DoS is not at all a flaw but rather a "feature" that was built in to this model by design. Nevertheless, content providers with one-to-many content have always been wary of this "feature." The guaranteed single-source nature of SSM is a perfect fit for content such as radio and television, where suppression of all other sources is highly desired.

To launch this same type of DoS attack in SSM, a malicious source must spoof the source address of the SSM channel. Moreover, the spoofing source must be on the same path as the real source. Otherwise, the RPF checks performed in each router will determine that the malicious traffic is received on an interface that is not the RPF interface of the real source. As we learned earlier, multicast traffic that is received by a router on an interface other than the RPF interface is always discarded. Thus this type of DoS attack is not impossible, but it is far more difficult to launch in SSM.

After learning of all the wonders of SSM, the usual response is "Sounds too good to be true! What's the catch?" The short answer is that there really is no catch. The long answer involves state, availability, and source discovery.

Recall from Chapter 3 that the SPT always takes the most efficient path but creates more state than the RPT. However, because the predominant implementations of PIM-SM switch from the RPT to the SPT immediately, this SPT state is created anyway. In fact, SSM creates slightly less state in this case because the RPT is never joined in the first place, so no (*,G) state is ever created.

The second caveat to consider with SSM is availability. SSM receivers must support IGMPv3 and have SSM-aware applications. The availability of SSM applications should not be much of a concern. Application developers usually make modifications very quickly when it means that their products will become more powerful and prevalent.

Support of IGMPv3 is a function of the operating system. Without kernel modifications, all Windows operating systems earlier than Windows XP do not support IGMPv3. It may take some time before the majority of hosts on the Internet are enabled for IGMPv3.

Finally, it is important to remember that SSM is really providing only a subset of ASM functionality. While this subset supports the majority of applications believed to be most viable in the near future, plenty of useful applications still rely on many-to-many communication.

Because SDR relies on the ASM SAP mechanism, it cannot function in its current form in an SSM-only environment. Likewise, videoconference and online gaming applications that rely on many-to-many mechanisms must be redesigned to use *many* one-to-many connections to operate in SSM. This change of paradigm should not be too difficult to achieve because the application layer affords the most amount of flexibility to accomplish the task of source discovery.

6.2 IGMPv3 IN SSM

As we have discussed throughout, routers use IGMP to discover directly connected group members. This section details the new features in version 3 of IGMP, which add the ability for a host to subscribe to or unsubscribe from an SSM channel. It is important to note that IGMPv3 is not used solely for SSM. IGMPv3 introduces two new source-filtering modes, *exclude* mode and *include* mode, and only one of them provides SSM functionality.

As stated in Chapter 2, exclude mode enables a host to request traffic for a group from all sources except those specified. Include mode enables a host to request traffic for a group from only specified sources. Include mode with a single specified source is used to support SSM.

To enable SSM functionality, IGMPv3 modifies the format of various messages to enable a host to specify the source address of interest in addition to the group address. IGMPv3 must be running on the host and on the host's directly connected router for SSM functionality to work.

The format of IGMPv3 **Membership Report messages** enables the host to specify both the source address and group address, fully describing the SSM channel. IGMPv3 reports have the following format:

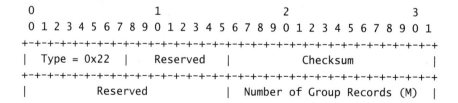

```
+-+-+-+-+-+-+-+-+-+-+-+-+-+-+-+-+-+-+-+-+-+-+-+-+-+-+-+-+-+-+-+-+
|                                                              |
.                                                              .
.                     Group Record [1]                         .
.                                                              .
|                                                              |
+-+-+-+-+-+-+-+-+-+-+-+-+-+-+-+-+-+-+-+-+-+-+-+-+-+-+-+-+-+-+-+-+
|                                                              |
.                                                              .
.                     Group Record [2]                         .
.                                                              .
|                                                              |
+-+-+-+-+-+-+-+-+-+-+-+-+-+-+-+-+-+-+-+-+-+-+-+-+-+-+-+-+-+-+-+-+
|                                 .                            |
.                                 .                            .
|                                 .                            |
+-+-+-+-+-+-+-+-+-+-+-+-+-+-+-+-+-+-+-+-+-+-+-+-+-+-+-+-+-+-+-+-+
|                                                              |
.                                                              .
.                     Group Record [M]                         .
.                                                              .
|                                                              |
+-+-+-+-+-+-+-+-+-+-+-+-+-+-+-+-+-+-+-+-+-+-+-+-+-+-+-+-+-+-+-+-+
```

Where each Group record has the following format:

```
+-+-+-+-+-+-+-+-+-+-+-+-+-+-+-+-+-+-+-+-+-+-+-+-+-+-+-+-+-+-+-+-+
|  Record Type  |   Reserved    |     Number of Sources (N)    |
+-+-+-+-+-+-+-+-+-+-+-+-+-+-+-+-+-+-+-+-+-+-+-+-+-+-+-+-+-+-+-+-+
|                        Multicast Address                     |
+-+-+-+-+-+-+-+-+-+-+-+-+-+-+-+-+-+-+-+-+-+-+-+-+-+-+-+-+-+-+-+-+
|                      Source Address [1]                      |
+-                                                            -+
|                      Source Address [2]                      |
+-                                                            -+
.                                 .                            .
.                                 .                            .
.                                 .                            .
+-                                                            -+
|                      Source Address [N]                      |
+-+-+-+-+-+-+-+-+-+-+-+-+-+-+-+-+-+-+-+-+-+-+-+-+-+-+-+-+-+-+-+-+
```

When a host subscribes to an SSM channel, it sends an IGMPv3 Membership Report message with a single Group record. That Group record specifies the multicast and source address of the channel and is record type 5 (ALLOW_NEW_SOURCES).

As with previous versions of IGMP, the router with the lowest IP address on the subnet is elected querier. The querier periodically sends out IGMPv3 **General Query messages**. These messages do not include any source or group information and are used to check whether interested listeners still exist for both ASM and SSM groups. One of the hosts that has subscribed to an SSM channel responds to every general query with an IGMPv3 Membership Report message with a single Group record. That Group record specifies the multicast group and source address of the channel and is record type 1 (MODE_IS_INCLUDE).

When a host unsubscribes from an SSM channel, it sends an IGMPv3 Membership Report message with a single Group record. That Group record specifies the group and source address of the channel and is record type 6 (BLOCK_OLD_SOURCES).

When the router that was elected querier receives this report describing the host's intent to unsubscribe from the SSM channel, it checks to see if any other hosts on the subnet are still interested in the channel by sending an IGMPv3 Group-and-Source-Specific Query message. If another host has subscribed to the SSM channel, it responds with an IGMPv3 Membership Report message with record type 1 (MODE_IS_INCLUDE). If no other hosts respond, the router stops forwarding the channel onto the LAN.

This following table summarizes the IGMPv3 Membership Report record types and their use for SSM:

Function	Record Type	Record Type Value
Subscribe	ALLOW_NEW_SOURCES	5
Maintain subscription	MODE_IS_INCLUDE	1
Unsubscribe	BLOCK_OLD_SOURCES	6

Note: With regard to ASM, there is no Leave-Group message in IGMPv3 as in IGMPv2. Its functionality is replaced by IGMPv3 Membership Report messages with record type 6 (BLOCK_OLD_SOURCES).

6.2.1 IGMP VERSION COMPATIBILITY

According to the spec, IGMPv3 is backward compatible with earlier versions. In general, a mix of IGMP versions among hosts on a LAN is permissible, while a mix of IGMP versions among routers on a LAN is not recommended.

An IGMPv3-speaking router can successfully provide ASM service to hosts running earlier versions of IGMP. If an IGMPv3 router receives an IGMPv1 or v2 message from a host, it maintains compatibility with that version for that group. However, a host running a previous version of IGMP is not generally aware of the address range reserved for SSM. Thus a host could send a v1 or v2 report message for a group in the SSM range. An SSM router ignores this message because it does not include source-specific information.

If one router on a LAN is configured for IGMPv3, it is recommended that all other routers on the LAN be configured for IGMPv3 as well. If a mixture of IGMP versions is running on the routers sharing a LAN, the querying router must drop to the lowest version of IGMP that is running on a router on the LAN. In this case, the IGMPv3-capable hosts on the subnet revert back to the version of the query messages, thus losing SSM capability.

6.3   PIM-SM IN SSM

Because it was already capable of building SPTs, PIM-SM required very little to be added to support SSM. The additions to PIM-SM for SSM primarily involved defining behavior in the SSM address range.

When a host subscribes to an SSM channel through IGMPv3, the directly connected PIM-SM router (the receiver's DR) initiates the creation of the SPT by sending an (S,G) Join message to its RPF neighbor for the source. The SPT is built hop by hop until it either reaches a router already on the SPT or a router connected to the source itself. Once the SPT is built, data packets for the SSM channel are delivered to the subscribing host.

Shared tree behavior is prohibited for groups in the SSM range. Accordingly, SSM routers must never send (*,G) Joins for groups in the 232/8 range. If an SSM router receives a (*,G) Join for a group in 232/8 (presumably from an ill-behaving router), it ignores the message. Likewise, it ignores nonsource-specific IGMP reports for groups in this range.

The DR for a source must not send Register messages for groups in 232/8. An RP ignores all Register messages and never creates, sends, or accepts an MSDP SA message for a group in this range.

For the most part, this behavior was possible on Juniper Networks and Cisco Systems routers prior to the existence of SSM by configuring filters and policy. Recently, these implementations have simply added commands that enforce SSM behavior in the SSM range in a much simpler and friendlier way. Thus it can be said that these implementations have always supported SSM for all router roles except the receiver's DR, even before SSM came into being.

Likewise, any domain that supports ASM can support SSM with the addition of this minor configuration. Thus the investment of building an RP-based ASM infrastructure does not go to waste, as both of these models can be supported side-by-side.

Finally, the potential of SSM-only deployments is very attractive for networks with engineers who are unfamiliar with multicast. By simply turning on PIM-SM on all router interfaces and configuring the commands that ensure SSM behavior in 232/8, a network can support SSM. The effort required to design, deploy, and operate such a network is minimal. An SSM-only network is also an ideal stepping-stone for deploying an ASM network. In this case, SSM provides the "training wheels" for engineers to become familiar with multicast, which prepares them to handle the far more complex ASM world.

Multiprotocol Extensions for BGP (MBGP)

This chapter describes in detail how routers use MBGP to transfer route information used for the reverse path forwarding (RPF) checks of the PIM and MSDP protocols. RPF checks can be performed on the same routing table used by the router to forward unicast traffic. However, splitting these two functions over two separate tables provides the flexibility to enforce different policies for unicast and multicast traffic and to create incongruent topologies for each.

7.1 OVERVIEW

MBGP is used to populate a separate routing table dedicated for the RPF mechanisms used when forwarding multicast packets, forwarding certain PIM-SM messages, and deciding whether to accept MSDP Source-Active (SA) messages.

The reason for having a dedicated multicast RPF table is to achieve an incongruent next-hop selection for unicast versus multicast RPF routes; that is to say, the next hop used to route unicast packets to prefix P can be different from the next hop used for multicast RPF checks.

This incongruence is advantageous in two situations:

- To avoid routers not capable of multicast routing as multicast RPF next hops but still use them as unicast forwarding next hops
- To use different links and routers for multicast and unicast traffic—for example, where ISPs publicly peer at a Multicast Internet Exchange (MIX) to exchange multicast traffic only

It is completely possible to use PIM-SM and MSDP for multicast routing without MBGP, as long as the next hops for any prefix P can be the same for both unicast forwarding and multicast RPF. However, it is wise to use MBGP from the start, even if it appears that incongruent paths are not a necessity. Topology changes, additional MSDP peers, and so on can potentially lead to such a need in the future. Using MBGP does not force you to have incongruent paths. And if the need arises, it is much easier to modify the policy of an existing MBGP setup than it is to convert from standard BGP to MBGP throughout your network and with all your external peers.

Figure 7-1 shows an example of a common topology where MBGP is quite useful. In this figure, we see that without MBGP, routers in AS 100 using standard BGP for RPF checks would typically select a path through AS 400 to get to

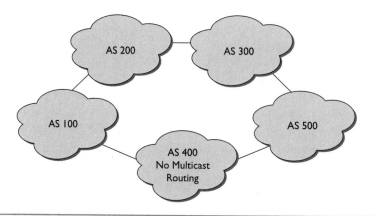

Figure 7-1 Topology with incongruent unicast and multicast paths

sources in AS 500. Because AS 400 is not multicast-enabled, multicast sources in AS 500 would be blackholed for receivers in AS 100. With MBGP, RPF could select the path through AS 200 and AS 300, while unicast routing could continue to use AS 400 to reach AS 500 destinations.

Furthermore, while it is possible to control the unicast and multicast topologies within a domain, the world outside your own autonomous system is a much trickier place. Many of the current deployments on the Internet have used multicast RPF topologies significantly different from those used for unicast routing, especially when connecting to other domains. In practice, this means multicast **multihoming** without MBGP can easily lead to multicast black holes, where RPF selects a path that is not multicast-enabled.

The specification document for MBGP is RFC 2858, "Multiprotocol Extensions for BGP-4." The specification is generic in that the extensions can be used to tag routes for any network layer protocol (IPv4, IPv6, VPN-IPv4, IPX, and so on). Most initial implementations of MBGP supported its use only for distributing information for the IPv4 address family (for both unicast forwarding and multicast RPF). More recently, MBGP has been used to distribute routing information for layer 2- and layer 3-based VPNs.

Because MBGP is an extension to the **BGP4** protocol, it contains all of the features and robustness of BGP, which is a critical feature for ISPs, where engineers are already very familiar and comfortable with BGP. By simply extending the capabilities of a well-understood routing protocol, less training and fewer changes are needed for ISPs to support it. BGP was an excellent candidate for these capabilities. The extensibility built into the original BGP4 specification (RFC 1771) allowed additional path attributes to be added to the BGP Update message. MBGP defines two new path attributes, MP_REACH_NLRI and MP_UNREACH_NLRI. These attributes are explained in section 7.4.

The key concept to understand is that MBGP does not build the incoming and outgoing interface lists for forwarding packets destined to multicast groups. This misconception is common. The building of the IIF and OIL for multicast groups is the function provided by a multicast routing protocol, such as PIM-SM. MBGP does not carry any information related to multicast addresses. You will never find a class D address in an MBGP message. Rather, MBGP merely populates the routing table that a multicast routing protocol like PIM-SM uses when performing RPF checks.

7.1.1 OTHER WAYS TO POPULATE THE MULTICAST RPF TABLE

There are ways other than MBGP to get information into the multicast RPF table of a router. One way is to import directly connected routes into the multicast RPF table, which is an important step because it is the way to generate information for MBGP updates. The routes for directly connected sources should always be imported into the multicast RPF table.

Additionally, if the router is serving as an RP, the local RP address should be placed in the multicast RPF table, which enables MBGP to distribute this information to other peers. Other routers that receive this information then can send PIM-SM Join/Prune messages to their RPF neighbor for both RPT and SPT construction.

The simplest thing to do is to import all directly connected routes into the multicast RPF table. Importing all directly connected routes should not hurt anything. That way if multicast sources crop up where none was expected, multicast routing works without a hitch.

7.1.1.1 Static Routes Static routes provide another way to insert routes into the multicast RPF table. Separate static routes can be defined for the same destination, one for the unicast routing table and one for the multicast RPF table. This enables the network operator to statically configure the RPF neighbor for a source or an RP address, overriding the information in the unicast routing table.

The use of static routes for multicast RPF suffers from the same drawbacks as using static routes for unicast routing. Network topology is constantly changing. Dynamic routing protocols automatically adapt to such changes, but static routes require human intervention when topology changes occur. Thus the use of dynamic routing protocols to populate the multicast RPF table is preferred over static routing for the same reasons that dynamic protocols are preferred for uni-cast routing.

7.1.1.2 DVMRP   As mentioned in Chapter 3, DVMRP has a built-in mecha-nism for populating its own multicast RPF table. DVMRP can be run in route-exchange-only (sometimes called *unicast-only*) mode, and PIM can leverage this information for use in determining RPF neighbors.

Our interest here in DVMRP is not in its ability to set up forwarding state for mul-ticast packets. Instead, we are interested in using DVMRP to populate the dedi-cated multicast RPF table, which is then used by protocols such as PIM-SM and MSDP. To be used this way, DVMRP should be switched to unicast routing mode .

DVMRP uses a distance-vector algorithm on the reverse path to the sender to de-termine the shortest path for multicast packets to take. This unicast routing mode works much like RIP. One difference is that DVMRP's maximum network diameter is 32 compared with RIP's 16. A DVMRP metric of 32 equals infinity (that is, the network is unreachable).

It is important to note DVMRP does not tag routes as belonging to either the multicast RPF or the unicast table. Instead, all unicast routes learned from DVMRP are automatically assumed to belong to the multicast RPF table. DVMRP routes are never used to forward unicast packets.

DVMRP suffers from the same drawbacks as other distance-vector protocols. Most notably, convergence is much slower, and the metric of hop count is very limiting compared with that found in link-state routing protocols. Most produc-tion networks run a **link-state protocol** as their IGP (either IS-IS or OSPF). It is also preferable to run a link-state protocol to populate the multicast RPF table with the addresses of sources and RPs within an AS.

7.1.1.3 Link-State Protocols   MBGP, and BGP in general, is much more adept at making inter-AS-path decisions. Static routing and DVMRP have lim-ited usefulness in real networks. IS-IS's use of TLV (type-length values) fields to carry its information makes it more easily extensible than OSPF. Multitopology

Routing in IS-IS (M-ISIS) is specified in an Internet-Draft and is discussed in detail in Chapter 8. M-ISIS currently is the best IGP choice for a multicast-enabled network.

A huge advantage of running a multicast-intelligent IGP, such as M-ISIS, is that the BGP next hop of an MBGP route might not be directly connected. In this situation, MBGP does a **recursive lookup** on the information from the IGP to determine the directly connected next hop. If the IGP is not multicast-intelligent, the IGP's best path to the BGP next hop possibly is not a multicast-capable path. With a multicast-intelligent IGP such as M-ISIS, this problem can be avoided. Unicast packets take the true best path, while multicast distribution trees are set up on the best multicast-capable path.

At the time of writing, no comparable extensions to the OSPF protocol are available. **Multicast Extensions to OSPF (MOSPF)**, defined in RFC 1584, is a multicast routing protocol (like PIM or DVMRP). MOSPF does not provide an equivalent function to M-ISIS; it does not solely populate the multicast RPF table. Discussion of MOSPF is outside the scope of this book, as this protocol has not been widely implemented or deployed.

7.1.2 JUNIPER NETWORKS AND CISCO SYSTEMS CONVENTIONS

There is a fundamental difference between the way Juniper Networks and Cisco Systems implement routing tables.

7.1.2.1 Juniper Networks Conventions In Juniper Network's **JUNOS** operating system, various routing tables are built, each for a specific purpose and a specific routed protocol (for example, IPv4, IPv6, MPLS [Multiprotocol Label Switching], or ISO **CLNS [Connectionless Network Service]**). Each routing table can be populated with information from various routing protocols. A specific routing table, named "inet.2," is used for RPF checks. The inet.2 table can be populated by various routing protocols including static routes, DVMRP, MBGP, and M-ISIS. The route used for an RPF check of source address, S, is the route with the longest mask in the inet.2 table that encompasses S. If more than one routing protocol provides the route with the longest mask, the route from the preferred protocol—the one with the lower preference value—is selected as the active route.

> **Note:** Comparing route metrics of two different routing protocols is like comparing apples and oranges. When multiple routing protocols provide a route to a prefix and the mask lengths are equal, the active route is selected based on protocol preference rather than route metric. In the JUNOS operating system, protocol preference is termed *preference.* In Cisco Internetwork Operating System (IOS), protocol preference is termed *administrative distance.* In both cases, a lower value is preferred.

Use the command `show route table inet.2` to show the multicast RPF table on a Juniper Networks router. The following commands provide more specific RPF information:

- **`show multicast rpf`:** Shows the RPF interface on which multicast data packets must arrive
- **`show pim source`:** Displays RPF neighbors to which PIM Join/Prune messages are sent
- **`test msdp rpf-peer`:** Displays the MSDP RPF peer from which SA messages are accepted

7.1.2.2 Cisco Systems Conventions In Cisco's operating system, IOS, each routing protocol has its own routing table. An RPF check can use any routing protocol's routing table. When doing an RPF check for source address, S, the routing tables are scanned in order of protocol preference. The route used for the RPF check is the one from the most preferred protocol that provides a route that encompasses S. It is important to note this route might not be the one with the longest mask.

In IOS, the MBGP table can be displayed with the `show ip mbgp` command. Because the multicast RPF route can come from sources other than MBGP (that is, from a unicast routing table, DVMRP routing table, or static mroutes), use the `show ip rpf <source address>` command to determine which source of information is used.

7.1.3 RECURSIVE LOOKUP FOR BGP NEXT HOPS

The BGP next hop, N, for a prefix, P, is not necessarily the address of a directly connected neighbor. For unicast routing, a router resolves the directly connected next hop by recursing on the unicast routing table. The next hop of the best matching route (longest prefix match, then lowest preference/administrative distance) for N is used as the forwarding next hop for P.

For multicast RPF routes learned via MBGP, the process of recursing to a connected next hop is implementation specific. On Juniper Networks routers, inet.2 is first scanned to see if a route encompasses the BGP next hop. If one exists, this route is used. If not, inet.0 is scanned for the best matching route.

On Cisco Systems routers, the recursed next hop is taken from the protocol routing table with the lowest administrative distance that has a route encompassing prefix P. For example, the route 10.0.0.0/14, learned via MBGP, will be selected over the route 10.0.0.0/16, learned via BGP, when performing an RPF check. Notice that unlike the recursion on the unicast routing table, the longest prefix match rule does not take effect; administrative distance is considered prior to prefix length.

7.2 BGP AND RELATED TERMINOLOGY

This chapter assumes the reader has working knowledge of BGP and specifically the use of BGP for interdomain routing of IP unicast packets. This section contains a brief overview of BGP to enable discussion of MGBP using consistent terminology.

The Internet is made up of thousands of heterogeneous internetworks, each maintained by a separate organization. An internetwork maintained by a single operating group is termed an autonomous system (AS). Each AS has a primary interior gateway protocol (IGP) that handles the routing of IP unicast packets within the AS. OSPF (Open Shortest Path First), IS-IS (Intermediate System to Intermediate System), and RIP (Routing Information Protocol) are examples of IGPs.

In order to exchange routes with other ASs, an exterior gateway protocol (EGP) is required. BGP4 is the EGP used in the Internet for routing IPv4 unicast packets across multiple autonomous systems and is defined in RFC 1771.

Three main functions separate the various IGPs and BGP:

- BGP can handle a much larger number of routes.
- BGP has a much more versatile array of attributes that can be used for enforcing policies.
- BGP is focused on routing packets by means of AS hops, not router hops.

Note: In this book, BGP and BGP4 refer to the same thing, with the "4" simply indicating the current version of Border Gateway Protocol and the specific version of the protocol we refer to.

IGPs are very trusting of the information received from their neighbors. They assume neighboring routers are part of their own domain and therefore share the same routing policy. BGP assumes the opposite is true because the information it receives from external peers is from a different organization. BGP tries to ensure the credibility and stability of that information.

Connections between BGP speakers of different ASs are referred to as *external* links. BGP connections between BGP speakers within the same AS are referred to as *internal* links. Similarly, a peer in a different AS is referred to as an *external peer*, while a peer in the same AS may be described as an *internal peer*.

7.3 BGP INTERNALS—FOUNDATION FOR UNDERSTANDING MBGP

A router configured to send and receive route information via BGP is known as a **BGP speaker**. To exchange route information, a BGP speaker forms adjacencies with peer routers. **BGP peers** establish a TCP session using **port number** 179.

Both peers attempt to open a connection to port 179, but only one connection is kept up for the peer adjacency. The peer initiating the connection uses a random port number on its side of the **BGP session**. All BGP packets have the following format:

```
+-+-+-+-+-+-+-+-+-+-+-+-+-+-+-+-+-+-+-+-+-+-+-+-+-+-+
| IP Header | TCP Header  | BGP Header  | BGP Message |
+-+-+-+-+-+-+-+-+-+-+-+-+-+-+-+-+-+-+-+-+-+-+-+-+-+-+
```

The BGP header contains three fields:

- **Marker:** Can be used for authentication and synchronization of the BGP session
- **Length:** Indicates the total length of the message, including the BGP header, in octets
- **Type:** Indicates the type of message to follow

BGP has four types of messages:

- Open
- Update
- Notification
- Keepalive

An explanation of how these messages are used requires an understanding of the BGP adjacency finite state machine. The clearest way to explain this state machine is to walk through the flow when everything works properly—that is, the connection comes up and routes are exchanged. The following example describes what happens when two routers, router A and router B, are configured as BGP peers for the first time.

1. Router A CONNECT; router B IDLE
    Router A is configured, identifying router B as a potential BGP peer. This configuration shifts router A into the CONNECT state, and it tries to initiate a TCP connection with router B on port 179.

2. **Router A ACTIVE; router B IDLE**

   This connection fails because router B has yet to be configured. This failure shifts router A into ACTIVE state. In ACTIVE state, router A listens on port 179 for a connection initiated by router B. Every few seconds, router A again attempts to initiate a TCP session.

3. **Router A ACTIVE; router B CONNECT**

   Router B is configured, identifying router A as a BGP peer. This configuration shifts router B into the CONNECT state; then router B tries to initiate a TCP connection with router A on port 179.

4. **Router A OPENSENT; router B OPENSENT**

   This connection succeeds. Each side sends out an Open message and changes its state to OPENSENT.

5. **Router A OPENCONFIRM; router B OPENCONFIRM**

   Upon the receipt of the Open message from the peer, each side checks the message for errors. If everything checks out all right, a Keepalive message is sent, and the state is changed to OPENCONFIRM.

6. **Router A ESTABLISHED; router B ESTABLISHED**

   Upon the receipt of the Keepalive message, each peer switches to ESTABLISHED state. In ESTABLISHED state, the peers are free to exchange Update messages containing route information. Keepalive messages are sent periodically to ensure that the connection is still up.

If anything goes wrong during the previously described process, a Notification message is sent, and the router shifts back to IDLE state.

When discussing MBGP, we are primarily concerned with the Update message. The following diagram depicts the various fields in the BGP Update message:

```
+-------------------------------------------------------+
| Unfeasible Routes Length (2 octets)                   |
+-------------------------------------------------------+
| Withdrawn Routes (variable)                           |
+-------------------------------------------------------+
| Total Path Attribute Length (2 octets)                |
+-------------------------------------------------------+
```

```
| Path Attributes (variable)                          |
+----------------------------------------------------+
| Network Layer Reachability Information (variable)   |
+----------------------------------------------------+
```

BGP considers every route to be a destination with the attributes of a path to that destination. The **Network Layer Reachability Information (NLRI) field** contains a list of destination prefixes that share the same path attributes. Path attributes are used by each router for next-hop selection when more than one path to the destination prefix is learned via BGP. The following depicts the Path Attributes field:

```
0                     1
 0 1 2 3 4 5 6 7 8 9 0 1 2 3 4 5
+-+-+-+-+-+-+-+-+-+-+-+-+-+-+-+-+
|  Attr. Flags |Attr. Type Code|
+-+-+-+-+-+-+-+-+-+-+-+-+-+-+-+-+
```

The following are examples of BGP path attributes:

- ORIGIN
- AS_PATH
- NEXT_HOP
- LOCAL_PREF
- ATOMIC_AGGREGATE
- AGGREGATOR
- MULTI_EXIT_DISC (MED)
- **COMMUNITY**

Path attributes fall into four categories:

- Well-known mandatory
- Well-known discretionary
- Optional transitive
- Optional nontransitive

Well-known attributes are recognized by the BGP implementations of all router vendors. Well-known mandatory attributes are included in every BGP Update message, whereas well-known discretionary attributes are not required to be incorporated in every Update message.

Both categories of well-known attributes are transferred to other BGP peers. ORIGIN, AS_PATH, and NEXT_HOP are well-known mandatory attributes. LOCAL_PREF and ATOMIC_AGGREGATE are well-known discretionary attributes.

In addition to well-known attributes, each path may contain one or more optional attributes. It is not required or expected that all BGP implementations support all optional attributes.

If a router receives a BGP Update message containing an unrecognized optional attribute, the optional attribute is quietly ignored, and the NLRI is accepted and passed on to other BGP peers. "Quietly ignored" means no Notification message is sent, and the BGP session is not torn down. The handling of the unrecognized optional attribute depends on whether it is transitive or nontransitive.

Unrecognized optional **transitive** path attributes are passed along to other BGP peers. Unrecognized optional **nontransitive** path attributes are not passed along to other BGP peers. For example, AGGREGATOR is an optional transitive attribute. MULTI_EXIT_DISC (MED—multiple exit discriminator) is an optional nontransitive attribute.

7.3.1 NLRI

The NLRI field is used to convey IP address prefix and subnet mask information. The NLRI consists of multiple instances of two fields, Length and Prefix. The Length field indicates the length in bits of the IP address prefix. The Prefix field contains IP address prefixes followed by enough trailing bits to make the end of the field fall on an octet boundary. Note that the value of the trailing bits is irrelevant.

7.3.2 BGP ROUTE SELECTION

RFC 1771 does not define any hard-and-fast rules about BGP route selection. Therefore, each router vendor's implementation may be slightly different. The following is an example of a route-selection process. When two or more BGP routes are being compared, the first attribute that is different for the two paths eliminates the loser.

1. Highest LOCAL_PREF value
2. Shortest AS_PATH length (fewest AS hops)
3. Lowest ORIGIN code (IGP = 0, EGP = 1, incomplete = 2)
4. If neighbor AS is same, then lowest MED metric
5. Prefer strictly internal paths
6. Prefer strictly external paths
7. Lowest IGP metric
8. Lowest peer router ID

7.4 EXTENDING BGP: MBGP

MBGP is not a separate protocol but an extension of BGP, so the specifics of MBGP peering are similar to conventional BGP peering. RFC 2858 defines the multiprotocol extensions for BGP4, and the extensions are implemented as optional path attributes. A standard BGP Update message may contain multiple destination prefixes that share the same path attributes such as AS_PATH, NEXT_HOP, MED, and so on.

As previously stated, a BGP Update message contains a single instance of each path attribute, plus a list of prefixes that share those particular attribute values. This strategy is unlike that of most IGPs, whose updates contain a list of prefixes, each listed with its own attributes.

BGP's method of exchanging updates leads to the efficient use of bandwidth for a protocol with so many attributes, especially considering that many of the attributes are optional and do not pertain to every prefix.

MBGP adds two new path attributes called MP_REACH_NLRI and MP_UNREACH_NLRI. MP_REACH_NLRI is used instead of the standard BGP NLRI for prefixes from protocols other than IPv4 or for IPv4 prefixes intended for a routing table other than the unicast **forwarding table**. The MP_UNREACH_NLRI attribute is used in place of the Withdrawn Routes field of the standard BGP UPDATE message to indicate that the specified prefixes are unreachable.

MBGP can be used to carry forwarding information for any protocol that has a prefix-mask hierarchical address space. Possible protocols include **IPX** (Novell's **Internetwork Packet Exchange**) and IPv6. The most popular implementation of MBGP currently is for multicast routing. This application is so popular that it is common to hear MBGP translated to "Multicast Border Gateway Protocol."

7.5 MBGP INTERNALS

An MBGP speaker must have an IPv4 address in order to establish sessions to its peers, even if it is only exchanging routing information for protocols other than IPv4. BGP4 has three attributes that are IPv4 specific:

- NEXT_HOP
- AGGREGATOR
- NLRI

MBGP does not specify a way to use other protocols' addresses in the AGGREGATOR attribute. It is possible to **aggregate** prefixes of other network layer protocols, but the router performing the route aggregation is denoted by its IPv4 address in the AGGREGATOR attribute for the path.

MBGP does add the ability to associate other network layer protocols' prefix addresses with next-hop information specific to that protocol. None of the other BGP path attributes is specific to IPv4, so the path attributes are used "as is" for non-IPv4 MBGP reachability information.

MBGP uses the numbers assigned to address families in RFC 1700. The assigned numbers are listed in Table 7-1.

Table 7-1 MBGP Address Family Numbers

Number	Description
0	Reserved
1	IPv4
2	IPv6
3	NSAP
4	HDLC (8-bit multidrop)
5	BBN 1822
6	802 (includes all 802 media plus Ethernet "canonical format")
7	E.163
8	E.164 (SMDS, Frame Relay, ATM)
9	F.69 (Telex)
10	X.121 (X.25, Frame Relay)
11	IPX
12	AppleTalk
13	DECnet IV
14	Banyan Vines
65535	Reserved

These numbers are referred to as **address family identifiers (AFIs)**. MBGP also uses subsequent address family identifiers (SAFIs) to provide additional information about the type of the NLRI included in the MBGP Update message. The SAFIs for IPv4 are as follows:

- **1:** NLRI used for unicast forwarding
- **2:** NLRI used for multicast forwarding
- **3:** NLRI used for both unicast and multicast forwarding

Most MBGP implementations will continue to use the standard BGP NLRI and Withdrawn Routes fields instead of the new BGP attributes with AFI = 1/SAFI = 1 for IPv4 routes used for unicast forwarding. SAFI = 3 is useful in minimizing routing table size and the amount of control messages when the topologies are congruent.

7.5.1 BGP CAPABILITIES NEGOTIATION

Various BGP implementations incorporate different optional capabilities of the BGP protocol. An example of a capability that might not be supported in every implementation of BGP is the route refresh option described in RFC 2918. Even within a single vendor's implementation, it may be possible to toggle whether some of these options are enabled or disabled. An example of a capability that can be toggled on or off is MBGP, the primary topic of this chapter.

When two routers running BGP bring up a session with each other, they are able to exchange information about what capabilities they have enabled. The routers can then make an intelligent choice of the capabilities they should disable for the session, based on the absence of that capability in the peer's announcement. This process is known as **capabilities negotiation** and is defined in RFC 2842.

If a BGP implementation does not support capabilities negotiation, the BGP session is torn down when an option is not understood by one of the peers. When a router recognizes that the other side has torn down the session, it might try to guess which capability caused the problem and try to reconnect without one or more of the options. This process is inefficient and may not always result in the session coming up.

The capabilities negotiation process enables the routers to communicate with each other about exactly which option is causing the problem and enables them to set up the session on the initial attempt. It avoids the up-and-down thrashing of the BGP session and stops the guessing game.

BGP Open messages have an optional parameters field. This field contains a list of optional parameters encoded as a <parameter type, parameter length, parameter value> triplet as shown in the first diagram on the next page.

```
0                   1
0 1 2 3 4 5 6 7 8 9 0 1 2 3 4 5
+-+-+-+-+-+-+-+-+-+-+-+-+-+-+-+
|  Parm. Type  | Parm. Length |
+-+-+-+-+-+-+-+-+-+-+-+-+-+-+-+
|  Parameter Value (variable)  |
+-+-+-+-+-+-+-+-...          +
```

RFC 2842 introduces a new optional parameter for BGP Open messages named *capabilities* (parameter type 2). This parameter is used by the capabilities negotiation process to convey the list of capabilities supported by the speaker. The parameter contains one or more triples <capability code, capability length, capability value> nested inside of the Parameter Value field. The following diagram shows an example capabilities optional parameter with a single capability triple:

```
0                   1
0 1 2 3 4 5 6 7 8 9 0 1 2 3 4 5
+-+-+-+-+-+-+-+-+-+-+-+-+-+-+-+
|     0x02     | Parm. Length |
+-+-+-+-+-+-+-+-+-+-+-+-+-+-+-+
|  Cap. Code   | Cap. Length  |
+-+-+-+-+-+-+-+-+-+-+-+-+-+-+-+
|  Capability Value (variable) |
+-+-+-+-+-+-+-+-...          +
```

A particular capability, as identified by its capability code, may occur more than once within the capabilities parameter.

7.5.1.1 How Capability Negotiation Is Used for MBGP MBGP-speaking peers can use the capability negotiation procedure to determine whether both peers support MBGP. It can also be used to determine which address families and subsequent address families each router supports. To indicate multiprotocol capabilities, the Capability Code field in the capabilities optional parameter is set to 1, and the Capability Length field is set to 4. The capability value is encoded as follows:

```
 0                   1
 0 1 2 3 4 5 6 7 8 9 0 1 2 3 4 5
+-+-+-+-+-+-+-+-+-+-+-+-+-+-+-+-+
|              AFI              |
+-+-+-+-+-+-+-+-+-+-+-+-+-+-+-+-+
|     Res.      |     SAFI      |
+-+-+-+-+-+-+-+-+-+-+-+-+-+-+-+-+
```

- **AFI:**   Address family identifier (16 bits)
- **Res.:**   Reserved field that is set to 0 (8 bits)
- **SAFI:** Subsequent address family identifier (8 bits)

A router that supports multiple AFI/SAFI includes each AFI/SAFI as a separate capability in the capabilities optional parameter. A router does not advertise routes for a specific AFI/SAFI unless it received that AFI/SAFI in the peer's Open message. The following diagram is an example of a capabilities optional parameter for a router that supports MBGP with both the unicast (AFI/SAFI 1/1) and multicast RPF (AFI/SAFI 1/2) address families:

```
 0                   1
 0 1 2 3 4 5 6 7 8 9 0 1 2 3 4 5
+-+-+-+-+-+-+-+-+-+-+-+-+-+-+-+-+
|Parm. Type = 2 |Parm. Length=12|
+-+-+-+-+-+-+-+-+-+-+-+-+-+-+-+-+
| Cap. Code = 1 |Cap. Length = 4|
+-+-+-+-+-+-+-+-+-+-+-+-+-+-+-+-+
|             AFI = 1           |
+-+-+-+-+-+-+-+-+-+-+-+-+-+-+-+-+
|   Res. = 0    |   SAFI = 1    |
+-+-+-+-+-+-+-+-+-+-+-+-+-+-+-+-+
| Cap. Code = 1 |Cap. Length = 4|
+-+-+-+-+-+-+-+-+-+-+-+-+-+-+-+-+
|             AFI = 1           |
+-+-+-+-+-+-+-+-+-+-+-+-+-+-+-+-+
|   Res. = 0    |   SAFI = 2    |
+-+-+-+-+-+-+-+-+-+-+-+-+-+-+-+-+
```

Example of Using Capability Negotiation for MBGP Imagine a BGP session between two peers, router A and router B. Router A is configured for both unicast (AFI/SAFI 1/1) and multicast RPF (AFI/SAFI 1/2) address families. Router B is configured for only the unicast address family. If a BGP session is started between router A and router B, then router A recognizes the fact that router B is not interested in AFI/SAFI 1/2 because router B did not include that address family in its capabilities optional parameter of its Open message. Router A suppresses advertisements for prefixes of the multicast RPF address family, even though it is configured to send these updates.

7.5.2 NEW PATH ATTRIBUTES IN MBGP

MBGP introduces two new BGP path attributes to carry the NLRI and withdrawn route information for protocols other than IPv4 unicast forwarding. These attributes are the Multiprotocol Reachable NLRI (MP_REACH_NLRI) and the Multiprotocol Unreachable NLRI (MP_UNREACH_NLRI). MP_REACH_NLRI is path attribute type code 14, and MP_UNREACH_NLRI is type code 15. Both are optional nontransitive attributes. The standard BGP Withdrawn Routes field and NLRI field are most likely empty in MBGP Update messages that include either of the new attributes.

7.5.2.1 Multiprotocol Reachable NLRI The Multiprotocol Reachable NLRI attribute is used to advertise one or more routes to a peer that shares the same path attributes. The Multiprotocol Reachable NLRI attribute conveys the equivalent of BGP next hop for the address family carried in the message. This isn't too interesting for IPv4 multicast RPF routes, but it is essential for non-IPv4 address families. MP_REACH_NLRI also enables a router to report some or all of its local IP addresses. These local addresses are known as subnetwork point of attachments (SNPAs). The SNPA functionality is not used when exchanging route information for the multicast SAFI. The following diagram shows the layout of a MP_REACH_NLRI for multicast forwarding:

```
+----------------------------------------------------------+
| Address Family Identifier (2 octets) = 0x0001            |
+----------------------------------------------------------+
| Subsequent Address Family Identifier (1 octet) = 0x02    |
+----------------------------------------------------------+
```

```
| Length of Next-Hop Network Address (1 octet) = 0x04   |
+-------------------------------------------------------+
| Network Address of Next-Hop (4 octets)                |
+-------------------------------------------------------+
| Number of SNPAs (1 octet) = 0x00                      |
+-------------------------------------------------------+
| Network Layer Reachability Information (variable)     |
+-------------------------------------------------------+
```

The NLRI field is a list of one or more destination prefixes encoded in the following manner:

```
+--------------------------+
|    Length (1 octet)      |
+--------------------------+
|    Prefix (variable)     |
+--------------------------+
```

The Length field indicates the length in bits of the address prefix. The Prefix field contains address prefixes followed by enough trailing bits to make the end of the field fall on an octet boundary. The value of trailing bits is irrelevant. A length and prefix of zero indicate a prefix that matches all addresses.

A BGP Update message with the MP_REACH_NLRI always has ORIGIN and AS_PATH attributes. In IBGP exchanges, such a message also carries the LOCAL_PREF attribute.

7.5.2.2 Multiprotocol Unreachable NLRI   The MP_UNREACH_NLRI attribute is used to indicate a previously advertised route is no longer reachable and the route should be withdrawn. The following diagram shows the format of this attribute when used for multicast RPF routes:

```
+-------------------------------------------------------+
| Address Family Identifier (2 octets) = 0x0001         |
+-------------------------------------------------------+
| Subsequent Address Family Identifier (1 octet) = 0x02 |
+-------------------------------------------------------+
| Withdrawn Routes (variable)                           |
+-------------------------------------------------------+
```

The Withdrawn Routes field has the exact same format as the NLRI field in the MP_REACH_NLRI attribute. An Update message that contains the MP_UNREACH_ NLRI attribute usually does not carry any other path attributes.

7.6 Using MGBP for Multicast Routing

While MBGP is not used to feed the (S,G) and (*,G) tables used for forwarding multicast packets out the correct interfaces, MBGP can indirectly influence the flow of multicast traffic. PIM Join/Prune messages are sent to a router's RPF neighbor. Upon receiving a Join, a router adds the interface on which the Join was received to the outgoing interface list for the multicast group. Thus, by populating the routing table used to determine the RPF neighbor, MBGP can influence which direction the multicast packets take through the network.

The primary application for MBGP is to create different topologies for unicast and multicast traffic. A benefit exists, however, of having MBGP running in the case of congruent topologies. Although both unicast and multicast packets traverse the same links, disparate policies can be applied to unicast and multicast BGP routes.

7.6.1 Manipulation of Path Attributes

Path attributes can be manipulated separately for both unicast and multicast paths. In particular, this section illustrates how routers use MBGP to transfer unicast route information employed specifically for the RPF checks of the PIM-SM and MSDP protocols.

MBGP can be used to achieve incongruent routing within a domain. Doing so typically requires manual manipulation of the NEXT_HOP attribute across IBGP sessions, which can be an administrative burden and can reduce redundancy. Recall the primary purpose of BGP is to provide policy-based routing between two ASs. BGP relies on the underlying IGP to make routing decisions within a particular AS. For this reason, it is much easier to manipulate the IGP to support disparate routing topologies for unicast and multicast within an AS. Chapter 8 describes how M-ISIS can be used for this purpose.

Using MBGP to achieve incongruent routing across ASs is much cleaner, and there are plenty of options (for example, MED, LOCAL_PREF, and AS_PATH prepending). In this example, the LOCAL_PREF attribute is manipulated to accomplish the goal.

We start out with congruent routing. The local router has two EBGP peers. They are 10.0.0.1 in AS 100 and 10.0.1.1 in AS 200. Both of these peers are advertising a SAFI = 1 and 2 route to 192.168.1.0/24. The route learned from 10.0.0.1 is chosen as the active route for both unicast forwarding and multicast RFP because its router ID is lower (indicated with the asterisk).

```
kalamata> show route 192.168.1.0/24

Unicast Routing Table
192.168.1.0/24    *[BGP/170] , localpref 100, from 10.0.0.1
                    AS path: 100 300 I > via so-6/1/0.0
                   [BGP/170] , localpref 100, from 10.0.1.1
                    AS path: 200 300 I > via so-6/2/0.0

Multicast RPF Table
192.168.1.0/24    *[BGP/170] , localpref 100, from 10.0.0.1
                    AS path: 100 300 I > via so-6/1/0.0
                   [BGP/170] , localpref 100, from 10.0.1.1
                    AS path: 200 300 I > via so-6/2/0.0
```

To achieve incongruent routing, a policy is applied to the multicast RPF route learned from 10.0.1.1. This policy sets the LOCAL_PREF for that route to 110. This change causes the preferred route for multicast RPF to be different from the route preferred for unicast forwarding. Notice that the route through 10.0.1.1 is now the active route for multicast RPF.

```
kalamata> show route 192.168.1.0/24

Unicast Routing Table
192.168.1.0/24    *[BGP/170] , localpref 100, from 10.0.0.1
                    AS path: 100 300 I > via so-6/1/0.0
                   [BGP/170] , localpref 100, from 10.0.1.1
                    AS path: 200 300 I > via so-6/2/0.0
```

```
Multicast RPF Table
192.168.1.0/24    *[BGP/170] , localpref 110, from 10.0.1.1
                    AS path: 200 300 I > via so-6/2/0.0
                   [BGP/170] , localpref 100, from 10.0.0.1
                    AS path: 100 300 I > via so-6/1/0.0
```

This chapter has presented a thorough discussion of multiprotocol extensions to the Border Gateway Protocol. Chapter 8 continues with a treatment of Multi-topology Routing for Intermediate Systems to Intermediate Systems (M-ISIS).

Multitopology Routing in Intermediate System to Intermediate System (M-ISIS)

This chapter describes Multitopology Routing in IS-IS (M-ISIS), which extends the capabilities of the IS-IS routing protocol. These extensions have enabled M-ISIS to evolve into a general-purpose tool for providing multiple-topology support for technologies such as in-band management, multicast, and IPv6. As we did in Chapter 7 with MBGP, we focus on how M-ISIS can be used to create two separate virtual topologies, one for unicast and another for multicast.

In interdomain unicast routing, recursive routing is used to select the best path to a destination. When a BGP-learned route is selected as the best path to a destination, an IGP such as OSPF or IS-IS determines the path to the BGP next hop of the selected BGP route. Thus BGP generally makes routing decisions *between* different autonomous systems, while an IGP makes routing decisions *within* an autonomous system.

M-ISIS and MBGP can be used side-by-side to build a dedicated multicast RPF table, much as IS-IS and BGP have traditionally coexisted. M-ISIS provides the ability to create incongruent topologies within the AS, whereas MBGP provides this ability between ASs.

At the time of writing, Juniper Networks routers support M-ISIS, while Cisco Systems routers do not.

8.1 OVERVIEW OF IS-IS

IS-IS is the most common IGP found in the networks of the world's largest ISPs, for reasons that are mainly due to circumstance. In the early 1990s, the first large ISPs such as UUNet, MCI, and Sprint were beginning to build IP backbones and needed to select an IGP. Because a link-state routing protocol was desired, IS-IS, developed by ISO (International Organization for Standardization), and OSPF, developed by IETF, were the main candidates.

At that time, Cisco Systems had just implemented a link-state routing protocol for Internetwork Packet Exchange (IPX) called **NetWare Link Services Protocol (NLSP)**. Because NLSP is very similar to IS-IS, Cisco Systems software developers rewrote the IS-IS code at the same time. The newer, more stable implementation of IS-IS was selected by these ISPs, where it continues to run today.

Over time, some have suggested that IS-IS is more stable for large carrier networks than its rival, OSPF. However, the operation of both is very similar, and there is nothing inherently better about one than the other. Further, with years of evolution and deployment experience, software implementations of both protocols by router vendors such as Juniper Networks and Cisco Systems have matured to be equally stable. In spite of this, the IS-IS versus OSPF debate continues to provide intense discussion among the fervent partisans of each.

8.1.1 IS-IS BACKGROUND

The Intermediate System to Intermediate System (IS-IS) routing protocol is specified in ISO 10589 (republished as RFC 1142). The ISO standard only describes how IS-IS can be used to route ISO's **Connectionless Network Protocol (CLNP)** packets. RFC 1195 integrated IS-IS as a routing protocol capable of carrying IPv4 prefixes. In ISO terminology, an intermediate system is a *router*. A host in ISO terms is known as an *end system*. The following lists some of the specification documents for IS-IS:

- ISO/IEC 10589, "IS-IS Intra-Domain Routing Information Exchange Protocol"
- RFC 1195, "Use of OSI IS-IS for Routing in TCP/IP and Dual Environments"
- RFC 2763, "Dynamic Hostname Exchange Mechanism for IS-IS"

- RFC 2966, "Domain-wide Prefix Distribution with Two-Level IS-IS"
- RFC 2973, "IS-IS Mesh Groups"
- draft-ietf-isis-traffic-04.txt, "IS-IS Extensions for Traffic Engineering"
- draft-ietf-isis-wg-multi-topology-02.txt, "M-ISIS: Multi Topology Routing in IS-IS"

Unlike most other unicast IP routing protocols, IS-IS is rarely documented outside of the standards themselves. Thus, in this chapter, we provide some detail of how IS-IS works at a core level to ensure that subsequent sections in this chapter on multitopology extensions make sense.

As stated earlier, IS-IS, like OSPF, is a link-state routing protocol. Because OSPF tends to be better understood throughout the networking community, we compare IS-IS to the operation of OSPF throughout this chapter. With an understanding of OSPF, learning other link-state protocols such as IS-IS becomes straightforward. IS-IS and OSPF strive for the same goal, simply approaching it from different angles.

As with OSPF, each IS-IS-speaking router generates a **link-state advertisement (LSA)** that includes information for all of its directly connected networks. It places its own LSA in its **link-state database**. An IS-IS-speaking router establishes adjacencies with its directly connected neighbors. When the adjacency comes up, both neighbors send the entire contents of their link-state database to each other.

From that point forward, incremental updates are exchanged whenever the contents of the link-state database change. When an IS-IS network has completely converged, every router's link-state database is identical. To decide on the best path through the network, each router runs Dijkstra's algorithm, also known as the **shortest path first (SPF) algorithm**, and inserts the best route into its routing table.

Although IS-IS and OSPF operate in a similar fashion, they were developed by separate organizations, so the Internet community forever will be plagued with two sets of terms that describe similar or identical items. For instance, LSA is an

OSPF term; in IS-IS, a link-state advertisement is known as a **link-state protocol data unit (LSP)**.

The following two components typically provide the most confusion for those who understand OSPF and are trying to learn IS-IS:

- ISO addresses
- Areas and levels

To mitigate the confusion, these two topics are discussed at some length in this chapter.

8.1.2 ISO ADDRESSES

IS-IS packets run natively on top of any layer 2 network as ISO packets. This is in contrast to OSPF packets, which are native IP packets. IS-IS messages travel over only a single hop, so ISO routing capability is not required in an IS-IS network. Every IS-IS-speaking router must have an ISO address configured on one of its attached interfaces (preferably the **loopback interface**) for the router to be able to send and receive IS-IS messages.

The logical interfaces on the router must be configured to accept ISO packets, but only one ISO address is required per router. The logical interfaces can borrow the ISO address from the loopback interface in a similar fashion to IP unnumbered interfaces (RFC 1812). ISO addresses in IS-IS use the **network service access point (NSAP)** address format and can vary in length from 8 to 20 bytes. An ISO address has the following format:

```
 0 1 2 3 4 5 6 7 8 9 0 1 2 3 4 5 6 7 8 9 0 1 2 3 4 5 6 7 8 9 0 1
+-+-+-+-+-+-+-+-+-+-+-+-+-+-+-+-+-+-+-+-+-+-+-+-+-+-+-+-+-+-+-+-+
|   AFI = 0x49  |                Domain Identifier              |
+-+-+-+-+-+-+-+-+-+-+-+-+-+-+-+-+-+-+-+-+-+-+-+-+-+-+-+-+-+-+-+-+
|                Domain Identifier (continued)                  |
+-+-+-+-+-+-+-+-+-+-+-+-+-+-+-+-+-+-+-+-+-+-+-+-+-+-+-+-+-+-+-+-+
|                Domain Identifier (continued)                  |
+-+-+-+-+-+-+-+-+-+-+-+-+-+-+-+-+-+-+-+-+-+-+-+-+-+-+-+-+-+-+-+-+
|Domain ID(cont)|          System Identifier (sysID)            |
```

```
+-+-+-+-+-+-+-+-+-+-+-+-+-+-+-+-+-+-+-+-+-+-+-+-+-+-+-+-+-+-+
|    System Identifier (sysID) (continued)    |n-selector=0x00|
+-+-+-+-+-+-+-+-+-+-+-+-+-+-+-+-+-+-+-+-+-+-+-+-+-+-+-+-+-+-+
```

The first byte is the **authority and format indicator (AFI)**. The AFI is used to describe the organization that assigned the address and the meaning of the fields that follow. Because IS-IS packets remain within an organization and are not routed across the Internet, ISO addresses do not need to be assigned by a central authority (unlike public IP addresses that are assigned by IANA).

An AFI field equal to 0x49 designates what is known as *local AFI*. Local AFI defines a structure that can be used by anyone within a private network. The octets following the AFI byte are specific to the IS-IS domain and can be structured by the network administrator.

> **Note:** NSAP addresses are also used within **Asynchronous Transfer Mode (ATM)**. ATM uses three different AFI values; each indicates a different authoritative assignment organization and address format. The possible values are 0x39 for DCC-formatted ATM end-system addresses (AESA), 0x45 for E.164-formatted AESA addresses, and 0x47 for **ICD**-formatted (**international code designator**-formatted) AESA addresses.

The next 12 bytes of the address are known as the *domain identifier*. The combination of the AFI and the domain identifier form the IS-IS area number. Routers within the same area share the same area number. IS-IS areas are not directly comparable to OSPF areas. The distinction between the two is covered in the next section.

The following six bytes represent the system identifier (sysID). The sysID of each router in an area must be unique. One common technique used to ensure uniqueness is to use one of the IP addresses assigned to the router expressed in binary-coded decimal. For example, IP address 192.168.85.16 corresponds to sysID 0x1921.6808.5016.

The final byte is known as the *n-selector*. For an IS-IS router, the value should always be 0x00. An n-selector equal to 0x00 indicates that the address is a special type called a **network entity title (NET)**.

8.1.3 IS-IS AREAS AND LEVELS

As stated in the previous section, each IS-IS-speaking router is assigned an ISO address. This address is used for two purposes:

- To send and receive ISO packets
- To identify the area in which the router resides

References to IS-IS areas use decimal numbers to imply an AFI of 49 and leading zeros in the domain identifier. For example, IS-IS area 10 corresponds to area number 0x49.0000.0000.000A.

IS-IS areas and OSPF areas serve slightly different roles. In OSPF every nonbackbone area has its own link-state database and at least one router that is also connected to the special backbone area (area 0). The routers within a nonbackbone area that connect to area 0 are known as **area border routers (ABRs)**. The ABR is responsible for leaking routes in both directions between area 0 and its other areas. Policy can be applied to filter and summarize advertisements in both directions at the ABR.

In IS-IS, areas and levels are used to provide roughly the same functionality. An IS-IS router can be a *level 1 (L1)* router, a *level 2 (L2)* router, or a *level 1/level 2 (L1/L2)* router. A router can be in only one area, but levels can be configured on a per interface basis. If directly connected routers are in the same area and the link between them is configured for L1, they build an L1 adjacency. If the link between directly connected routers is configured for L2, they build an L2 adjacency. Note that L2 routers do not have to be in the same area. On links where conditions for both are met, level 1 *and* level 2 adjacencies are built.

As with OSPF, IS-IS uses areas to limit the size of the link-state database. The link-state database of a L1 router contains information about the L1 routers only in its own area. Because L1 routers can route only *within* their own area, traffic is sent to routers in L2 to reach other areas. L2 routers provide connectivity between different areas, similarly to OSPF routers in area 0. L2 routers maintain a level 2 link-state database, which, again like the area 0 in OSPF, must be contiguous.

L1/L2 routers are similar to OSPF ABRs. With both a level 1 and a level 2 link-state database, L1/L2 routers are responsible for leaking routes in both directions between the databases. To reach routers in other areas, L1 routers send traffic to an L1/L2 router. Policy can be applied to filter and summarize advertisements in both directions at the L1/L2 router.

Figure 8-1 shows the location of level 1 and level 2 adjacencies in a multiple-area IS-IS network.

> **Note:** Using multiple areas within an IS-IS or OSPF domain is not required as long as wise deployment guidelines are followed. IS-IS and OSPF should carry routes only for router loopback addresses and backbone links. All other routes, including customer networks and links to customer routers, should be carried in BGP. Deployments of both protocols exist that can handle the world's largest networks with a single area. In fact, most IS-IS deployments use only one area (and level).

8.1.4 TYPE LENGTH VALUES (TLVS)

It is relatively easy to extend the capabilities of the IS-IS protocol because its messages are built using structures known as TLVs. TLVs get their name from having three fields.

The first field is a fixed-length Type field. Its value is well known and determines the format of the Value field. If a router receives a message and does not have knowledge of a type for one of the TLV's Type fields, the router silently ignores the TLV for that field and processes the remainder of the message. The TLVs are structured so that if one TLV is unrecognized, it does not lead to the misinterpretation of the information held in other TLVs.

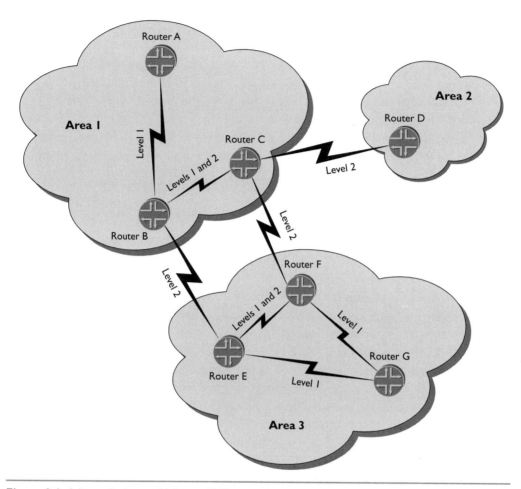

Figure 8-1 Adjacencies in a multiple-area IS-IS network

The Length field specifies the length of the Value field. The Value field contains the relevant information for the TLV itself. The Value field can also contain other TLVs (known as *sub-TLVs*).

8.2 SPECIFICS OF IS-IS

In this section, we discuss several important IS-IS topics, including the use of packets, establishing adjacencies on point-to-point links, determination of designated routers on multiaccess networks, and exchanging link-state information with neighbors.

8.2.1 IS-IS PACKETS

Every IS-IS packet (or PDU in OSI-speak) begins with a list of mandatory fields specific to that packet type. The fixed PDU fields are followed by various TLVs. Some TLVs apply to certain PDUs and not to others. IS-IS uses the following packets to exchange protocol information:

- **Level 1 IS-IS Hello PDU (IIH):** Used on LANs to discover the identity of neighboring level 1 IS-IS systems, elect a designated intermediate system, and keep up the adjacencies.
- **Level 2 IS-IS Hello PDU (IIH):** Used on LANs to discover the identity of neighboring level 2 IS-IS systems, elect a designated intermediate system, and keep up the adjacencies.
- **Point-to-Point Hello (IIH) PDU:** Used on point-to-point links to discover the identity of the neighboring IS-IS system, determine whether the neighbor is a level 1 or level 2 router, and keep up the adjacency. This message is the only one that is not level dependent. The same packet format is used for both levels.
- **Level 1 link-state PDU (LSP):** Contains information about the state of adjacencies to neighboring level 1 IS-IS systems. LSPs are flooded periodically throughout an area.
- **Level 2 link-state PDU (LSP):** Contains information about the state of adjacencies to neighboring level 2 IS-IS systems. LSPs are flooded periodically.
- **Level 1 Complete Sequence Number PDU (CSNP):** Used to synchronize level 1 link-state databases when adjacency first comes up and periodically thereafter.
- **Level 2 Complete Sequence Number PDU (CSNP):** Used to synchronize level 2 link-state databases when adjacency first comes up and periodically thereafter.
- **Level 1 Partial Sequence Number PDU (PSNP):** Used to request one or more level 1 LSPs that were detected to be missing from a level 1 CSNP. The local

router sends a level 1 PSNP to the neighbor that transmitted the incomplete level 1 CSNP. That router, in turn, forwards the missing level 1 LSPs to the requesting router.

- **Level 2 Partial Sequence Number PDU (PSNP):** Used to request one or more level 2 LSPs that were detected to be missing from a level 2 CSNP. The local router sends a level 2 PSNP to the neighbor that transmitted the incomplete level 2 CSNP. That router, in turn, forwards the missing level 2 LSPs to the requesting router.

8.2.2 IS-IS NEIGHBOR STATE MACHINE ON POINT-TO-POINT LINKS

To establish adjacencies on point-to-point links, each side declares the other side to be reachable if a Hello packet is heard. Once this occurs, each side then sends a CSNP to trigger database synchronization.

8.2.3 IS-IS ON MULTIACCESS NETWORKS

On broadcast networks, a single router is elected as the **designated intermediate system (DIS)**. A DIS is elected independently for each level. The DIS on a LAN that has both level 1 and level 2 adjacencies can be the same router, but it is not required.

An IS-IS DIS is functionally similar to an OSPF designated router (DR). Like the OSPF DR, the DIS acts as the spokesperson for the LAN. The DIS is the only router that builds an LSP for the LAN itself, which is known as the *pseudonode*. Unlike OSPF, IS-IS does not provide a backup DIS capability. A backup is not necessary because all IS-IS routers on a LAN become adjacent with one another. When the DIS becomes unavailable, a new DIS is elected. In OSPF, by contrast, all routers on a LAN become adjacent only with the DR and backup DR.

DIS priority is transmitted in the Hello packets. If a new router appears on a LAN with a higher DIS priority, it becomes the new DIS. This also differs from OSPF, where DR-ship is "sticky." In OSPF, once a router is elected DR, it remains so unless it disappears. In OSPF, the DR is typically the first router that comes up.

IS-IS's preemptive DIS behavior, on the other hand, provides deterministic DIS selection.

8.2.4 EXCHANGING LINK-STATE INFORMATION WITH NEIGHBORS

Each side of an IS-IS adjacency sends a CSNP when the adjacency first comes up and when a change is detected in the link-state database. The CSNP contains a summary of each LSP in the database (essentially the LSP's name, a checksum, and an age), but it does not carry any network layer reachability information. When a router receives a CSNP, it checks to see whether the information contained within corresponds to its own link-state database. If the local router recognizes that its neighbor is missing or has an older version of an LSP, the local router sends the latest version of the LSP to the neighbor.

If the local router notices that it is missing an LSP or its neighbor has a newer version of an LSP, the local router sends a PSNP to its neighbor requesting that LSP. The neighbor responds to the PSNP with the appropriate LSP.

This procedure happens throughout the network and eventually all L1 routers in each area have the exact same level 1 link-state database. Likewise, all L2 routers have the exact same level 2 link-state database.

8.2.5 INTERAREA LEAKING

An L1/L2 router sets the ATTACHED bit (ATT) in its L1 LSP. Setting this bit informs all L1 routers in this area that the L1/L2 router can be used to reach other areas. L1 routers install a default route toward the closest router that generated an LSP with the ATT bit set. The operation of the ATT bit provides similar functionality to OSPF *totally stubby areas*, in that only a default route is injected into the area and more specific routes are suppressed.

RFC 2966, "Domain-wide Prefix Distribution with Two-Level IS-IS," introduces a way to enable IS-IS areas to behave similarly to OSPF *stub* and *not-so-stubby areas*. Like an OSPF ABR, an IS-IS L1/L2 router that supports RFC 2966 can inject route information from other areas into its own area. With interarea leaking, an L1 router no longer has to send traffic destined for other areas to its own closest L1/L2 router. Instead, an L1 router can send interarea traffic to the L1/L2 router closest to the destination, which reduces the potential for suboptimal routing.

8.2.6 EXTENDING TLVs

The flexibility of TLVs makes IS-IS much easier to extend than OSPF for such added capabilities as multiple topologies, IPv6, and traffic engineering. Enabling IS-IS to carry a new type of information is as simple as adding and defining a new TLV.

M-ISIS introduces new TLVs, but no new PDU types are required. This can be compared to adding new attributes to the existing BGP Update message, which also did not require any new message formats. Table 8-1 shows the TLVs applicable to each PDU.

In the rest of this section, we discuss the IS-IS TLVs upon which the new M-ISIS TLVs build. The new M-ISIS TLVs are discussed in section 8.4.2.

The Extended IS Reachability (TLV 22) is defined in an Internet-Draft titled "IS-IS Extensions for Traffic Engineering" (draft-ietf-isis-traffic-04.txt). TLV 22 adds the ability for IS-IS to carry information, such as link color and bandwidth, that is used in traffic engineering. The format of TLV 22 is as follows:

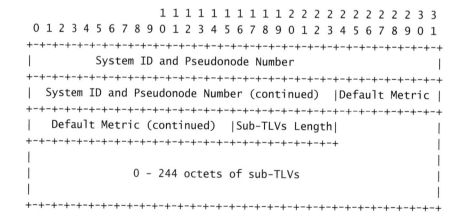

Table 8-1 TLVs for PDUs

IS-IS TLVs			LAN HELLO		P2P HELLO	LSP		CSNP		PSNP	
		TLV Number of the PDU →	15	16	17	18	20	24	25	26	27
TLV Name	TLV #	PDU Name → Source	L1	L2		L1	L2	L1	L2	L1	L2
Area Address	1	ISO 10589	X	X	X	X	X				
IS Reachability	2	ISO 10589				X	X				
IS Neighbors	6	ISO 10589	X	X							
Padding	8	ISO 10589	X	X	X						
LSP Entry	9	ISO 10589						X	X	X	X
Authentication	10	ISO 10589 draft-ietf-isis-hmac-03.txt	X	X	X	X	X	X	X	X	X
Checksum	12	draft-ietf-isis-wg-snp-checksum-02.txt	X	X	X			X	X	X	X
Extended IS Reachability	22	draft-ietf-isis-traffic-04.txt				X	X				
IP Internal Reachability	128	RFC 1195				X	X				
Protocols Supported	129	RFC 1195	X	X	X	X	X				
IP External Reachability	130	RFC 1195					X				
IP Interface Address	132	RFC 1195	X	X	X	X	X				
TE IP Router ID	134	draft-ietf-isis-traffic-04.txt				X	X				
Extended IP Reachability	135	draft-ietf-isis-traffic-04.txt				X	X				
Dynamic Hostname Resolution	137	RFC 2763				X	X				
IPv6 Interface Address	232	draft-ietf-isis-ipv6-02.txt	X	X	X	X	X				
IPv6 Reachability	236	draft-ietf-isis-ipv6-02.txt				X	X				
P2P Adjacency	240	draft-ietf-isis-3way-04.txt			X						

The valid sub-TLVs are as follows:

Sub-TLV Type	Length (octets)	Name
3	4	Administrative group (color)
6	4	IPv4 interface address
8	4	IPv4 neighbor address
9	4	Maxim link bandwidth
10	4	Reservable link bandwidth
11	32	Unreserved bandwidth
18	3	TE default metric
250–254		Reserved for Cisco-specific extensions
255		Reserved for future expansion

The Extended IP Reachability (TLV 135) is defined in the same Internet-Draft as TLV 22. TLV 135 extends the capability of TLV 128. The Metric field in TLV 128 is only 6 bits wide, providing a range of possible cost metrics from 0 through 63. TLV 135 increases this range to 0 through 16,777,215 with a new Metric field that is expanded to 32 bits. TLV 135 also introduces a bit known as the *up/down bit*. This bit indicates that the route has been leaked from level 2 to level 1, which prevents the route from being leaked back into level 2, thus potentially causing routing loops. The format for TLV 135 is as follows:

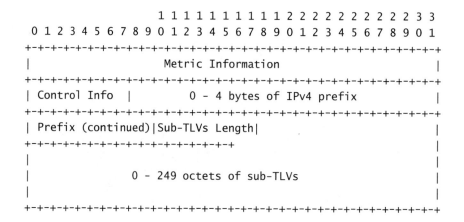

```
                       1 1 1 1 1 1 1 1 1 1 2 2 2 2 2 2 2 2 2 2 3 3
   0 1 2 3 4 5 6 7 8 9 0 1 2 3 4 5 6 7 8 9 0 1 2 3 4 5 6 7 8 9 0 1
  +-+-+-+-+-+-+-+-+-+-+-+-+-+-+-+-+-+-+-+-+-+-+-+-+-+-+-+-+-+-+-+-+
  |                      Metric Information                       |
  +-+-+-+-+-+-+-+-+-+-+-+-+-+-+-+-+-+-+-+-+-+-+-+-+-+-+-+-+-+-+-+-+
  | Control Info  |       0 - 4 bytes of IPv4 prefix             |
  +-+-+-+-+-+-+-+-+-+-+-+-+-+-+-+-+-+-+-+-+-+-+-+-+-+-+-+-+-+-+-+-+
  | Prefix (continued)|Sub-TLVs Length|                          |
  +-+-+-+-+-+-+-+-+-+-+-+-+-+-+-+-+-+-+                           |
  |                                                              |
  |               0 - 249 octets of sub-TLVs                     |
  |                                                              |
  +-+-+-+-+-+-+-+-+-+-+-+-+-+-+-+-+-+-+-+-+-+-+-+-+-+-+-+-+-+-+-+-+
```

The one-byte Control Information field consists of the following:

- One bit of up/down information
- One bit indicating the existence of sub-TLVs
- Six bits of prefix length

8.3   OVERVIEW OF M-ISIS

The multitopology extensions to IS-IS provide four main features:

- A way to tag Hello packets as belonging to certain topologies
- A means of tagging LSP information as being specific to a topology
- Separate SPF calculations for each topology
- Backward compatibility with legacy IS-IS implementations

IS-IS is already "multiprotocol" because it can carry routing information for both ISO and IPv4 network addresses. M-ISIS gives IS-IS the added ability of being able to view the underlying topology in a different way for each independent IP topology. Each of these **multitopologies (MTs)** views the cost of each link throughout the network independently from other MTs.

Similar to the multiprotocol extensions to BGP, M-ISIS can be used for purposes other than populating a dedicated multicast RPF table. For example, each topology can have overlapping IP prefixes, so it might be possible to employ M-ISIS in some VPN schemes.

M-ISIS is backward compatible with standard IS-IS implementations. The protocol overcomes the following two challenges in order to achieve backward compatibility:

- Establishing IS-IS adjacencies
- Advertising prefixes within each MT

Level boundaries are consistent across all MTs, which enables only one adjacency to be required for each level the router is exchanging with each of its peers. For example, two level 1 neighbors running M-ISIS establish only a single level 1 adjacency; they need not have a separate adjacency for each MT in which they both participate.

MT 0 is a special MT. It is equivalent to the standard IS-IS topology. LSPs tagged with MT 0 are placed in the same link-state database as untagged LSPs. Tagging an LSP with MT 0 is optional if it is the only MT on the interface. Untagged routes are considered to be in MT 0.

MT 3 is reserved for multicast RPF topology. LSPs tagged with MT 3 are placed in the link-state database dedicated to the multicast RPF topology. The router runs the SPF algorithm separately on each MT link-state database to determine the best paths for each prefix in that MT.

The best routes, determined by running the SPF algorithm on the MT 3 link-state database, are placed in the dedicated multicast RPF routing table. From this routing table, they are used for the RPF checks of such protocols as PIM-SM and MSDP. Figure 8-2 presents a conceptual view of the information flow within a router running MBGP and M-ISIS.

The next section discusses specific issues in implementing M-ISIS.

8.4 SPECIFICS OF M-ISIS

M-ISIS adds functionality to various parts of the base IS-IS protocol. Affected parts include the forming of adjacencies and advertising of prefixes. New IS-IS TLVs are specified to enable the new functionality.

8.4.1 FORMING ADJACENCIES

On point-to-point links, an M-ISIS adjacency is associated with a set of MTs. In their Hello packets, both routers advertise the MTs they have configured for the

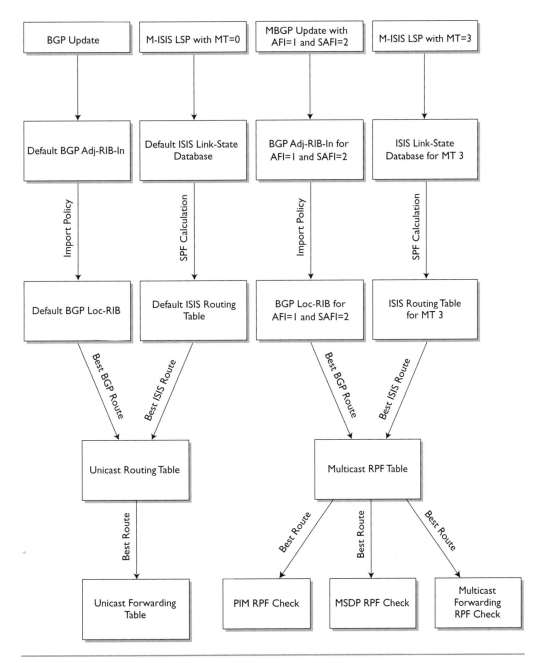

Figure 8-2 Information flow for a router running MGBP and M-ISIS

interface. The set of MTs associated with the adjacency consists of those present in both routers' Hellos. If the two routers do not share any MTs, the adjacency does not need to be formed. Absence of M-ISIS TLVs in the Hello is interpreted as MT 0.

Broadcast media present more complications for backward-compatible M-ISIS adjacencies. All M-ISIS routers on a LAN announce that they are MT-capable in their Hellos. To maintain backward compatibility, the DIS function is not MT-enabled; that is to say, the pseudonode LSP created by the DIS does not contain any MT information. On a LAN with mixed M-ISIS and legacy IS-IS speakers, the DIS can be any of the routers. Even if the DIS is MT-capable, it does not include MT information in the pseudonode LSP. Because of this operation, it is possible to make a graceful transition from a legacy IS-IS network to an M-ISIS network.

8.4.2 M-ISIS TLVs

The M-ISIS draft defines three new TLVs:

- **TLV 222:** Multitopology Intermediate Systems TLV
- **TLV 229:** Multitopology TLV
- **TLV 235:** Multitopology Reachable IPv4 Prefixes TLV

TLV 222 leverages the format and functionality of TLV 22 (Extended IS Reachability). TLV 222 is found only in LSPs. The format of the Value field for the multicast topology is as follows:

```
                      1 1 1 1 1 1 1 1 1 1 2 2 2 2 2 2 2 2 2 2 3 3
    0 1 2 3 4 5 6 7 8 9 0 1 2 3 4 5 6 7 8 9 0 1 2 3 4 5 6 7 8 9 0 1
   +-+-+-+-+-+-+-+-+-+-+-+-+-+-+-+-+-+-+-+-+-+-+-+-+-+-+-+-+-+-+-+-+
   |0|0|0|0|      MT ID = 3        |                               |
   +-+-+-+-+-+-+-+-+-+-+-+-+-+-+-+-+                               +
   |                                                               |
   |    0 - 251 octets of various structures used in TLV 22        |
   |                                                               |
   +-+-+-+-+-+-+-+-+-+-+-+-+-+-+-+-+-+-+-+-+-+-+-+-+-+-+-+-+-+-+-+-+
```

TLV 229 lists the MT ID numbers in which the local router is participating. This TLV is applicable to all Hello PDUs and LSP fragment 0. For a router that supports unicast and multicast topologies, the format of the Value field is as follows:

```
                              1 1 1 1 1 1 1 1 1 1 2 2 2 2 2 2 2 2 2 2 3 3
        0 1 2 3 4 5 6 7 8 9 0 1 2 3 4 5 6 7 8 9 0 1 2 3 4 5 6 7 8 9 0 1
        +-+-+-+-+-+-+-+-+-+-+-+-+-+-+-+-+-+-+-+-+-+-+-+-+-+-+-+-+-+-+-+-+
        |0|0|0|0|      MT ID = 0           |0|A|0|0|      MT ID = 3         |
        +-+-+-+-+-+-+-+-+-+-+-+-+-+-+-+-+-+-+-+-+-+-+-+-+-+-+-+-+-+-+-+-+
```

The Value field is divided into 2-byte sections for each supported MT. The most significant 4 bits are control bits. The least-significant 12 bits are the MT ID. The control bits are composed of (from most significant to least significant):

• One bit indicating the existence of sub-TLVs: always zero because no sub-TLVs are defined
• One bit representing the ATTACH bit for the MT: only valid in LSP fragment #0 and for MTs other than ID #0; otherwise, it is set to zero and ignored
• Two reserved bits: both set to zero and ignored

The 12 least-significant bits are the MT ID. If a router does not advertise the TLV 229, MT ID = 0 is assumed, but if TLV 229 is announced, MT ID = 0 must be explicitly included (it is no longer assumed).

TLV 235 leverages the format and functionality of TLV 135 (Extended IP Reachability). Like TLV 222, TLV 235 is found only in LSPs. The format of the Value field for the multicast topology is as follows:

```
                              1 1 1 1 1 1 1 1 1 1 2 2 2 2 2 2 2 2 2 2 3 3
        0 1 2 3 4 5 6 7 8 9 0 1 2 3 4 5 6 7 8 9 0 1 2 3 4 5 6 7 8 9 0 1
        +-+-+-+-+-+-+-+-+-+-+-+-+-+-+-+-+-+-+-+-+-+-+-+-+-+-+-+-+-+-+-+-+
        |0|0|0|0|      MT ID = 3         |                               |
        +-+-+-+-+-+-+-+-+-+-+-+-+-+-+-+-+                               +
        |                                                               |
        |     0 - 251 octets of various structures used in TLV 135      |
        |                  and/or new sub-TLV 117                       |
        |                                                               |
        +-+-+-+-+-+-+-+-+-+-+-+-+-+-+-+-+-+-+-+-+-+-+-+-+-+-+-+-+-+-+-+-+
```

The new sub-TLV 117 has a length of four octets. It is used to designate the MT prefix color. The MT prefix color can be used to designate other MT routing tables into which this prefix should be installed.

The following values are reserved for the 12-bit MT ID value:

- **MT ID 0:**   IPv4 Unicast Topology
- **MT ID 1:**   Network Management Topology
- **MT ID 2:**   IPv6 Unicast Topology
- **MT ID 3:**   IPv4 Multicast RPF Topology
- **MT ID 8191:** Experimental/Proprietary Features

8.5 EXAMPLES OF USING M-ISIS

Within the realm of multicast routing, there are two main uses of M-ISIS. The first is to set up a separate RPF topology for sources inside an autonomous system. The second is to set up a multicast-specific topology for resolving MBGP next hops for routes to sources outside the local AS; these routes are learned from IBGP peers that are not directly connected. Figure 8-3 shows a generic example of the this second usage.

In Figure 8-3, the routers in AS 200 learn the route to the multicast source in AS 100 over two External BGP (EBGP) connections: one between routers C and D and one between routers B and E. Both of these connections are MBGP-enabled. These two routes have identical path attributes except for the BGP next hop.

Router F receives the two BGP routes to the source with AFI/SAFI equal to 1/1 (unicast routes) and two BGP routes to the source with AFI/SAFI equal to 1/2 (multicast RPF routes). Router F places the unicast routes in its BGP **Loc-RIB** for unicast routes, and it places the multicast RPF routes in its BGP Loc-RIB for multicast RPF routes.

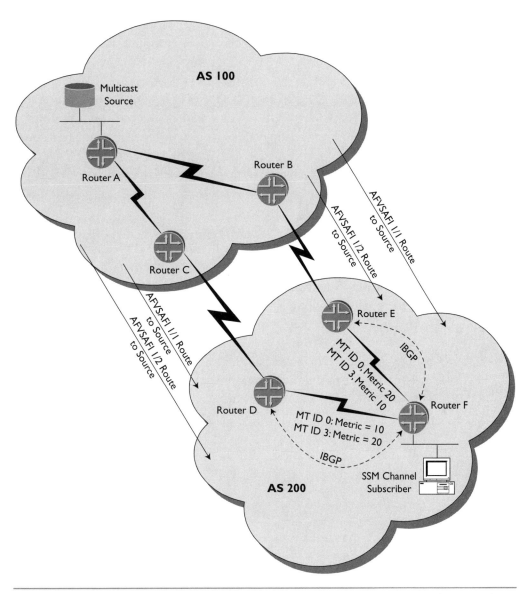

Figure 8-3 M-ISIS used to resolve MBGP next hops (Routers D and E use a next-hop self-export policy for their IBGP peers.)

Lookups for BGP-learned routes are done recursively using an IGP. When a router runs the BGP path selection algorithm to select the best BGP route, it uses the IGP to determine the best path to the BGP next hop of the BGP route.

In this example, router F learns its routes to the BGP next hops (via D and E) in IS-IS. M-ISIS is used here to provide different metrics over the same links for each topology. In the unicast routing table, the IS-IS route to router D has a metric of 10, and the route to router E has a metric of 20. In the multicast RPF table, the IS-IS route to router D has a metric of 20, and the route to router E has a metric of 10.

Because BGP next hop is the only path attribute that is different between the two BGP routes, path selection is determined by the shortest IGP metric to the BGP next hop. For the unicast routing table, the BGP route via router D is selected because it has the lower IS-IS (MT = 0) metric. For the multicast RPF table, the BGP route via router E is selected because it has the lower M-ISIS (MT = 3) metric. Thus router E is the RPF neighbor of router F for the multicast source.

Other reasons to use M-ISIS include detouring around routers not capable of forwarding multicast packets and using **generic routing encapsulation (GRE)** tunnels exclusively for multicast while routing unicast hop by hop.

Configuring and Verifying Multicast Routing on Juniper Networks Routers

Juniper Networks produces various router platforms targeted for deployment in the core and at the edge of ISP networks. The JUNOS operating system runs Juniper Networks routers. The commands described in this chapter give a general understanding of the minimum configuration needed to enable multicast in JUNOS software. This chapter does not describe every possible multicast command. The full technical documentation for configuring JUNOS software is available at *http://www.juniper.net/techpubs/software.html*.

All of Juniper Networks platforms keep the route control function and the packet-forwarding function on completely separate hardware modules. The **Routing Engine** (**RE**) handles the route control function. The **Packet Forwarding Engine** (**PFE**) handles the packet-forwarding function. The RE is a single module. Some platforms can house two Routing Engines, but one is always in backup mode. The PFE is composed of multiple hardware modules: mainly, the Physical Interface Cards (PICs), the Flexible PIC Concentrators (FPCs), and the packet-switching board (the abbreviation for the latter depends on the platform).

The RE has an external management Ethernet interface named **fxp0**. This interface can be used for remote access and monitoring, but it is not used as a transit interface. The RE has an internal Ethernet interface named **fxp1** that it uses to communicate with all the other modules in the chassis. The RE uses the **Trivial Network Protocol (TNP)** for internal communication, so there is no need to configure an IP address on fxp1. The M160 platform has two internal Ethernet interfaces, the second one being fxp2. All of the external interfaces on the router other than the RE's fxp0 interface are termed *PFE interfaces*. The PFE interfaces can be used for transit IP and Multiprotocol Label Switching (MPLS) traffic as well as IP and ISO Connectionless Network Service (CLNS—used for IS-IS) traffic destined for the RE.

9.1   CONFIGURING IGMP AND PIM

The following sections describe how to configure and manage JUNOS software to support multicast routing within a domain.

9.1.1 ENABLING INTERFACES FOR IGMP AND PIM

Without any configuration, none of the router's interfaces is enabled for PIM or IGMP. Enabling PIM on the router automatically enables IGMP on all LAN interfaces. Use the following configuration to enable IGMP and PIM-SM with the version 2 packet format on all nonmanagement interfaces:

```
protocols {
    igmp {
        interface fxp0.0 {
            disable;
        }
    }
    pim {
        interface all {
            mode sparse;
            version 2;
        }
        interface fxp0.0 {
            disable;
        }
    }
}
```

```
user@m20-a> show pim interfaces
Name            Stat Mode     V State  Priority  DR address   Neighbors
fe-3/3/0.3      Up   Sparse   2 DR     1         10.0.3.1             0
lo0.0           Up   Sparse   2 DR     1         10.0.5.3             0
t3-1/0/0.0      Up   Sparse   2 P2P                                  0

user@m20-a> show igmp interface
Interface         State        Querier       Timeout  Version  Groups
fxp0.0            Disabled                          0        2       0
fxp1.0            Disabled                          0        2       0
t3-1/0/0.0        Disabled                          0        2       0
fe-3/3/0.3        Up           10.0.3.1         None        2       0

Configured Parameters:
IGMP Query Interval (1/10 secs): 1250
IGMP Query Response Interval (1/10 secs): 100
IGP Last Member Query Interval (1/10 secs): 10
IGMP Robustness Count: 2

Derived Parameters:
IGMP Membership Timeout (usecs): 260000000
IGMP Other Querier Present Timeout (usecs): 255000000
```

Notice that enabling PIM on the t3-1/0/0.0 interface does not automatically enable IGMP because this interface is a point-to-point interface and is most likely
not connected to any end hosts that could become group members. If a point-to-
point interface needs to speak IGMP, it can be explicitly enabled.

Even if a router is attached to a LAN that has only IGMP-speaking hosts and no
other PIM-speaking routers, the interface connected to that LAN must still run
PIM for the router to function properly. If PIM is disabled on an interface, IGMP
shows the UP state, but group membership reports will not be processed cor-
rectly. Use the show igmp group command to show the groups joined by directly
connected hosts.

```
user@m20-a> show igmp group
Interface       Group        Source      Last Reported   Timeout
fe-3/3/0.3      224.0.0.2    0.0.0.0     10.0.3.2            193
fe-3/3/0.3      224.0.0.22   0.0.0.0     10.0.3.2            193
local           224.0.0.2    0.0.0.0     0.0.0.0               0
```

9.1.2 SSM GROUP RANGE

By default, Juniper Networks routers assume the SSM range is 232.0.0.0/8, but you can configure the SSM range to be something other than 232.0.0.0/8. For example, to configure the SSM range to be 235.0.0.0/8, use the following configuration:

```
routing-options {
    multicast {
        ssm-groups {
            235.0.0.0/8;
        }
    }
}
```

With this command, shared tree behavior is prohibited for groups configured as SSM groups. The router rejects any control messages for the groups in the SSM range that are not source-specific. Examples of messages that would be discarded for groups in the SSM range are IGMP group-specific reports and PIM (*,G) Joins.

In the output of the following command, notice that ASM groups have 0.0.0.0 in the Source column, whereas SSM groups have the IP address of the source.

```
user@m20-a> show igmp group
Interface      Group          Source           Last Reported    Timeout
fe-0/0/0.0     224.0.0.2      0.0.0.0          192.168.14.144   193
fe-0/0/0.0     224.0.0.22     0.0.0.0          192.168.14.142   193
fe-2/0/1.0     232.232.10.10  192.168.195.42   192.168.195.34   0
fe-2/0/1.0     232.232.10.10  192.168.195.62   192.168.195.34   0
fe-2/0/1.0     232.232.10.11  192.168.195.62   192.168.195.34   0
local          224.0.0.2      0.0.0.0          0.0.0.0          0
```

9.1.3 THE TUNNEL PIC AND THE PE AND PD INTERFACES

On Juniper Networks routers, the encapsulation and decapsulation of data packets into tunnels (GRE or **IP-IP—IP in IP Tunneling**) is executed in hardware. The data packets never touch the RE. Most other vendors' routers perform this function in the software running on the route processor. The advantage of doing it in hardware in the PFE is that packets can be encapsulated or decapsulated and forwarded at a much faster rate. Additionally, because the RE does not have to process these packets, routing control processes are not adversely affected.

In order to create tunnel interfaces on a Juniper router, a Tunnel PIC must be installed. The Tunnel PIC serves as a placeholder for the packet memory in the FPC. If a native data packet comes into the router and its next hop resolves to a tunnel interface, the packet is forwarded by the packet-switching board to the Tunnel PIC. The packet is encapsulated in the appropriate header, and the Tunnel PIC loops it back to the packet-switching board. Then it is forwarded out a physical interface based on the destination IP address in the tunnel header.

PIM Register messages encapsulate and decapsulate data packets similarly to GRE tunnels. The PIM Register function is also performed in hardware. A Tunnel PIC is required if a router is going to encapsulate or decapsulate data packets into or out of Register messages. Thus, all RPs and all PIM-SM designated routers (DRs) that are directly connected to a source require a Tunnel PIC.

To determine whether a tunnel PIC is installed, use the following command:

```
user@m20-b> show chassis hardware | match "fpc|tunnel"
FPC 0             REV 01    710-001292    AB4751
  PIC 3           REV 01    750-002982    HF2515                    1x Tunnel
FPC 2             REV 09    710-000175    AA4843
```

The preceding output shows that a Tunnel PIC is installed in PIC slot 3 of the FPC in FPC slot 0. If PIM-SM is configured and this router is serving as RP, a virtual interface, named pd (which is short for "PIM Register decapsulation interface"), will be configured. The following configuration and two commands show that this router is acting as an RP:

```
user@m20-b> show pim rps
RP address      Type        Holdtime Timeout Active groups Group prefixes
10.0.1.1        bootstrap        150  None                0 224.0.0.0/4

10.0.1.1        static             0  None                0 224.0.0.0/4

user@m20-b> show interfaces terse | match 10.0.1.1
lo0.0           up    up    inet  10.0.1.1        --> 0/0
```

The following command shows the newly created pd interface that is used for decapsulating Register messages. The 0/3/0 indicates the location of the Tunnel PIC.

```
user@m20-b> show pim interfaces
Name            Stat Mode    V State   Priority  DR address   Neighbors
ge-0/0/0.0      Up   Sparse  2 DR      1         10.0.5.2             0
lo0.0           Up   Sparse  2 DR      1         10.0.1.1             0
pd-0/3/0.32768  Up   Sparse  2 P2P                                   0
```

If a router running PIM-SM is using another router as an RP and it has a tunnel PIC installed, it will create a virtual interface named pe (which is short for "PIM Register encapsulation interface"). The pe interface does not appear until the RP is discovered. The 4/1/0 in the following output indicates the position of the Tunnel PIC:

```
user@m40-a> show pim rps
RP address   Type        Holdtime   Timeout   Active groups   Group prefixes
10.0.1.1     bootstrap        150       108               0   224.0.0.0/4

user@m40-a> show chassis hardware | match "fpc|tunnel"
FPC 1           REV 10   710-000175   AA7674
FPC 2           REV 10   710-000175   AA7619
FPC 4           REV 01   710-001292   AF0103
  PIC 1         REV 01   750-001323   AG1832           1x Tunnel
FPC 5           REV 01   710-001292   AD4141

user@m40-a> show pim interfaces
Name            Stat Mode    V State    Priority  DR address   Neighbors
ge-4/2/0.0      Up   Sparse  2 NotDR    1         10.0.5.2             1
lo0.0           Up   Sparse  2 DR       1         10.0.2.1             0
pe-4/1/0.32769  Up   Sparse  2 P2P                                    0
```

9.1.4 CONFIGURING STATIC GROUP-TO-RP MAPPING

To configure a router to be a statically defined RP, use the following configuration, where 10.0.1.1 is the IP address of one of this router's interfaces (preferably lo0.0):

```
protocols {
    pim {
        rp {
```

```
            local {
                address 10.0.1.1;
            }
        }
    }
}
```

To configure a non-local RP address for an RP that expects PIMv2 Register messages, use the following configuration:

```
protocols {
    pim {
        rp {
            static {
                address 10.0.1.1;
                version 2;
            }
        }
    }
}
```

By default, both the rp local and rp static set the RP for all groups in the 224.0.0.0/4 range. It is possible to specify a more specific range for an RP. For example, the following configuration sets the local router to be RP for groups in 224.0.0.0/5 and a nonlocal RP address (10.0.1.2) for groups in the 234.0.0.0/8 group range:

```
protocols {
    pim {
        rp {
            local {
                address 10.0.1.1;
                range 224.0.0.0/5;
            }
            static {
                address 10.0.1.2;
                version 2;
                range 234.0.0.0/8;
            }
        }
    }
}
```

9.1.5 CONFIGURING THE PIM BOOTSTRAP MECHANISM

To configure the bootstrap mechanism in a PIM-SM domain, select which rout-ers are candidate RPs and which routers are candidate BSRs. A single router can be both a candidate RP and candidate BSR. You need at least one candidate RP and one candidate BSR for the bootstrap mechanism to work. All the interfaces within the PIM-SM domain must run PIM version 2.

To configure a router as a candidate RP, use the following configuration:

```
protocols {
    pim {
        rp {
            local {
                address 10.0.1.1;
            }
        }
    }
}
```

To configure a router as a candidate BSR, use the following configuration:

```
protocols {
    pim {
        rp {
            bootstrap-priority 50;
            }
        }
    }
}
```

The value of the bootstrap-priority can be 0–255. The default is 0, which means that the router is not a candidate BSR. Turning on PIM tracing with the option of flagging RP-related messages on a router that is the elected BSR yields the follow-ing messages:

```
Apr 5 06:26:36 PIM RECV 10.0.1.1 -> 10.0.2.1 V2 CandidateRP sum 0xe963 len 22
Apr 5 06:27:32 PIM RECV 10.0.1.1 -> 10.0.2.1 V2 CandidateRP sum 0xe963 len 22
Apr 5 06:27:36 PIM SENT 10.0.5.1 -> 224.0.0.13 V2 Bootstrap sum 0x69ed len 36
Apr 5 06:27:36 PIM RECV 10.0.1.1 -> 10.0.2.1 V2 CandidateRP sum 0xe963 len 22
Apr 5 06:28:34 PIM RECV 10.0.1.1 -> 10.0.2.1 V2 CandidateRP sum 0xe963 len 22
Apr 5 06:28:36 PIM SENT 10.0.5.1 -> 224.0.0.13 V2 Bootstrap sum 0x2ded len 36
```

```
Apr 5 06:28:36 PIM RECV 10.0.1.1 -> 10.0.2.1 V2 CandidateRP sum 0xe963 len 22
Apr 5 06:29:34 PIM RECV 10.0.1.1 -> 10.0.2.1 V2 CandidateRP sum 0xe963 len 22
Apr 5 06:29:36 PIM SENT 10.0.5.1 -> 224.0.0.13 V2 Bootstrap sum 0xf1ec len 36
Apr 5 06:29:36 PIM RECV 10.0.1.1 -> 10.0.2.1 V2 CandidateRP sum 0xe963 len 22
```

The interfaces that connect to other PIM-SM domains should have BSR filters configured to prevent BSR messages from leaking across domain boundaries. The following configuration prevents BSR messages from entering or leaving the router through interface so-0/0/0:

```
protocol {
    pim {
        rp {
            bootstrap-import bsr-import-filter
            bootstrap-export bsr-export-filter
        }
    }
}
policy-options {
    policy-statement bsr-import-filter {
        from interface so-0/0/0.0;
        then reject;
    }
    policy-statement bsr-export-filter {
        from interface so-0/0/0.0;
        then reject;
    }
}
```

9.1.6 CONFIGURING AUTO-RP

The steps to configure auto-RP are as follows:

1. On all routers, configure sparse-dense mode on all PIM-enabled interfaces:

```
protocols {
    pim {
        interface all {
            mode sparse-dense;
        }
    }
}
```

2. On all routers, configure 224.0.1.39 and 224.0.1.40 as dense groups. Only groups that are configured as dense groups are forwarded according to dense mode operation.

```
protocols {
    pim {
        dense-groups {
            224.0.1.39/32;
            224.0.1.40/32;
        }
    }
}
```

3. In a PIM domain running auto-RP, each router falls into one of four categories. The following lists each category along with its configuration:

- **Discovery:** Listen for auto-RP Mapping messages:

```
protocols {
    pim {
        rp {
            auto-rp discovery;
        }
    }
}
```

- **Announce-only:** Transmit auto-RP Announcement messages and listen for auto-RP Mapping messages:

```
protocols {
    pim {
        rp {
            local {
                address 10.0.1.1;
            }
            auto-rp announce;
        }
    }
}
```

- **Mapping-only:** Listen for auto-RP Announcement messages, perform RP-to-group mapping function, and transmit auto-RP Mapping messages:

```
protocols {
    pim {
        rp {
            auto-rp mapping;
        }
    }
}
```

- **Announce and mapping:** Perform combined tasks of both announce-only and mapping-only categories:

```
protocols {
    pim {
        rp {
            local {
                address 10.0.1.1;
            }
            auto-rp mapping;
        }
    }
}
```

The following command shows the RPs learned through auto-RP as well as a static entry if the router is configured as a local RP:

```
user@m20-b> show pim rps
RP address    Type       Holdtime  Timeout  Active groups  Group prefixes
10.0.1.1      auto-rp         150      148              2  224.0.0.0/4

10.0.1.1      static            0     None              2  224.0.0.0/4
```

A domain running auto-RP needs at least one router providing the announce functionality and one router providing the mapping functionality. The same router can provide both announce and mapping functions. Here is a sample of messages in a PIM trace file on a router configured for announce-only:

```
Jan 30 04:59:21 PIM RECV 10.0.2.1+496 -> 224.0.1.40 AutoRP v1 mapping hold
150 rpcount 1 len 20 rp 10.0.1.1 version 2 groups 1 prefixes 224.0.0.0/4
Jan 30 04:59:25 PIM SENT 10.0.1.1 -> 224.0.1.39+496 AutoRP v1 announce hold
150 rpcount 1 len 20 rp 10.0.1.1 version 2 groups 1 prefixes 224.0.0.0/4
Jan 30 04:59:25 PIM RECV 10.0.1.1+496 -> 224.0.1.39 AutoRP v1 announce hold
150 rpcount 1 len 20 rp 10.0.1.1 version 2 groups 1 prefixes 224.0.0.0/4
Jan 30 05:00:19 PIM RECV 10.0.2.1+496 -> 224.0.1.40 AutoRP v1 mapping hold
150 rpcount 1 len 20 rp 10.0.1.1 version 2 groups 1 prefixes 224.0.0.0/4
Jan 30 05:00:24 PIM SENT 10.0.1.1 -> 224.0.1.39+496 AutoRP v1 announce hold
150 rpcount 1 len 20 rp 10.0.1.1 version 2 groups 1 prefixes 224.0.0.0/4
Jan 30 05:00:24 PIM RECV 10.0.1.1+496 -> 224.0.1.39 AutoRP v1 announce hold
150 rpcount 1 len 20 rp 10.0.1.1 version 2 groups 1 prefixes 224.0.0.0/4
```

At the boundaries of a domain running auto-RP, the auto-RP control messages should be administratively scoped, which prevents them from leaking into other domains. Use the following configuration to prevent auto-RP leaking:

```
routing-options {
    multicast {
        scope s0 {
            prefix 224.0.1.39/32;
            interface t3-5/2/0.0;
        }
        scope s1 {
            prefix 224.0.1.40/32;
            interface t3-5/2/0.0;
        }
    }
}
```

The following command shows that the 224.0.1.39 group is administratively scoped on interface t3-5/2/0.0:

```
user@m40-a> show pim join extensive
Group           Source          RP              Flags
224.0.1.39      10.0.2.1                        dense
    Upstream interface: local
    Downstream interfaces:
```

```
local
t3-5/2/0.0 (Administratively scoped)
ge-4/2/0.0
```

9.1.7 CONFIGURING ANYCAST RP

Anycast RP can use any RP-set mechanism (that is, static, bootstrap, or auto-RP) to distribute the RP-to-group mapping. Anycast RP with static group-to-RP mapping is the most common strategy used by ISPs because it provides load balancing and redundancy in the simplest and most intuitive manner. Anycast RP requires additional configuration only on the routers that are serving as the RPs. All other routers are configured with the standard static RP configuration pointing to the shared anycast address.

To configure anycast RP, perform the following steps on each RP:

1. Configure two addresses on the lo0.0 interface. One is unique to the router, and the other is the shared anycast address. Make the unique address the primary address for the interface to insure that protocols such as OSPF and BGP select it as router ID.

```
interfaces {
    lo0 {
        unit 0 {
            family inet address 10.0.0.1/32 {
                primary;
            }
            family inet address 10.0.0.2/32;
        }
    }
}
```

2. Use the shared anycast address as the local RP address:

```
protocols {
    pim {
        rp {
            local {
```

```
            address 10.0.0.2;
        }
      }
    }
}
```

3. Use the unique address as the local address for the MSDP sessions to the other RPs in the domain:

```
protocols {
    msdp {
        local-address 10.0.0.1;
        peer 10.0.0.3;
        peer 10.0.0.4;
    }
}
```

9.1.8 MONITORING PIM JOIN STATE AND MULTICAST FORWARDING

Once PIM is enabled on all the routers and the RP has been discovered through one of the aforementioned mechanisms, the network is ready to carry multicast traffic. The command used to show PIM Join state is show pim join extensive. The two scenarios described in the following sections examine the output of this command during different phases of PIM operation.

9.1.8.1 Scenario 1: RPT is Set Up, No Active Sources The following is the output for a router sitting along the RPT between the RP and a group member. At this point, no active sources are sending to the group.

```
user@m20-b> show pim join extensive 226.1.1.1
Group          Source     RP              Flags
226.1.1.1      0.0.0.0    10.0.2.1        sparse,rptree,wildcard
    Upstream interface: ge-0/0/0.0
    Upstream State: Join to RP
    Downstream Neighbors:
        Interface: ge-0/1/0.0
            10.0.4.1        State: Join   Flags: SRW  Timeout: 196
```

The source is displayed as 0.0.0.0, which indicates that this state is (*,G). The address 10.0.4.1 is the address of the PIM neighbor that sent the (*,G) Join message. The upstream interface is the RPF interface for the RP address, which is confirmed by the following command:

```
user@m20-b> show multicast rpf 10.0.2.1
Multicast RPF table: INET.2


Source prefix      Protocol   RPF interface    RPF neighbor
10.0.2.1/32        IS-IS      ge-0/0/0.0       10.0.5.1
```

Here is the output showing the Join state on the RP. Notice that the upstream interface is local.

```
user@m40-a> show pim join extensive 226.1.1.1
Group          Source      RP            Flags
226.1.1.1      0.0.0.0     10.0.2.1      sparse,rptree,wildcard
     Upstream interface: local
     Upstream State: Local RP
     Downstream Neighbors:
         Interface: ge-4/2/0.0
             10.0.5.2          State: Join    Flags: SRW   Timeout: 162
```

9.1.8.2 Scenario 2: A Source Is Active, a Host Joins the Group

Later The following is the output on the PIM-SM DR connected to a source for a group that has no members:

```
user@m20-b> show pim join extensive 227.1.1.1
Group          Source          RP            Flags
227.1.1.1      10.0.4.1                       sparse
     Upstream interface: ge-0/1/0.0
     Upstream State: Local Source
     Downstream Neighbors:
```

The upstream interface is the RPF interface for the source as shown with the following commands:

```
user@m20-b> show multicast rpf 10.0.4.1
Multicast RPF table: INET.2
```

```
Source prefix       Protocol   RPF interface    RPF neighbor
10.0.4.0/30         Direct     ge-0/1/0.0

user@m20-b> show pim source 10.0.4.1
RPF Address    Prefix/length    Upstream interface  Neighbor address
10.0.4.1       10.0.4.0/30      ge-0/1/0.0          Direct
```

The PIM statistics show that Register messages were sent and Register-Stop messages were received:

```
user@m20-b> show pim statistics
PIM Message type        Received        Sent     Rx errors
V2 Hello                    5488        5483         0
V2 Register                    0          32         0
V2 Register Stop              32           0         0
```

Without any members, the RP has no Join state for the group.

```
user@m40-a> show pim join extensive 227.1.1.1
Group            Source          RP              Flags
```

The fact that the DR has registered this source to the RP is kept in the RP's Register state. To view the RP's Register state, use the following command:

```
user@m40-a> show pim rps extensive
RP: 10.0.2.1
Learned from 10.0.2.1 via: auto-rp
Time Active: 20:26:14
Holdtime: 150 with 107 remaining
Device Index: 39
Subunit: 32768
Interface: pd-4/1/0.32768
Group Ranges:
        224.0.0.0/4
Active groups using RP:

Register State for RP:
Group         Source        FirstHop        RP Address      State
227.1.1.1     10.0.4.1      10.0.1.1        10.0.2.1        Receive
```

If a host joins the group, the RP receives a (*,G) Join message for 227.1.1.1. The RP sets up (*,G) Join state for 227.1.1.1. The RP scans its PIM Register state and MSDP Source-Active cache looking for any active sources for the group. For each source it finds, it sets up (S,G) state, copying the downstream neighbors from the (*,G) entry and forwards an (S,G) Join message toward the source.

Here is the output on the PIM-SM DR connected to a source after a host has joined the group. This router sits along the SPT, so it has no (*,G) state.

```
user@m20-b> show pim join extensive 227.1.1.1
Group            Source          RP              Flags
227.1.1.1        10.0.4.1                        sparse
    Upstream interface: ge-0/1/0.0
    Upstream State: Local Source
    Downstream Neighbors:
        Interface: ge-0/0/0.0
            10.0.5.1          State: Join   Flags: S   Timeout: 198
```

This command shows traffic statistics based on group and source:

```
user@m20-b> show multicast usage
Group            Sources Packets
227.1.1.1        1       3101
224.0.1.40       1       1440
224.0.1.39       1       1343

Prefix           /len Groups Packets
10.0.4.1         /32  1      3101
10.0.2.1         /32  2      2783
```

The following sequence of commands illustrates how PIM Join state is transferred to the PFE, so packets entering the router are forwarded out the correct interfaces. The first command shows the multicast route that is installed based on the PIM (S,G) Join state:

```
user@m20-b> show multicast route extensive group 227.1.1.1
Group        Source prefix   Act Pru NHid  Packets   IfMismatch Timeout
227.1.1.1    10.0.4.1        /32 AF  30    1734      0          319
    Upstream interface: ge-0/1/0.0
    Session name: Unknown
```

The following command shows the entry in the multicast routing table (inet.1):

```
user@m20-b> show route table inet.1 detail 227.1.1.1/32

inet.1: 3 destinations, 3 routes (3 active, 0 holddown, 0 hidden)
+ = Active Route, - = Last Active, * = Both

227.1.1.1.10.0.4.1/64 (1 entry, 1 announced)
        *PIM    Preference: 105
                Next hop type: Multicast
                State: <Active Int>
                Local AS:    100
                Age: 33:27
                Task: PIM.master
                Announcement bits (1): 0-KRT
                AS path: I
```

The following command shows the entry in the RE's copy of the IPv4 forwarding table:

```
user@m20-b> show route forwarding-table matching 227.1.1.1/32
Routing table:: inet
Internet:
Destination            Type RtRef InIf Flags Nexthop Type Index NhRef Netif
224.0.0.0/4            user 2     0    0x1a          rslv 27    3
227.1.1.1.10.0.4.1/64  user 0     6    0x1e          mcrt 30    1
```

The following command shows the entry in the PFE's copy of the IPv4 forwarding table:

```
user@m20-b> show pfe route ip
Destination                      NH IP Addr      Type     NH ID Interface
-------------------------------- --------------- -------- ----- ---------
227.1.1.1.10.0.4.1/64                            MultiRT     30 ge-0/1/0.0
```

The following command shows the entry in next-hop database stored in the PFE:

```
user@m20-b> show pfe next-hop
```

```
Nexthop Info:
    ID    Type    Interface  Protocol         Encap  Next Hop Addr   MTU
   -----  ------  ---------- --------  ----------- -------------  -----
    30   MultiRT  -            IPv4          -  -                 0
            ge-0/0/0.0       IPv4     Ethernet
```

9.2 CONFIGURING MSDP

The following shows the configuration of an MSDP speaker with a unique IP address 10.0.0.1 (preferably on lo0.0) peering with two other MSDP-speaking routers:

```
protocols {
    msdp {
        local-address 10.0.0.1;
        peer 10.0.0.3;
        peer 10.0.0.4;
    }
}
```

Use the following command to display the MSDP Source-Active cache:

```
user@m20-a> show msdp source-active
Group address    Source address  Peer address   Originator    Flags
224.0.1.11       10.222.100.32   10.9.201.205   10.222.1.5    Accept
                                 10.9.201.254   10.222.1.5    Reject
                                 10.9.202.2     10.222.1.5    Reject
                                 10.9.202.253   10.222.1.5    Reject
```

From this output, it can be inferred that 10.9.201.205 is the RPF peer for originator 10.222.1.5 because the Flags column shows that it is the only peer from which the router accepted the SA. Another way to show the RPF peer for a particular originator address is as follows:

```
user@m20-a> test msdp rpf-peer 10.222.1.5
MSDP peer is 10.9.201.205 for Originator 10.222.1.5/32
```

To configure peers in an MSDP mesh group, use the following configuration:

```
protocols {
    msdp {
        local-address 10.0.0.1;
        group g {
            mode mesh-group;
            peer 10.0.0.3;
            peer 10.0.0.4;
        }
    }
}
```

To configure a default peer, use the following configuration:

```
protocols {
    msdp {
        local-address 10.0.0.1;
        peer 10.0.0.3 {
            default-peer;
        }
    }
}
```

The following is an example of an SA filter in which SA messages for the 229.9.9.9 group are discarded:

```
protocols {
    msdp {
        peer 10.0.0.3 {
            import msdp-p;
        }
    }
}
policy-options {
    policy-statement msdp-p {
        term 10 {
            from {
                route-filter 229.9.9.9/32 exact;
            }
            then reject;
```

```
        }
    }
}

user@m20-a> show msdp source-active
Group address  Source address  Peer address  Originator   Flags
229.9.9.9      10.129.2.2      10.129.3.3    10.129.3.2   Accept,Filtered
```

MSDP policies can also match on the MSDP peer address and the source address in the SA. Care should be taken when using SA filters in transit domains. Preventing SAs from being flooded to other domains can lead to multicast "blackholes."

9.3   CONFIGURING A DEDICATED RPF TABLE

In JUNOS software, the primary IPv4 unicast routing table is inet.0. This table imports routes from the unicast routing protocols running on the router. By default, PIM and MSDP use inet.0 for their RPF checks. JUNOS software has another routing table, inet.2, that is reserved for use as a dedicated multicast RPF table. The following demonstrates how to configure PIM and MSDP to use inet.2 as the dedicated multicast RPF table:

```
routing-options {
    rib-groups {
        mcast-rpf-rib {
            import-rib inet.2;
        }
    }
}
protocols {
    msdp {
        rib-group inet mcast-rpf-rib;
    }
    pim {
        rib-group inet mcast-rpf-rib;
    }
}
```

A **routing information base (RIB)** is a routing table. A RIB group associates zero or more import RIBs with zero or one export RIBs. This association does not have any meaning until you apply the RIB group to a routing protocol. The RIB group is interpreted differently depending on the protocol. PIM and MSDP use the first import RIB listed in the configuration as their respective RPF tables. Any other RIBs listed in the RIB group are ignored by PIM and MSDP.

The previously shown configuration tells PIM and MSDP to use inet.2 for their RPF checks. It does not place any routes in inet.2. To verify that the PIM is now using inet.2 as its RPF table, use the following command:

```
user@m20-a> show multicast rpf
Multicast RPF table: INET.2

Source prefix     Protocol   RPF interface    RPF neighbor
```

At this point, PIM is using inet.2 as its RPF table, but there are no routes in inet.2. The first step in building an RPF table is to get the directly connected routes into inet.2, as illustrated in Figure 9-1. Use the following configuration to do so:

```
routing-options
    interface-routes {
        rib-group inet if-rib;
    }
    rib-groups {
        if-rib {
            import-rib [ inet.0 inet.2 ];
        }
    }
}
```

To show that the interface routes are now in inet.2, use the following command. Note that inet.2 is not the default multicast RPF RIB; you must configure the PIM RIB group as described previously (the initial configuration shown in section 9.3) in order to make inet.2 the RPF RIB.

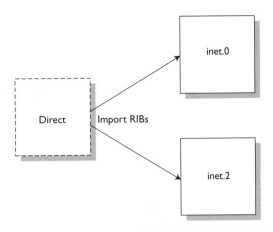

Figure 9-1 Use of RIB groups for interface routes

```
user@m20-a> show multicast rpf
Multicast RPF table: INET.2

Source prefix    Protocol    RPF interface    RPF neighbor
10.0.5.0/24      Direct      ge-4/2/0.0
10.0.5.1/32      Local
127.0.0.1/32
172.29.1.0/24    Direct      fxp0.0
172.29.1.5/32    Local
```

The RIB group configured for the interface routes takes on a completely different meaning from those used by PIM and MSDP. All connected routes are placed into each of the RIBs listed as import RIBs in the interface routes' RIB group.

With the directly connected routes in inet.2, you can add other routes to inet.2 with a variety of different protocols. Static routes can be added to inet.2 with the following configuration:

```
routing-options {
    rib inet.2 {
        static {
```

```
            route 192.0.0.0/8 next-hop 10.0.5.254;
        }
    }
}

user@m20-a> show route 192/8

inet.2: 6 destinations, 6 routes (5 active, 0 holddown, 1 hidden)
+ = Active Route, - = Last Active, * = Both

192.0.0.0/8           *[Static/5] 00:00:06
                      > to 10.0.5.254 via ge-4/2/0.0
```

The JUNOS software also implements the concept of configuration groups. These groups can be used to apply a template configuration to multiple parts of the configuration file. Doing so comes in handy when you want to add a static route to both inet.0 and inet.2, but you do not want to type the static route configuration twice. The following configuration illustrates this application of configuration groups:

```
groups {
    dual-statics {
        routing-options {
            rib <inet.*> {
                static {
                    route 172.0.0.0/8 next-hop 10.0.5.254;
                }
            }
        }
    }
}
routing-options {
    rib inet.0 {
        apply-groups dual-statics;
    }
    rib inet.2 {
        apply-groups dual-statics;
    }
}

user@m20-a> show route 172/8
```

```
inet.0: 10 destinations, 10 routes (9 active, 0 holddown, 1 hidden)
+ = Active Route, - = Last Active, * = Both

172.0.0.0/8            *[Static/5] 00:00:11
                       > to 10.0.5.254 via ge-4/2/0.0

inet.2: 8 destinations, 8 routes (7 active, 0 holddown, 1 hidden)
+ = Active Route, - = Last Active, * = Both

172.0.0.0/8            *[Static/5] 00:00:11
                       > to 10.0.5.254 via ge-4/2/0.0
```

You can perform similar configurations for aggregate and generated routes.

9.3.1 CONFIGURING MBGP

By default, the router establishes BGP sessions as unicast-only (that is, AFI = 1, SAFI = 1). To configure a specific neighbor as an MBGP peer, use the following configuration:

```
protocols {
    bgp {
        family inet {
            any;
        }
        group g {
            type internal;
            neighbor 10.0.2.1;
        }
    }
}
```

An alternative is to explicitly configure the RIB groups for both unicast and multicast RPF routes. This configuration yields identical results to the preceding configuration but is shown here to help illustrate the behavior of the family inet any command:

```
routing-options {
    rib-groups {
        bgp-unicast-rg {
```

```
                export-rib inet.0;
                import-rib inet.0;
            }
            bgp-multicast-rg {
                export-rib inet.2;
                import-rib inet.2;
            }
        }
    }
}
protocols {
    bgp {
        family inet {
            unicast {
                rib-group bgp-unicast-rg;
            }
            multicast {
                rib-group bgp-multicast-rg;
            }
        }
    }
}
```

Import RIBs can be used to install routes learned from BGP neighbors into one or more routing tables. The export RIB is the table used when BGP extracts routes to advertise to peers. MBGP adds another level of complexity because it enables import and export RIBs to be set independently for both unicast and multicast NLRIs. Figure 9-2 shows the logical data flow between the protocol and RIBs when configuring MBGP.

The following command shows that the local router is exchanging both unicast and multicast RPF NLRI information with the 10.0.2.1 neighbor:

```
user@m20-b> show bgp neighbor | match "peer:|nlri"
Peer: 10.0.2.1+179    AS 65000  Local: 10.0.1.1+2152   AS 65000
  NLRI advertised by peer: inet-unicast inet-multicast
  NLRI for this session: inet-unicast inet-multicast
```

When MBGP is enabled, received routes tagged as IPv4 multicast RPF routes (that is, AFI = 1, SAFI = 2,3) are placed into the inet.2 RIB. Active BGP routes in

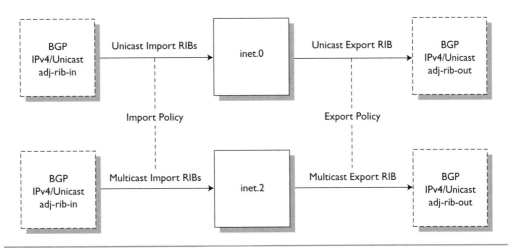

Figure 9-2 Default RIB groups for MBGP

inet.2 are advertised to BGP peers, based on the standard BGP route advertisement rules. To specify separate policies for unicast and multicast RPF routes, BGP export and import policies can be configured referencing the inet.0 and inet.2 tables. For example, the following policy sets the local preference to 100 for unicast routes but to 200 for multicast RPF routes:

```
policy-options policy-statement mbgp-p
term 10 {
    from rib inet.0;
    then {
        local-preference 100;
    }
}
term 20 {
    from rib inet.2;
    then {
        local-preference 200;
    }
}
```

The following configuration applies the policy as the import policy for the 10.0.2.1 neighbor:

```
protocols {
    bgp {
        group g {
            neighbor 10.0.2.1 {
                import mbgp-p;
            }
        }
    }
}
```

Keep in mind that policy is always applied between a routing protocol and a RIB. You can never apply policy directly between two RIBs nor directly between two protocols.

9.3.2 CONFIGURING M-ISIS

M-ISIS can be used to place routes learned from IS-IS into both inet.0 and inet.2. Additionally, each M-ISIS interface can have a separate metric for both the unicast and multicast RPF. Here is an example M-ISIS configuration:

```
protocols {
    isis {
        multicast-topology;
        interface ge-0/0/0.0 {
            level 1 disable;
            level 2 {
                metric 50;
                multicast-metric 25;
            }
        }
        interface ge-0/1/0.0 {
            level 1 disable;
            level 2 {
                metric 25;
                multicast-metric 50;
            }
        }
```

```
        }
    }
}
```

This configuration enables level 2-only M-ISIS on two Gigabit Ethernet interfaces. It sets the unicast metric on ge-0/0/0.0 to 50 and the multicast metric to 25. It sets the unicast metric on ge-0/1/0.0 to 25 and the multicast metric to 50. This configuration can be used to influence the active route chosen in inet.0 and inet.2.

Figure 9-3 shows the logical data flow between the protocol and RIBs when configuring M-ISIS.

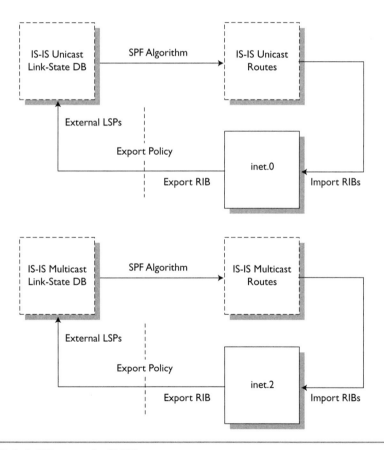

Figure 9-3 Default RIB groups for M-ISIS

9.3.3 CONFIGURING OSPF TO PLACE ROUTES IN INET.2

OSPF does not have multitopology capabilities, but it is possible to place the routes learned via OSPF in both inet.0 and inet.2. It is not possible to apply separate routing metrics or policy for unicast and multicast with OSPF. Importing OSPF routes into inet.0 and inet.2 can be used to enable the success of RPF checks for sources within the domain learned via OSPF, while applying separate policy for interdomain unicast and multicast routes learned via MBGP. To place OSPF routes in both inet.0 and inet.2, use the following configuration statements in addition to the base OSPF configuration:

```
routing-options {
    rib-groups {
        ospf-rib {
            export-rib inet.0;
            import-rib [ inet.0 inet.2 ];
        }
    }
}
protocols {
    ospf {
        rib-group ospf-rib;
    }
}
```

The following command output shows that the OSPF-learned routes are placed in inet.2:

```
user@m20-a> show route table inet.2 protocol ospf

inet.2: 7 destinations, 7 routes (7 active, 0 holddown, 0 hidden)
+ = Active Route, - = Last Active, * = Both

10.0.0.0/30        *[OSPF/10] 14:22:39, metric 11
                    > to 172.17.4.111 via fxp0.0
                      to 172.17.4.112 via fxp0.0
10.10.0.1/32       *[OSPF/10] 14:22:39, metric 10
                    > to 172.17.4.112 via fxp0.0
```

```
10.10.0.2/32        *[OSPF/10] 14:22:39, metric 10
                     > to 172.17.4.111 via fxp0.0
10.10.14.0/24       *[OSPF/10] 14:22:39, metric 1
                     > via so-2/0/0.0
172.1.1.1/32         *[OSPF/10] 14:22:39, metric 11
                     > to 172.17.4.110 via fxp0.0
10.61.0.10/32       *[OSPF/10] 14:22:39, metric 1
                     > via so-2/0/0.0
10.61.0.82/32       *[OSPF/10] 14:22:39, metric 0
                     > via so-2/0/2.0
```

Figure 9-4 shows the logical data flow between the protocol and RIBs when configuring a RIB group for OSPF.

9.3.4   CONFIGURING DVMRP TO PROVIDE RPF INFORMATION TO PIM

In JUNOS software, you can configure DVMRP to provide RPF information to PIM. This mode of operation is known as *unicast-only mode* because DVMRP is not used to set up forwarding state for multicast traffic. When used in this fashion, DVMRP is essentially equivalent to RIP except DVMRP places its routes into

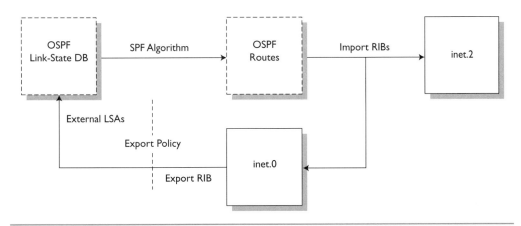

Figure 9-4 Using nondefault OSPF RIB groups to place routes in inet.2

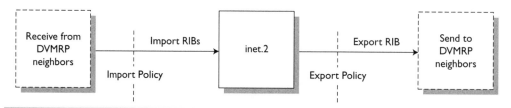

Figure 9-5 Using nondefault DVMRP RIB groups to place routes in inet.2

the dedicated multicast RPF table (inet.2). Use the following configuration to enable DVMRP in unicast-only mode on an interface:

```
routing-options {
    rib-groups {
        dvmrp-rg {
            export-rib inet.2;
            import-rib inet.2;
        }
    }
}
protocols {
    dvmrp {
        rib-group inet dvmrp-rg;
        interface all {
            mode unicast-routing;
        }
    }
}
```

To display all of the routes in inet.2 learned from DVMRP, use the following command:

```
show route protocol dvmrp table inet.2
```

Figure 9-5 shows the logical data flow between the protocol and RIBs when configuring DVMRP in unicast-only mode.

This chapter has shown the reader practical means for configuring and verifying multicast routing on Juniper Network routers. Chapter 10 continues by providing similar guidelines for configuring multicast routing on Cisco Systems routers.

Configuring and Verifying Multicast Routing on Cisco Systems Routers

Cisco Systems produces a wide variety of router platforms. The IOS (Internetwork Operating System) runs on most Cisco router platforms. The commands described in this chapter provide a general understanding of the minimum configuration needed to enable multicast in IOS. This chapter does not describe every possible multicast command. The full technical documentation for configuring IOS software is available at *http://www.cisco.com/univercd/cc/td/doc/product/software/index.htm.*

Chapter 10 assumes the reader has experience configuring IOS software and understands such terms as *global configuration mode* and *interface configuration mode.* Experience configuring multicast routing features in the IOS software is not assumed.

Note: The organization of this chapter parallels Chapter 9, which describes JUNOS software.

10.1 CONFIGURING PIM AND IGMP

In this section, we provide practical configuration guidelines for PIM and IGMP on IOS platforms.

10.1.1 ENABLING INTERFACES FOR IGMP AND PIM

The first step when configuring IOS software for multicast is to enable multicast routing on the entire router with the following command in global configuration mode:

```
ip multicast-routing
```

Enabling PIM on an interface automatically enables IGMP for that interface. Use the following command in interface configuration mode to enable PIM-SM and IGMP:

```
ip pim sparse-mode
```

Use the following command to show which interfaces have PIM enabled:

```
Router# show ip pim interface
```

Address	Interface	Mode	Neighbor Count	Query Interval	DR
10.92.37.6	Ethernet0	Sparse	2	30	10.92.37.33
10.92.36.129	Ethernet1	Sparse	2	30	10.92.36.131
10.1.37.2	Tunnel0	Sparse	1	30	0.0.0.0

Use the following command to show which interfaces have IGMP enabled:

```
Router# show ip igmp interface

Ethernet0 is up, line protocol is up
  Internet address is 10.92.37.6, subnet mask is 255.255.255.0
  IGMP is enabled on interface
  IGMP query interval is 60 seconds
```

```
    Inbound IGMP access group is not set
    Multicast routing is enabled on interface
    Multicast TTL threshold is 0
    Multicast designated router (DR) is 10.92.37.33
    No multicast groups joined
Ethernet1 is up, line protocol is up
  Internet address is 10.92.36.129, subnet mask is 255.255.255.0
  IGMP is enabled on interface
  IGMP query interval is 60 seconds
  Inbound IGMP access group is not set
  Multicast routing is enabled on interface
  Multicast TTL threshold is 0
  Multicast designated router (DR) is 10.92.36.131
  No multicast groups joined
Tunnel0 is up, line protocol is up
  Internet address is 10.1.37.2, subnet mask is 255.255.0.0
  IGMP is enabled on interface
  IGMP query interval is 60 seconds
  Inbound IGMP access group is not set
  Multicast routing is enabled on interface
  Multicast TTL threshold is 0
  No multicast groups joined
```

Use the following command to show the groups joined by directly connected hosts:

```
Router# show ip igmp groups
```

```
IGMP Connected Group Membership
Group Address     Interface    Uptime     Expires   Last Reporter
224.0.255.1       Ethernet0    18:51:41   0:02:15   10.92.37.192
224.2.226.60      Ethernet0    1:51:31    0:02:17   10.92.37.192
224.2.127.255     Ethernet0    18:51:45   0:02:17   10.92.37.192
226.2.2.2         Ethernet1    18:51:47   0:02:35   10.92.36.128
224.2.0.1         Ethernet0    18:51:43   0:02:14   10.92.37.192
225.2.2.2         Ethernet0    18:51:43   0:02:21   10.92.37.33
225.2.2.2         Ethernet1    18:51:47   0:02:55   10.92.36.124
225.2.2.4         Ethernet0    18:18:02   0:02:20   10.92.37.192
225.2.2.4         Ethernet1    18:23:32   0:02:41   10.92.36.128
```

10.1.2 SSM GROUP RANGE

To configure the SSM range to be 232.0.0.0/8, use the following command in global configuration mode:

```
ip pim ssm default
```

You can also configure the SSM range to be something other than 232.0.0.0/8. For example, to configure the SSM range to be 235.0.0.0/8, use the following commands in global configuration mode:

```
ip pim ssm range 4
access-list 4 permit 235.0.0.0 0.255.255.255
```

In the access-list statement, 0.255.255.255 is the wild card mask equivalent to a 255.0.0.0 (8-bit) subnet mask. To calculate a wild card mask, swap all the bits of the subnet mask.

With the following command, shared tree behavior is prohibited for groups configured in the SSM range. The router rejects any control messages for the groups in the SSM range that are not source-specific. Examples of messages that are discarded for groups in the SSM range are IGMP group-specific reports and PIM (*,G) Joins.

10.1.3 CONFIGURING STATIC RP

This section covers the configuration steps necessary when you are using static configuration to set the RP in your PIM-SM domain. If a particular router is serving as the static RP for the domain, no RP mapping configuration is needed on that router. A Cisco Systems router serving as a static RP does not need to be configured as such. Currently in IOS software, when a router receives a (*,G) Join message containing an RP address that matches one of the router's local addresses for which PIM is configured, the router believes it is the RP and honors the Join. Thus, IOS software has no equivalent to JUNOS software's `rp local` command.

Non-RP routers need to be configured with the IP address of the RP. For example, to set the address 10.92.37.33 as the RP for all multicast groups, use the following command in global configuration mode:

```
ip pim rp-address 10.92.37.33 override
```

The preceding command sets the RP address to 10.92.37.33 for all groups in the 224.0.0.0/4 range. The override keyword forces the router to ignore any auto-RP or BSR mapping announcements. If override is omitted and a router hears an auto-RP or BSR announcement that conflicts with the static address, the router uses the RP address learned via auto-RP or BSR. The override keyword should always be used so that auto-RP or BSR messages that may have accidentally leaked into a domain cannot remap the router.

It is possible to specify a more specific range for an RP. For example, to set the local router (10.0.1.1) to be the RP for groups in 224.0.0.0/8 and to set a nonlocal RP address (10.92.37.33) for groups in the 235.0.0.0/8 group range, use the following commands in global configuration mode:

```
ip pim rp-address 10.92.37.33 1
access-list 1 235.0.0.0 0.255.255.255
```

Notice that no configuration is necessary to set the local router to be RP for the groups in the 224.0.0.0/8 range. The local router is the RP for this range by virtue of all other routers in its PIM-SM domain having the following commands in global configuration mode:

```
ip pim rp-address 10.92.37.33 1
access-list 1 235.0.0.0 0.255.255.255
ip pim rp-address 10.0.1.1 2
access-list 2 224.0.0.0 0.255.255.255
```

10.1.4 CONFIGURING THE PIM-SM BOOTSTRAP MECHANISM

To configure the bootstrap mechanism in a PIM-SM domain, select which routers are candidate RPs and which routers are candidate BSRs. A single router can be both a candidate RP and a candidate BSR. You need at least one candidate RP and one candidate BSR for the bootstrap mechanism to work. All of the interfaces within the PIM-SM domain must run PIM version 2. The interfaces that connect to other PIM-SM domains should run PIM version 1 or be configured as PIM borders so that Candidate RP and Bootstrap messages are not leaked to the other domain.

To configure a router to announce itself as a candidate RP for groups in the 239.0.0.0/8 range using the IP address of its loopback 0 interface, use the following commands in global configuration mode:

```
ip pim rp-candidate loopback 0 group-list 4
access-list 4 permit 239.0.0.0 0.255.255.255
```

To configure a router as a candidate BSR using the IP address of its loopback 0 interface and setting a bootstrap priority of 50, use the following command in global configuration mode:

```
ip pim bsr-candidate loopback 0 50
```

The value of the bootstrap priority can be 0 to 255. The default is 0, and the router with the largest preference is elected BSR.

To keep Bootstrap messages from traversing an interface connected to a neighboring PIM-SM domain, use the following command in interface configuration mode:

```
ip pim border
```

Use the following command to turn on debugging for PIM BSR messages:

```
debugging ip pim bsr
```

10.1.5 CONFIGURING AUTO-RP

A domain running auto-RP needs at least one router providing the announce functionality and one router providing the mapping functionality. The same router can provide both announce and mapping functions. In IOS software, 224.0.1.39 and 224.0.1.40 are automatically set to be dense groups when any interfaces on the router are enabled for sparse-dense mode. The steps to configure auto-RP are as follows:

1. On all routers, configure sparse-dense mode on all PIM-enabled interfaces. Use the following command in interface configuration mode:

   ```
   ip pim sparse-dense-mode
   ```

On an interface configured for sparse-dense mode, any ASM group that does not have an RP is automatically considered a dense group. If a Cisco Systems router somehow loses its group-to-RP mapping, it considers all groups to be dense. Likewise, if the RP(s) in a domain becomes unreachable, all Cisco Systems routers in that domain flood all groups according to dense mode. This behavior is fundamentally different from the way sparse-dense mode operates in Juniper Networks routers. In JUNOS software, only groups that are explicitly configured in dense mode are forwarded densely.

2. In a PIM domain running auto-RP, each router falls into one of four categories. The following lists each category along with its configuration:

- **Discovery:** The IOS software automatically listens for auto-RP Mapping messages. No configuration is necessary.

- **Announce-only:** Transmit auto-RP Announce messages and listen for auto-RP Mapping messages. Use the following commands in global configuration mode:

```
ip pim send-rp-announce loopback 0 scope 255 group-list 5
access-list 5 permit 224.0.0.0 15.255.255.255
```

The scope parameter sets the IP TTL value in the auto-RP Announce messages transmitted by this router. Prior to the advent of administrative scoping of IP multicast, TTL was used as a mechanism to scope auto-RP control packets. Setting the scope parameter to 255 ensures that auto-RP messages can reach the farthest edges of a domain. To prevent leaking, the interfaces that connect to other PIM-SM domains should be set to administratively scope the two auto-RP group addresses.

- **Mapping-only:** Listen for auto-RP Announce messages, perform RP-to-group mapping function, and transmit auto-RP Mapping messages. Use the following command in global configuration mode:

```
ip pim send-rp-discovery scope 255
```

- **Announce and mapping:** Perform combined tasks of both Announce-only and Mapping-only categories. Use the following commands in global configuration mode:

```
ip pim send-rp-announce loopback 0 scope 255 group-list 5
access-list 5 permit 224.0.0.0 15.255.255.255
ip pim send-rp-discovery scope 255
```

Use the following command to show the RPs learned through auto-RP:

```
Router# show ip pim rp mapping
PIM Group-to-RP Mappings
Group(s) 224.0.1.39/32, uptime: 1w4d, expires: never
    RP 10.0.1.2
    Info source: local
Group(s) 224.0.1.40/32, uptime: 1w4d, expires: never
    RP 10.0.1.2
    Info source: local
Group(s): 224.0.0.0/4, uptime: 1d03h, expires: 00:02:28
    RP 10.0.0.1, PIMv2 v1
    Info source: 10.0.0.1
```

The first two groups are the auto-RP groups, which are treated as dense groups. Info source: 10.0.0.1 indicates that 10.0.0.1 is the mapping agent.

Use the following command to turn on debugging for PIM auto-RP messages:

```
debug ip pim auto-rp
```

At the edges of a domain running auto-RP, the auto-RP control messages should be administratively scoped, which keeps them from leaking into other domains. For example, if the Ethernet 0 interface connects to another PIM-SM domain, use the following commands in global configuration mode to scope the two groups used for auto-RP control messages:

```
access-list 1 deny 224.0.1.39 0.0.0.0
access-list 1 deny 224.0.1.40 0.0.0.0
access-list 1 permit 224.0.0.0 15.255.255.255
interface ethernet 0
 ip multicast boundary 1
```

10.1.6 CONFIGURING ANYCAST RP

Anycast RP can use any RP-set mechanism to distribute the RP-to-group mapping (that is, static, bootstrap, or auto-RP). Anycast RP with static group-to-RP mapping is the most common strategy used by ISPs because it provides load balancing and redundancy in the simplest and most intuitive manner. Anycast RP requires additional configuration only on the routers that are serving as the RPs. All other routers are configured with the standard static RP configuration pointing to the shared anycast address.

To configure anycast RP, perform the following steps on each RP:

1. Configure two addresses on a loopback interface. One is unique to the router, and the other is the shared anycast address. The unique address should be the primary address on the loopback interface. For example, if 192.168.1.1 is an address unique to the local router and 10.10.10.10 is the shared anycast address, use the following commands in global configuration mode:

```
interface loopback 0
  ip address 192.168.1.1 255.255.255.255
  ip address 10.10.10.10 255.255.255.255 secondary
  ip pim sparse-mode
```

Alternatively, two loopback interfaces can be used. In this example, loopback 0 contains the unique address of the router, while interface loopback 1 contains the shared anycast address:

```
interface loopback 0
  ip address 192.168.1.1 255.255.255.255
  ip pim sparse-mode
interface loopback 1
  ip address 10.10.10.10 255.255.255.255
  ip pim sparse-mode
```

2. Use the unique address as the local address for the MSDP sessions to the other RPs in the domain. Also, the originator ID command sets the RP address in all originating SA messages to the unique address, which prevents originating SA messages from being rejected by other anycast RPs because of RPF failures.

The following commands in global configuration mode create an MSDP peering with another anycast RP whose unique address is 192.168.1.2:

```
ip msdp peer 192.168.1.2 connect-source loopback 0
ip msdp originator-id loopback 0
```

10.1.7 MONITORING PIM JOIN STATE AND MULTICAST FORWARDING

Once PIM is enabled on all the routers and one of the RP mapping mechanisms is configured, the network is ready to carry multicast traffic. The command used to show PIM Join state is show ip mroute.

The following example shows the output of this command for all (*,G) and (S,G) state for the group 232.1.1.1. This router is treating 232.1.1.1 as an SSM group, so there is no RP for the group, and the (*,G) entry has no upstream or downstream interfaces listed.

```
Router# show ip mroute 232.1.1.1

IP Multicast Routing Table
Flags: D - Dense, S - Sparse, B - Bidir Group, s - SSM Group, C -
    Connected,
        L - Local, P - Pruned, R - RP-bit set, F - Register flag,
        T - SPT-bit set, J - Join SPT, M - MSDP created entry,
        X - Proxy Join Timer Running, A - Advertised via MSDP, U - URD,
        I - Received Source Specific Host Report
Outgoing interface flags: H - Hardware switched
Timers: Uptime/Expires
Interface state: Interface, Next-Hop or VCD, State/Mode

(*, 232.1.1.1), 4d21h/00:02:59, RP 0.0.0.0, flags:sSJP
  Incoming interface: Null, RPF nbr 0.0.0.0
  Outgoing interface list: Null

(10.69.214.1, 232.1.1.1), 4d21h/00:02:45, flags:CTI
  Incoming interface: Ethernet3/2, RPF nbr 10.108.1.1
  Outgoing interface list:
    Ethernet3/1, Forward/Sparse-Dense, 4d21h/00:02:45
```

The following output is an example of an ASM group for which the local router is serving as the RP, which is evidenced by the null incoming interface for the (*,G) entry. The output also shows us that the RPF neighbor for the 10.102.222.70 source is 10.1.196.13 and that the route used to decide it came from the MBGP routing table.

```
Router# show ip mroute 234.12.251.11
IP Multicast Routing Table
Flags: D - Dense, S - Sparse, B - Bidir Group, s - SSM Group, C -
    Connected,
    L - Local, P - Pruned, R - RP-bit set, F - Register flag,
    T - SPT-bit set, J - Join SPT, M - MSDP created entry,
    X - Proxy Join Timer Running, A - Advertised via MSDP, U - URD,
    I - Received Source Specific Host Report
Outgoing interface flags: H - Hardware switched
Timers: Uptime/Expires
Interface state: Interface, Next-Hop or VCD, State/Mode

(*, 234.12.251.11), 00:15:24/00:03:02, RP 10.190.196.253, flags: S
  Incoming interface: Null, RPF nbr 0.0.0.0
  Outgoing interface list:
    ATM3/0.3, Forward/Sparse-Dense, 00:15:24/00:03:02

(10.102.222.70, 234.12.251.11), 00:01:00/00:01:59, flags: M
  Incoming interface: ATM3/0.10, RPF nbr 10.1.196.13, Mbgp
  Outgoing interface list:
    ATM3/0.3, Forward/Sparse-Dense, 00:01:00/00:02:32
```

10.2 CONFIGURING MSDP

To configure an MSDP peer, use the following command in global configuration mode:

```
ip msdp peer 192.168.1.2 connect-source loopback 0
```

By default, the IOS software does not cache Source-Active state. To enable Source-Active caching, use the following command in global configuration mode:

```
ip msdp cache-sa-state
```

Use the following command to display the MSDP Source-Active cache:

```
Router# show ip msdp sa-cache

MSDP Source-Active Cache - 5 entries
(10.39.41.33, 238.105.148.0), RP 10.39.3.111, MBGP/AS 65000, 2d10h/00:05:33
(10.240.112.8, 224.2.0.1), RP 10.9.200.65, MBGP/AS 65001, 00:03:21/00:02:38
(10.69.10.13, 227.37.32.1), RP 10.39.3.92, MBGP/AS 65002, 05:22:20/00:03:32
(10.67.66.18, 234.0.0.1), RP 10.39.3.111, MBGP/AS 65002, 2d10h/00:05:35
(10.67.66.148, 234.0.0.1), RP 10.39.3.111, MBGP/AS 65002, 2d10h/00:05:35
```

The AS listed is the AS in which the originating RP resides according to the MBGP table.

To configure peers in an MSDP mesh group, use the following commands in global configuration mode:

```
ip msdp mesh-group mesh-group-01 192.168.1.2
ip msdp mesh-group mesh-group-01 192.168.1.3
```

The mesh-group-01 parameter is a user-assigned mesh group name. This string is not carried in MSDP messages, so it is significant only to the local router. A router can participate in multiple mesh groups, and the name is used to distinguish among them.

To configure a default peer, use the following command in global configuration mode:

```
ip msdp default-peer 192.168.1.2
```

To filter SA messages for the 229.9.9.9 group received from a particular peer (192.168.1.2) by defining an MSDP import policy, use the following commands in global configuration mode:

```
ip msdp sa-filter in 192.168.1.2 route-map msdp-import
route-map msdp-import permit 10
  match ip address 1
access-list 1 deny 229.9.9.9 0.0.0.0
access-list 1 permit any
```

Care should be taken when using SA filters in transit domains. Preventing SAs from being flooded to other domains can lead to multicast "blackholes."

10.3 CONFIGURING A DEDICATED RPF TABLE

In IOS, the following four routing tables are used for RPF:

- Unicast routing table (which includes tables for each unicast routing protocol)
- MBGP routing table
- DVMRP routing table
- Static mroute table

When performing an RPF check, the software searches each table to find the **longest-match** prefix. If it finds a matching prefix in more than one of the tables, it uses the protocol preference (known as *administrative distance* in IOS software) to determine the route that is used for RPF.

It is important to note that the RPF route-selection process is different from that of unicast routing. With unicast routing, the longest-match prefix is chosen even if a matching prefix with a shorter mask exists from a more preferred protocol. In the case of RPF, the same selection criteria are used on each of the four routing tables, and then the route from the most preferred protocol is selected regardless of mask length. For example, the route 10.0.0.0/14, learned via MBGP, will be selected over the route 10.0.0.0/16, learned via BGP, when performing an RPF check. Unlike the unicast routing table, the longest-match prefix rule does not take effect because administrative distance is considered prior to prefix length.

Table 10-1 lists the default protocol preferences (lower preference values are more preferred).

Table 10-1 Routing Preferences

Protocol	Preference
Directly connected	0
Static mroute	0
DVMRP	0
Static route	1
External MBGP	20
External BGP	20
OSPF	110
IS-IS	115
RIP	120
Local MBGP	200
Internal MBGP	200
Local BGP	200
Internal BGP	200

You can override the default preference for each protocol. For example, to change the preference value for Internal MBGP to 20, use the following commands in global configuration mode:

```
router bgp 65005
    distance bgp 20 20 200
```

The parameters in the distance bgp command are in the order external-internal-local. To change the preference of all DVMRP-learned routes to 100, use the following commands in global configuration mode:

```
access-list 1 permit 0.0.0.0 255.255.255.255
interface ethernet 0
  ip dvmrp accept-filter 1 100
```

You can check the route that is used as the RPF route for any address by using the following command:

```
Router # show ip rpf 10.69.10.13

RPF information for 10.69.10.13
  RPF interface: BRI0
  RPF neighbor: 10.69.121.10
  RPF route/mask: 10.69.0.0/255.255.0.0
  RPF type: unicast
```

The RPF Type field shows the routing table from which this route was selected. The possible values for RPF Type are unicast, DVMRP, MBGP, or static mroute.

Static mroutes are static routes that are used for multicast RPF but are not used for unicast forwarding. To configure a static mroute to 10.0.0.0/8 with a next hop of 172.16.1.1 and a preference (administrative distance) of 180, use the following command in global configuration mode:

```
ip mroute 10.0.0.0 255.0.0.0 172.16.1.1 180
```

> **Note:** It can be confusing that the show ip mroute command shows the PIM Join state instead of the contents of the ip mroute table. There is no way to show the contents of the mroute table, but it can be inferred from the configuration file and the output of show ip rpf.

Static mroutes have a default preference of 0. A static mroute to 0.0.0.0/0 prevents the unicast routing table and the MBGP table from ever being used for RPF, assuming that administrative distances are not modified.

10.3.1 CONFIGURING MBGP

By default, the router establishes BGP sessions as unicast-only (that is, AFI = 1, SAFI = 1). To configure a specific neighbor as an MBGP peer (AFI = 1, SAFI = 2), use the following configuration:

```
router bgp 65005
  neighbor 10.108.1.1 remote-as 65006 nlri multicast
```

Use the following command to show that the neighbor is configured to exchange both unicast and multicast RPF routes:

```
Router# show ip bgp neighbors 172.16.232.178

BGP neighbor is 172.16.232.178,  remote AS 65007, external link
  BGP version 4, remote router ID 192.168.3.3
  BGP state = Established, up for 1w1d
  Last read 00:00:53, hold time is 180, keepalive interval is 60 seconds
  Neighbor capabilities:
    Route refresh: advertised and received
    Address family IPv4 Unicast: advertised and received
    Address family IPv4 Multicast: advertised and received
  Received 12519 messages, 0 notifications, 0 in queue
  Sent 12523 messages, 0 notifications, 0 in queue
  Route refresh request: received 0, sent 0
  Minimum time between advertisement runs is 30 seconds

 For address family: IPv4 Unicast
  BGP table version 5, neighbor version 5
  Index 1, Offset 0, Mask 0x2
  Community attribute sent to this neighbor
  Inbound path policy configured
  Outbound path policy configured
  Route map for incoming advertisements is uni-in
  Route map for outgoing advertisements is uni-out
  3 accepted prefixes consume 108 bytes
  Prefix advertised 6, suppressed 0, withdrawn 0

 For address family: IPv4 Multicast
  BGP table version 5, neighbor version 5
  Index 1, Offset 0, Mask 0x2
  Inbound path policy configured
```

```
Outbound path policy configured
Route map for incoming advertisements is mul-in
Route map for outgoing advertisements is mul-out
3 accepted prefixes consume 108 bytes
Prefix advertised 6, suppressed 0, withdrawn 0
```

BGP-learned routes tagged as IPv4 multicast RPF routes (that is, AFI = 1, SAFI = 2,3) are placed into the MBGP routing table. The active route for each prefix in the MBGP routing table is advertised to MBGP peers, based on the standard BGP route advertisement rules.

To specify separate policy for unicast and multicast RPF routes, BGP export and import policies can be configured to reference the unicast BGP table and the MBGP table. For example, this policy sets the local preference to 100 for unicast routes but to 200 for multicast RPF routes for routes learned from the 10.108.1.1 neighbor:

```
route-map bgp-mbgp permit 10
  match nlri unicast
  set local-preference 100
route-map bgp-mbgp permit 20
  match nlri multicast
  set local-preference 200
router bgp 65005
  neighbor 10.108.1.1 remote-as 65005 nlri unicast multicast
  neighbor 10.108.1.1 route-map bgp-mbgp in
```

To display the contents of the MBGP table, use the following command:

```
Router# show ip mbgp
```

```
MBGP table version is 6, local router ID is 192.168.200.66
Status codes: s suppressed, d damped, h history, * valid, > best, i - internal
Origin codes: i - IGP, e - EGP, ? - incomplete
   Network           Next Hop        Metric LocPrf     Weight Path
*> 10.0.20.16/28     0.0.0.0              0            0 32768 i
*> 10.0.35.16/28     0.0.0.0              0            0 32768 i
*> 10.0.36.0/28      0.0.0.0              0            0 32768 i
*> 10.0.48.16/28     0.0.0.0              0            0 32768 i
*> 10.2.0.0/16       0.0.0.0              0            0 32768 i
*> 10.2.1.0/24       0.0.0.0              0            0 32768 i
```

```
*> 10.2.2.0/24       0.0.0.0          0      0 32768 i
*> 10.2.3.0/24       0.0.0.0          0      0 32768 i
*> 10.2.7.0/24       0.0.0.0          0      0 32768 i
*> 10.2.8.0/24       0.0.0.0          0      0 32768 i
*> 10.2.10.0/24      0.0.0.0          0      0 32768 i
*> 10.2.11.0/24      0.0.0.0          0      0 32768 i
*> 10.2.12.0/24      0.0.0.0          0      0 32768 i
*> 10.2.13.0/24      0.0.0.0          0      0 32768 i
```

10.3.2 CONFIGURING DVMRP TO PROVIDE RPF INFORMATION TO PIM

In IOS software, you can configure DVMRP to provide RPF information for PIM. This mode of operation is known as *unicast-only mode* because DVMRP is not used to set up forwarding state for multicast traffic. When used in this fashion, DVMRP is essentially equivalent to RIP, except DVMRP places its routes into a dedicated multicast RPF table. To enable DVMRP in unicast-only mode on an interface, use the following command in interface configuration mode:

```
ip dvmrp unicast-routing
```

To display the contents of the DVMRP routing table, use the following command:

```
Router# show ip dvmrp route

DVMRP Routing Table - 1 entry
10.68.0.0/16 [100/11] uptime 07:55:50, expires 00:02:52
    via 10.39.3.93, Tunnel3
```

The [100/11] signifies that this route has an administrative distance of 100 and a metric of 11. Like RIP, DVMRP uses hop count as its metric.

Having provided guidelines for IMR configuration with Juniper Networks and Cisco Systems routers in the previous two chapters, we provide in Chapter 11 a representative case study for native deployment of IMR by an ISP. In the case study, a feasible combination of Juniper Networks and Cisco Systems router configurations is presented.

Case Study: Service Provider Native Deployment

In this chapter, we combine all of the concepts we have discussed in previous chapters and describe a working model of IMR. Throughout this chapter, we illustrate the exact blueprint that is typically used by the world's largest ISPs when deploying native multicast.

Juniper Networks and Cisco Systems router configurations for all router roles in this example network are provided. Additionally, configurations are provided for the routers that a customer can use to connect to the example network.

While our example network supports both ASM and SSM, most of the "heavy lifting" of this design involves ASM support. In fact, the configuration needed to enable SSM in this network involves the addition of only one or two commands in each router, which illustrates how current ASM networks require so little to add support for SSM. At the end of this chapter, configurations for an SSM-only domain are provided for comparison.

11.1 NETWORK ARCHITECTURE

In the previous chapters, we described most of the design options that are *possible*. In this case study, the focus is on what is *recommended*. This practical architecture reflects all of the best current practices of deployment on the Internet.

11.1.1 PIM-SM

PIM-SM is the multicast routing protocol used in this network. The PIM-SM domain contains five statically mapped anycast RPs. As is the case in most native ISP deployments, static RP mapping is selected over BSR and auto-RP because it provides maximum simplicity. Anycast delivers RP load balancing and redundancy.

The number of RPs deployed in an ISP network typically ranges from four to eight. Fewer than four RPs in a domain may not supply enough redundancy or load balancing. More than eight RPs adds extra administrative burden with little benefit.

11.1.1.1 RP Placement To reduce the potential for suboptimal routing on the RPT, the routers selected as RPs should be well connected and in the core of the network. Because the RPT is usually short-lived, it is not essential to have centrally located RPs, but it makes more sense. In our example network, one core router from each of the five largest hub sites is chosen as RP. The names and unique IP addresses of the loopbacks of these routers are as follows:

- **NY-RP:** 10.1.1.1/32
- **Atlanta-RP:** 10.1.1.2/32
- **Chicago-RP:** 10.1.1.3/32
- **Denver-RP:** 10.1.1.4/32
- **LA-RP:** 10.1.1.5/32
- **Anycast RP address:** 10.1.1.100

PIM-SM is configured on all of the nonmanagement interfaces of all routers in the network. PIM borders are configured on all customer-facing links to prevent certain multicast traffic from leaking onto the service provider network. This type of traffic includes protocol and administratively scoped addresses.

Customers of this ISP have the choice of using the provider's RP or their own RP. Likewise, BGP customers may elect to run MBGP with the provider.

11.1.2 IGP

In our example network, configuration for IS-IS is provided with the equivalent OSPF configuration shown in *italics*. All routers in the domain are assumed to be level 2-only routers in the same area with congruent unicast and multicast topologies. Likewise, a single backbone area is the only OSPF area in the network. The IGP carries routing information for only the loopback and network-facing (that is, noncustomer-facing) interfaces of the ISP's routers. The anycast RP address is also carried by the IGP.

11.1.3 MBGP

MBGP is used to carry all other routes, including customer networks, static routes, and all directly connected routes. Because the unicast and multicast topologies are congruent, the unicast and multicast routing tables are identical.

11.1.4 MSDP

MSDP is used to create connections between internal and external RPs so that they can exchange information about the active sources in their respective domain and subdomains. Customers who choose to run their own RPs have an MSDP peering between their RP and the nearest RP of the provider. SA filters are configured on customer peerings to prevent customers from leaking SA messages that should not be on the Internet, including SAs with sources that are in private address space and groups that are administratively scoped or reserved for protocol use.

In this example, we reluctantly chose to put all anycast RPs in an MSDP mesh group. A mesh group is needed in this topology to prevent RPF-peer failures. Without the mesh group, external SA messages forwarded by one anycast RP may be discarded by the other four anycast RPs. For example, imagine NY-RP receives an SA message from a customer MSDP peering. The customer's RP, Cust-RP, originates the SA message.

Based on the first RPF rule of version 2 of the MSDP draft (Cust-RP is the originator), NY-RP determines that Cust-RP is the RPF peer, accepts the SA, and forwards the SA to the other four anycast RPs. If NY-RP is not advertising the active IBGP route for Cust-RP to LA-RP (RPF rule 3), LA-RP determines that NY-RP is not the MSDP RPF peer for Cust-RP and discards the SA. Because NY-RP is a router somewhere in the core of the network, this condition probably will not be met, and LA-RP (and possibly the other three anycast RPs) will not accept any SA messages coming from Cust-RP's domain.

With a mesh group, LA-RP always accepts any SA it receives from NY-RP. The disadvantage of mesh groups is that MSDP traceroute might not work properly, and the entire goal of RPF-peer forwarding is lost.

There are two alternatives to using a mesh group in this topology. First, create an MSDP peering between every anycast RP and every edge router that connects directly to customers. By setting up the external MSDP peering between Cust-RP and its nearest edge router, SA messages received by the anycast RPs from this edge router satisfy RPF rule 3. However, this complex topology of MSDP peerings would carry a great deal of administrative burden.

A second approach is to create an MBGP session along with the MSDP session between Cust-RP and NY-RP. This alternative makes NY-RP far more likely to advertise the active IBGP route for Cust-RP to the other anycast RPs, satisfying RPF rule 3. Once again, this solution adds far more administrative overhead than the simple mesh group option.

11.2 ISP ROUTER CONFIGURATIONS

This section shows relevant configurations for Juniper Networks and Cisco Systems routers acting as both RPs and non-RPs. In our example network, NY-RP and LA-nonRP are Juniper Networks routers, while LA-RP and NY-nonRP are Cisco Systems routers. On the Juniper Networks non-RP routers, interfaces so-0/0/0 and so-0/0/1 are backbone links, while interface t3-1/0/0 connects to a customer. On the Cisco non-RP routers, interfaces POS0/0/0 and POS0/0/1 are backbone links, while Serial1/0/0 connects to a customer.

To reduce repetition, MBGP, IS-IS, and OSPF configurations are shown only for the RP routers. Configuration for the non-RP routers would look the same.

11.2.1 ISP RP CONFIGURATION: JUNIPER NETWORKS

This configuration describes a Juniper Networks router acting as an RP in a typical service provider's network.

```
system {
    host-name NY-RP;
}
interfaces {
    so-0/0/0 {
        unit 0 {
            description "Backbone Link";
            family inet;
            family iso;
        }
    }
    lo0 {
        unit 0 {
            family inet {
                address 10.1.1.1/32 {       /*  Unique IP Address  */
                    primary;
                }
                address 10.1.1.100/32;      /*  Anycast RP Address  */
            }
            family iso {
                address 49.0001.0100.0100.1001.00; /* ISO Address */
            }
        }
    }
}
protocols {
    sap;                             /* Listen to SDR announcements */
    bgp {
        family inet {
            unicast;                        /* SAFI=1  */
            multicast;                /* SAFI=2  */
```

```
        }
        export static-connected;  /* Redistribute static and connected */
        group IBGP-Peers {         /* routes into BGP */
            type internal;
            local-address 10.1.1.1;
            neighbor 10.1.1.x;
        }
        group BGP-Customers {
            type external;
            neighbor 10.2.2.x {
                peer-as 65001;
            }
        }
    }
    isis {
        multicast-topology;               /* M-ISIS */
        level 1 disable;
        interface so-0/0/0.0 {
            level 2 {
                metric 10;                /* MT 0 metric */
                multicast-metric 10;      /* MT 3 metric */
            }
        }
        interface lo0.0 {
            level 2 passive;
        }
    }
}
msdp {
    rib-group inet mcast-rpf-rib;          /* Use inet.2 for MSDP RPF */
    local-address 10.1.1.1;
    group Anycast-RPs {
        mode mesh-group;
        peer 10.1.1.2;
        peer 10.1.1.3;
        peer 10.1.1.4;
        peer 10.1.1.5;
    }
    group Customer-RPs {                   /* SA filter for customer peerings */
        export SA-filter;
        import SA-filter;
        peer 10.2.2.x;
    }
```

```
      }
   ospf {
      rib-group ospf-rib;            /* Put OSPF routes in inet.2 */
      area 0.0.0.0 {
         interface so-0/0/0.0 {
            metric 10;
         }
         interface lo0.0 {
            passive;
         }
      }
   }
pim {
   rib-group inet mcast-rpf-rib;   /* Use inet.2 for PIM RPF */
   rp {
      bootstrap-import block-bsr;   /* Prevents BSR messages from */
      bootstrap-export block-bsr;   /* entering or leaving router */
      local {
         address 10.1.1.100;   /* I am the RP */
      }
   }
   interface all {                 /* Enable PIM-SM on all interfaces */
      mode sparse;
   }
   interface fxp0.0 {              /* ... except management interface */
      disable;
   }
   }
}
routing-options {
   interface-routes {              /* Put connected routes in inet.2 */
      rib-group inet if-rib;
   }
   static {
      rib-group static-rib;       /* Put static routes in inet.2 */
   }
   rib-groups {
     mcast-rpf-rib {   /* RIB group used for PIM and MSDP RPF */
         import-rib inet.2;
      }
      if-rib {          /* RIB group used for connected routes */
         import-rib [ inet.0 inet.2 ];
```

```
            }
            static-rib {   /* RIB group used for static routes */
                import-rib [ inet.0 inet.2 ];
            }
            ospf-rib {      /* RIB group used for OSPF */
                import-rib [ inet.0 inet.2 ];
            }
        }
    }
    autonomous-system 65000;
    }
}
policy-options {
    policy-statement SA-filter { /* SA filter for all customers */
        term BAD-groups {
            from {
                route-filter 224.0.1.2/32 exact;   /* SGI-Dogfight */
                route-filter 224.0.1.3/32 exact;   /* RWHOD */
                route-filter 224.0.1.22/32 exact; /* SVRLOC */
                route-filter 224.0.1.24/32 exact; /* MICROSOFT-DS */
                route-filter 224.0.1.35/32 exact; /* SVRLOC-DA */
                route-filter 224.0.1.39/32 exact; /* AutoRP Announce */
                route-filter 224.0.1.40/32 exact; /* AutoRP Discovery */
                route-filter 224.0.1.60/32 exact; /* HP-Dev-Disc */
                route-filter 224.0.2.2/32 exact;   /* Sun RPC */
                route-filter 229.55.150.208/32 exact; /* Norton Ghost */
                route-filter 232.0.0.0/8 orlonger;   /* SSM */
                route-filter 239.0.0.0/8 orlonger;   /* Admin-scoped */
            }
            then reject;
        }
        term BAD-Sources {
            from {                      /* Private address space */
                source-address-filter 10.0.0.0/8 orlonger;
                source-address-filter 127.0.0.0/8 orlonger;
                source-address-filter 172.16.0.0/12 orlonger;
                source-address-filter 192.168.0.0/16 orlonger;
            }
            then reject;
        }
        term everything-else {
            then accept;
        }
```

```
   }
   policy-statement static-connected { /* Redistribute static and */
      from protocol [ static direct ]; /* connected routes into BGP */
      then accept;
   }
   policy-statement block-bsr {          /* BSR input/output filter */
       then reject;
   }
}
```

11.2.2 ISP RP Configuration: Cisco Systems

This configuration describes a Cisco Systems router acting as an RP in a typical
service provider's network.

```
hostname LA-RP
ip multicast-routing
!
! Enable PIM-SM on all interfaces
! Listen to SDR sessions on one interface
!
interface Loopback0
 description Unique IP address
 ip address 10.1.1.5 255.255.255.255
 ip pim sparse-mode
 ip sdr listen
!
interface Loopback1
 description Anycast RP address
 ip address 10.1.1.100 255.255.255.255
 ip pim sparse-mode
!
interface POS0/0/0
 description Backbone link
 ip pim sparse-mode
 ip router isis ISP
 clns router isis ISP
 isis circuit-type level-2-only
 isis metric 10 level-2
 ip ospf cost 10
!
```

```
! ISIS config
!
router isis ISP
 passive-interface Loopback0
 passive-interface Loopback1
 summary-address 10.1.1.0 255.255.255.0
 net 49.0001.0100.0100.1005.00
 is-type level-2-only
!
! OSPF Config
!
router ospf 10
 passive-interface Loopback0
 passive-interface Loopback1
 network 10.1.1.0 0.0.0.255 area 0
!
! BGP Peerings
!
router bgp 65000
 no synchronization
 redistribute connected route-map static-connected-mbgp
 redistribute static route-map static-connected-mbgp
 neighbor ibgp-peers peer-group nlri unicast multicast
 neighbor ibgp-peers remote-as 65000
 neighbor ibgp-peers update-source Loopback0
 neighbor 10.1.1.x peer-group ibgp-peers
 neighbor 10.2.2.x remote-as 65001 nlri unicast multicast
 neighbor 10.2.2.x description MBGP Customer peering
!
! Static RP mapping and SSM address range
!
ip pim rp-address 10.1.1.100 override
ip pim ssm default
!
! Customer MSDP peering
!
ip msdp peer 10.2.2.x connect-source Loopback0
ip msdp sa-filter in 10.2.2.x list 101
ip msdp sa-filter out 10.2.2.x list 101
!
! Anycast RP MSDP peerings in mesh group
!
```

```
ip msdp peer 10.1.1.1 connect-source Loopback0
ip msdp peer 10.1.1.2 connect-source Loopback0
ip msdp peer 10.1.1.3 connect-source Loopback0
ip msdp peer 10.1.1.4 connect-source Loopback0
ip msdp mesh-group IMSDP 10.1.1.1
ip msdp mesh-group IMSDP 10.1.1.2
ip msdp mesh-group IMSDP 10.1.1.3
ip msdp mesh-group IMSDP 10.1.1.4
!
! Set the RP in originating SAs to unique address
! and cache SAs (both done by default on Juniper routers)
!
ip msdp originator-id Loopback0
ip msdp cache-sa-state
!
! MSDP SA filter
!
access-list 101 deny  ip any host 224.0.1.2 ! SGI "Dogfight" game
access-list 101 deny  ip any host 224.0.1.3  ! RWHOD
access-list 101 deny  ip any host 224.0.1.22 ! SVRLOC
access-list 101 deny  ip any host 224.0.1.24 ! MICROSOFT-DS
access-list 101 deny  ip any host 224.0.1.35 ! SVRLOC-DA
access-list 101 deny  ip any host 224.0.1.39 ! AutoRP Announce
access-list 101 deny  ip any host 224.0.1.40 ! AutoRP Discovery
access-list 101 deny  ip any host 224.0.1.60 ! HP Device Discovery
access-list 101 deny  ip any host 224.0.2.2  ! Sun RPC
access-list 101 deny  ip any host 229.55.150.208 ! Norton "Ghost"
access-list 101 deny  ip any 232.0.0.0 0.255.255.255 ! SSM
access-list 101 deny  ip any 239.0.0.0 0.255.255.255 ! Admin Scoped
! Private Address Space
access-list 101 deny   ip 10.0.0.0 0.255.255.255  any
access-list 101 deny   ip 127.0.0.0 0.255.255.255 any
access-list 101 deny   ip 172.16.0.0 0.15.255.255 any
access-list 101 deny   ip 192.168.0.0 0.0.255.255 any
access-list 101 permit ip any any
!
! Redistributes static and connected routes
! into MBGP
!
route-map static-connected-mbgp permit 10
 set nlri unicast multicast
!
```

11.2.3 ISP Non-RP Configuration: Juniper Networks

This configuration describes a Juniper Networks router acting as a non-RP in a typical service provider's network.

```
system {
    host-name LA-nonRP;
}
interfaces {
    so-0/0/0 {
        unit 0 {
            description "Backbone Link";
            family inet;
            family iso;
        }
    }
    so-0/0/1 {
        unit 0 {
            description "Backbone Link";
            family inet;
            family iso;
        }
    }
    t3-1/0/0 {
        unit 0 {
            description "Customer Link";
            family inet;
        }
    }
    lo0 {
        unit 0 {
            family inet;
            family iso;
        }
    }
}
protocols {
    sap;            /* Listen to SDR announcements */
    pim {
```

```
        rib-group inet mcast-rpf-rib;   /* Use inet.2 for PIM RPF */
        rp {
            bootstrap-import block-bsr; /* Prevents BSR messages from */
            bootstrap-export block-bsr; /* entering or leaving router */
              static {
                  address 10.1.1.100;   /* RP address */
              }
        }
        interface all {       /* Enable PIM-SM on all interfaces */
            mode sparse;
        }
        interface fxp0.0 {    /* ... except management interface */
            disable;
        }
      }
  }
}
routing-options {
    interface-routes {      /* Put connected routes in inet.2 */
        rib-group inet if-rib;
    }
    static {
        rib-group static-rib;    /* Put static routes in inet.2 */
    }
    rib-groups {
        mcast-rpf-rib {   /* RIB group used for PIM and MSDP RPF */
            import-rib inet.2;
        }
        if-rib {     /* RIB group used for connected routes */
            import-rib [ inet.0 inet.2 ];
        }
        static-rib {           /* RIB group used for static routes */
            import-rib [ inet.0 inet.2 ];
        }
        ospf-rib {             /* RIB group used for OSPF */
            import-rib [ inet.0 inet.2 ];
        }
    }
    multicast {    /* Boundaries between customers and provider */
        scope SGI-Dogfight {
            prefix 224.0.1.2/32;
            interface all;
```

```
        }
        scope RWHOD {
            prefix 224.0.1.3/32;
            interface all;
        }
        scope SVRLOC {
            prefix 224.0.1.22/32;
            interface all;
        }
        scope MICROSOFT-DS {
            prefix 224.0.1.24/32;
            interface all;
        }
        scope SVRLOC-DA {
            prefix 224.0.1.35/32;
            interface all;
        }
        scope AutoRP-Announce {
            prefix 224.0.1.39/32;
            interface all;
        }
        scope AutoRP-Discovery {
            prefix 224.0.1.40/32;
            interface all;
        }
        scope HP-Device-Discovery {
            prefix 224.0.1.60/32;
            interface all;
        }
        scope Sun-RPC {
            prefix 224.0.2.2/32;
            interface all;
        }
        scope Norton-Ghost {
            prefix 229.55.150.208/32;
            interface all;
        }
        scope Admin-Scope {
            prefix 239.0.0.0/8;
            interface all;
        }
    }
```

```
}
policy-options {
    policy-statement block-bsr {    /* BSR input/output filter */
        then reject;
    }
}
```

11.2.4 ISP Non-RP Configuration: Cisco Systems

This configuration describes a Cisco Systems router acting as a non-RP in a typical service provider's network.

```
hostname NY-nonRP
ip multicast-routing
!
! Enable PIM-SM on all interfaces
! Listen to SDR sessions on one interface
!
interface Loopback0
ip pim sparse-mode
 ip sdr listen
!
interface POS0/0/0
 description Backbone link
 ip pim sparse-mode
!
interface POS0/0/1
 description Backbone link
 ip pim sparse-mode
!
interface Serial1/0/0
 description Customer link
 ip pim sparse-mode
 ip multicast boundary 10  !  Apply boundary between customer and provider
!
! Static RP mapping and SSM address range
!
ip pim rp-address 10.1.1.100 override
ip pim ssm default
!
! Boundaries between customer and provider
```

```
!
access-list 10 deny   224.0.1.2  ! SGI "Dogfight" game
access-list 10 deny   224.0.1.3  ! RWHOD
access-list 10 deny   224.0.1.22 ! SVRLOC
access-list 10 deny   224.0.1.24 ! MICROSOFT-DS
access-list 10 deny   224.0.1.35 ! SVRLOC-DA
access-list 10 deny   224.0.1.39 ! AutoRP Announce
access-list 10 deny   224.0.1.40 ! AutoRP Discovery
access-list 10 deny   224.0.1.60 ! HP Device Discovery Protocol
access-list 10 deny   224.0.2.2  ! Sun RPC
access-list 10 deny   229.55.150.208 ! Norton "Ghost"
access-list 10 deny   239.0.0.0 0.255.255.255 ! Admin Scoped
access-list 10 permit any
!
```

11.3 CUSTOMER ROUTER CONFIGURATIONS

This section shows relevant router configurations for customers of our example ISP. Configurations for a customer who does not operate his own RP and uses the ISP's RP are shown first. Configuration for a customer RP follows.

In the customer RP scenario shown in sections 11.3.3 and 11.3.4, a single statically mapped RP is used. Configuration for a non-RP router in a customer domain with an RP is not shown. In that case, the configuration looks identical to that found in sections 11.3.1 and 11.3.2 with the exception of the IP address in the RP mapping command.

These configurations assume that the customer uses the standard unicast routing table for RPF. To populate a separate routing table for RPF, the same configuration shown for the ISP's RPs can be used.

11.3.1 CUSTOMER WITHOUT RP CONFIGURATION: JUNIPER NETWORKS

This configuration describes a Juniper Networks router acting as a non-RP in a typical customer network.

```
interfaces {
    t3-1/0/0 {
        unit 0 {
            description "To ISP";
        }
    }
}
protocols {
    sap;            /* Listen to SDR announcements */
    pim {
        rp {
            bootstrap-import block-bsr; /* Prevents BSR messages from */
            bootstrap-export block-bsr; /* entering or leaving router */
            static {
                address 10.1.1.100;    /* RP address of provider */
            }
        }
        interface all {       /* Enable PIM-SM on all interfaces */
            mode sparse;
        }
        interface fxp0.0 {   /* ... except management interface */
            disable;
        }
    }
}
routing-options {
    multicast {
        scope SGI-Dogfight {
            prefix 224.0.1.2/32;
            interface all;
        }
        scope RWHOD {
            prefix 224.0.1.3/32;
            interface all;
        }
        scope SVRLOC {
            prefix 224.0.1.22/32;
            interface all;
        }
        scope MICROSOFT-DS {
            prefix 224.0.1.24/32;
            interface all;
```

```
        }
        scope SVRLOC-DA {
            prefix 224.0.1.35/32;
            interface all;
        }
        scope AutoRP-Announce {
            prefix 224.0.1.39/32;
            interface all;
        }
        scope AutoRP-Discovery {
            prefix 224.0.1.40/32;
            interface all;
        }
        scope HP-Device-Discovery {
            prefix 224.0.1.60/32;
            interface all;
        }
        scope Sun-RPC {
            prefix 224.0.2.2/32;
            interface all;
        }
        scope Norton-Ghost {
            prefix 229.55.150.208/32;
            interface all;
        }
        scope Admin-Scope {
            prefix 239.0.0.0/8;
            interface all;
        }
    }
}
policy-options {
    policy-statement block-bsr {    /* BSR input/output filter */
        then reject;
    }
}
```

11.3.2 CUSTOMER WITHOUT RP CONFIGURATION: CISCO SYSTEMS

This configuration describes a Cisco Systems router acting as a non-RP in a typical customer network.

```
ip multicast-routing
!
! Enable PIM-SM on all interfaces
! Listen to SDR sessions on one interface
!
!
 interface Serial1/0/0
 description To ISP
 ip pim sparse-mode
 ip multicast boundary 10
 ip sdr listen
!
! Static RP mapping and SSM address range
!
ip pim rp-address 10.1.1.100 override
ip pim ssm default
!
! Domain Border
!
access-list 10 deny   224.0.1.2  ! SGI "Dogfight" game
access-list 10 deny   224.0.1.3  ! RWHOD
access-list 10 deny   224.0.1.22 ! SVRLOC
access-list 10 deny   224.0.1.24 ! MICROSOFT-DS
access-list 10 deny   224.0.1.35 ! SVRLOC-DA
access-list 10 deny   224.0.1.39 ! AutoRP AnnounceFS
access-list 10 deny   224.0.1.40 ! AutoRP Discovery
access-list 10 deny   224.0.1.60 ! HP Device Discovery Protocol
access-list 10 deny   224.0.2.2  ! Sun RPC
access-list 10 deny   229.55.150.208 ! Norton "Ghost"
access-list 10 deny   239.0.0.0 0.255.255.255 ! Admin Scoped
access-list 10 permit any
!
```

11.3.3 Customer RP Configuration: Juniper Networks

This configuration describes a Juniper Networks router acting as an RP in a typical customer network.

```
interfaces {
    t3-1/0/0 {
        unit 0 {
            description "Customer Link";
        }
    }
    lo0 {
        unit 0 {
            family inet {
                address 10.2.2.2/32
            }
        }
    }
}
protocols {
    sap;                        /* Listen to SDR announcements */
    msdp {
        local-address 10.2.2.2;
        peer 10.1.1.1 {         /* NY is the closest RP */
            export SA-filter;   /* SA filter for provider peering */
            import SA-filter;
        }
    }
    pim {
        rp {
            bootstrap-import block-bsr; /* Prevents BSR messages from */
            bootstrap-export block-bsr; /* entering or leaving router */
            local {
                address 10.2.2.2;       /* I am the RP */
            }
        }
        interface all {         /* Enable PIM-SM on all interfaces */
            mode sparse;
        }
```

```
            interface fxp0.0 {      /* ... except management interface */
                disable;
            }
        }
    }
    routing-options {
        multicast {
            scope SGI-Dogfight {
                prefix 224.0.1.2/32;
                interface all;
            }
            scope RWHOD {
                prefix 224.0.1.3/32;
                interface all;
            }
            scope SVRLOC {
                prefix 224.0.1.22/32;
                interface all;
            }
            scope MICROSOFT-DS {
                prefix 224.0.1.24/32;
                interface all;
            }
            scope SVRLOC-DA {
                prefix 224.0.1.35/32;
                interface all;
            }
            scope AutoRP-Announce {
                prefix 224.0.1.39/32;
                interface all;
            }
            scope AutoRP-Discovery {
                prefix 224.0.1.40/32;
                interface all;
            }
            scope HP-Device-Discovery {
                prefix 224.0.1.60/32;
                interface all;
```

```
        }
        scope Sun-RPC {
            prefix 224.0.2.2/32;
            interface all;
        }
        scope Norton-Ghost {
            prefix 229.55.150.208/32;
            interface all;
        }
        scope Admin-Scope {
            prefix 239.0.0.0/8;
            interface all;
        }
    }
}
policy-options {
    policy-statement SA-filter {/* SA filter for all customers */
        term BAD-groups {
            from {
                route-filter 224.0.1.2/32 exact; /* SGI-Dogfight */
                route-filter 224.0.1.3/32 exact; /* RWHOD */
                route-filter 224.0.1.22/32 exact; /* SVRLOC */
                route-filter 224.0.1.24/32 exact; /* MICROSOFT-DS */
                route-filter 224.0.1.35/32 exact; /* SVRLOC-DA */
                route-filter 224.0.1.39/32 exact; /* AutoRP Announce */
                route-filter 224.0.1.40/32 exact; /* AutoRP Discovery */
                route-filter 224.0.1.60/32 exact; /* HP-Dev-Disc */
                route-filter 224.0.2.2/32 exact; /* Sun RPC */
                route-filter 229.55.150.208/32 exact; /* Norton Ghost */
                route-filter 232.0.0.0/8 orlonger; /* SSM */
                route-filter 239.0.0.0/8 orlonger; /* Admin-scoped */
            }
            then reject;
        }
        term BAD-Sources {
            from { /* Private address space */
                source-address-filter 10.0.0.0/8 orlonger;
                source-address-filter 127.0.0.0/8 orlonger;
                source-address-filter 172.16.0.0/12 orlonger;
                source-address-filter 192.168.0.0/16 orlonger;
```

```
            }
            then reject;
        }
        term everything-else {
            then accept;
        }
    }
    policy-statement block-bsr { /* BSR input/output filter */
        then reject;
    }
}
```

11.3.4 Customer RP Configuration: Cisco Systems

This configuration describes a Cisco Systems router acting as an RP in a typical
customer network.

```
ip multicast-routing
!
! Enable PIM-SM on all interfaces
! Listen to SDR sessions on one interface
!
!
 interface Serial1/0/0
 description To ISP
 ip pim sparse-mode
 ip multicast boundary 10
!
interface Loopback0
 ip address 10.2.2.2 255.255.255.255
 ip pim sparse-mode
 ip sdr listen
!
! Static RP mapping and SSM address range
!
ip pim rp-address 10.2.2.2 override
ip pim ssm default
!
! NY is the closest RP
!
```

```
ip msdp peer 10.1.1.1 connect-source Loopback0
ip msdp sa-filter in 10.1.1.1 list 101
ip msdp sa-filter out 10.1.1.1 list 101
ip msdp cache-sa-state
!
! Domain Border
!
access-list 10 deny    224.0.1.2  ! SGI "Dogfight" game
access-list 10 deny    224.0.1.3  ! RWHOD
access-list 10 deny    224.0.1.22 ! SVRLOC
access-list 10 deny    224.0.1.24 ! MICROSOFT-DS
access-list 10 deny    224.0.1.35 ! SVRLOC-DA
access-list 10 deny    224.0.1.39 ! AutoRP Announce
access-list 10 deny    224.0.1.40 ! AutoRP Discovery
access-list 10 deny    224.0.1.60 ! HP Device Discovery Protocol
access-list 10 deny    224.0.2.2  ! Sun RPC
access-list 10 deny    229.55.150.208 ! Norton "Ghost"
access-list 10 deny    239.0.0.0 0.255.255.255 ! Admin Scoped
access-list 10 permit any
!
! MSDP SA filter
!
access-list 101 deny   ip any host 224.0.1.2  ! SGI "Dogfight" game
access-list 101 deny   ip any host 224.0.1.3  ! RWHOD
access-list 101 deny   ip any host 224.0.1.22 ! SVRLOC
access-list 101 deny   ip any host 224.0.1.24 ! MICROSOFT-DS
access-list 101 deny   ip any host 224.0.1.35 ! SVRLOC-DA
access-list 101 deny   ip any host 224.0.1.39 ! AutoRP Announce
access-list 101 deny   ip any host 224.0.1.40 ! AutoRP Discovery
access-list 101 deny   ip any host 224.0.1.60 ! HP Device Discovery
access-list 101 deny   ip any host 224.0.2.2  ! Sun RPC
access-list 101 deny   ip any host 229.55.150.208 ! Norton "Ghost"
access-list 101 deny   ip any 232.0.0.0 0.255.255.255 ! SSM
access-list 101 deny   ip any 239.0.0.0 0.255.255.255 ! Admin Scoped
! Private Address Space
access-list 101 deny   ip 10.0.0.0 0.255.255.255   any
access-list 101 deny   ip 127.0.0.0 0.255.255.255 any
access-list 101 deny   ip 172.16.0.0 0.15.255.255 any
access-list 101 deny   ip 192.168.0.0 0.0.255.255 any
access-list 101 permit ip any any
!
```

11.4 SSM-ONLY DOMAIN

Creating an SSM-only domain is a much simpler task because an RP-based infrastructure is not necessary. This option is likely to be attractive for network operators with limited multicast experience. Deploying an SSM-only domain requires nothing more than enabling PIM-SM on interfaces, defining the SSM address range, and creating boundaries between other domains.

Once again, these configurations assume the customer uses the standard unicast routing table for RPF. To populate a separate routing table for RPF, the same configuration shown for the ISP's RPs can be used.

11.4.1 SSM-ONLY CONFIGURATION: JUNIPER NETWORKS

This configuration describes a Juniper Networks router in a typical customer network that supports SSM-only.

```
interfaces {
    t3-1/0/0 {
        unit 0 {
            description "To ISP";
        }
    }
}
protocols {
    pim {
        rp {
            bootstrap-import block-bsr;  /* Prevents BSR messages from */
            bootstrap-export block-bsr;  /* entering or leaving router */
        }
        interface all {          /* Enable PIM-SM on all interfaces */
            mode sparse;
        }
        interface fxp0.0 {       /* ... except management interface */
            disable;
        }
    }
}
routing-options {
```

```
multicast {
    scope SGI-Dogfight {
        prefix 224.0.1.2/32;
        interface all;
    }
    scope RWHOD {
        prefix 224.0.1.3/32;
        interface all;
    }
    scope SVRLOC {
        prefix 224.0.1.22/32;
        interface all;
    }
    scope MICROSOFT-DS {
        prefix 224.0.1.24/32;
        interface all;
    }
    scope SVRLOC-DA {
        prefix 224.0.1.35/32;
        interface all;
    }
    scope AutoRP-Announce {
        prefix 224.0.1.39/32;
        interface all;
    }
    scope AutoRP-Discovery {
        prefix 224.0.1.40/32;
        interface all;
    }
    scope HP-Device-Discovery {
        prefix 224.0.1.60/32;
        interface all;
    }
    scope Sun-RPC {
        prefix 224.0.2.2/32;
        interface all;
    }
    scope Norton-Ghost {
        prefix 229.55.150.208/32;
        interface all;
```

```
        }
        scope Admin-Scope {
            prefix 239.0.0.0/8;
            interface all;
        }
    }
}
policy-options {
    policy-statement block-bsr {    /* BSR input/output filter */
        then reject;
    }
}
```

11.4.2 SSM-ONLY CONFIGURATION: CISCO SYSTEMS

This configuration describes a Cisco Systems router in a typical customer network that supports SSM-only.

```
ip multicast-routing
!
! Enable PIM-SM on all interfaces
!
 interface Serial1/0/0
 description To ISP
 ip pim sparse-mode
 ip multicast boundary 10
!
! SSM address range
!
ip pim ssm default
!
! Domain Border
!
access-list 10 deny    224.0.1.2  ! SGI "Dogfight" game
access-list 10 deny    224.0.1.3  ! RWHOD
access-list 10 deny    224.0.1.22 ! SVRLOC
access-list 10 deny    224.0.1.24 ! MICROSOFT-DS
access-list 10 deny    224.0.1.35 ! SVRLOC-DA
access-list 10 deny    224.0.1.39 ! AutoRP Announce
```

```
access-list 10 deny    224.0.1.40 ! AutoRP Discovery
access-list 10 deny    224.0.1.60 ! HP Device Discovery Protocol
access-list 10 deny    224.0.2.2  ! Sun RPC
access-list 10 deny    229.55.150.208 ! Norton "Ghost"
access-list 10 deny    239.0.0.0 0.255.255.255 ! Admin Scoped
access-list 10 permit any
!
```

Management Tools for Multicast Networks

This chapter provides an overview of the various tools available to monitor and troubleshoot multicast-enabled internets. Some of these tools run on the router itself, and some run on a separate host. Similar to unicast monitoring and troubleshooting tools, the multicast counterparts help to identify loss of connectivity and provide insight into the cause of that loss of connectivity.

12.1 SNMP MIBs

The **Simple Network Management Protocol (SNMP)** provides a means to help manage networks. SNMP is essentially the only network management protocol in use today.

SNMP uses Management Information Bases (MIBs) to establish a consistent language between all SNMP-speaking devices. A MIB is written in human-readable MIB language and is saved as a text file. Network management administrators must compile the MIBs that interest them into the proprietary binary format of their network management software. Once this is done, users can browse the MIBs using the network management software.

Public MIBs exist as RFCs. A MIB RFC provides a brief description of the intended use of the MIB and includes the contents of the MIB. If you need to compile a MIB in your network management software, you can copy and paste the RFC text, being careful to delete each page's header and footer.

You can usually find versions of public MIBs on Web sites in a ready-to-compile form. One such site is *http://www.aciri.org/fenner/mibs/mib-index.html*. Router vendors support a subset of the public MIBs available, depending on the protocols that run on their routers. Check your router vendor's technical documentation to determine the MIBs it supports. Juniper Networks lists the public MIBs it supports in its *Installation and System Management* guide.

In addition to public MIBs, many vendors provide proprietary MIBs for information specific to their products. Juniper Networks' proprietary MIBs are available at *http://www.juniper.net/techpubs/mibs.html*.

An SNMP daemon runs on each router, and SNMP software runs on one or more **network management systems (NMS)**. SNMP MIBs contain two types of entities, namely *traps* and *objects*. SNMP traps are pushed from the router to the NMS, without the NMS requesting the information. SNMP traps are sent when a specific event occurs (for example, a link or adjacency in the networks goes down).

MIB objects can be polled from the NMS. They can either be polled manually—a practice known as *MIB browsing*—or they can be polled periodically and used for graphs of historical data. You can find free NMS software on the Web. The authors' favorite is Active SNMP, which is available at *http://www.cs-care.com/ActiveSNMP/*.

When an NMS sends an SNMP request to a router, it identifies the MIB object in which it is interested by the object identifier (OID). OIDs are hierarchical, with each level separated by a dot in the standard notation. Each named level of hierarchy is assigned a number. The following lists where various MIBs are rooted:

- **Public MIBs:** .iso.org.dod.internet.mgmt.mib-2 = .1.3.6.1.2.1
- **Proprietary MIBs:** .iso.org.dod.internet.private.enterprises = .1.3.6.1.4.1
- **Experimental MIBs:** .iso.org.dod.internet.experimental = .1.3.6.1.3

To know where a MIB fits into the hierarchy, read the MODULE-IDENTITY section of the MIB. For example the MODULE-IDENTITY of the ipMRouteStdMIB MIB is the following:

```
ipMRouteStdMIB MODULE-IDENTITY
    LAST-UPDATED "200009220000Z" -- September 22, 2000
    ORGANIZATION "IETF IDMR Working Group"
    CONTACT-INFO
            " Dave Thaler
            Microsoft Corporation
            One Microsoft Way
            Redmond, WA  98052-6399
            US

            Phone: +1 425 703 8835
            EMail: dthaler@microsoft.com"
    DESCRIPTION
            "The MIB module for management of IP Multicast routing, but
            independent of the specific multicast routing protocol in
            use."
    REVISION      "200009220000Z" -- September 22, 2000
    DESCRIPTION
            "Initial version, published as RFC 2932."
    ::= { mib-2 83 }
```

The last line of the preceding output shows that this MIB fits into the MIB-2 hierarchy with OID 83. The following shows the full OID of the ipMRouteStdMIB (both named and numeric representation):

```
.iso.org.dod.internet.mgmt.mib-2.ipMRouteStdMIB = .1.3.6.1.2.1.83
```

12.1.1 MULTICAST ROUTING MIB (IPMROUTESTDMIB)

The IPv4 multicast routing MIB (ipMRouteStdMIB) is defined in RFC 2932. The MIB contains objects that are not specific to any protocol and are needed to manage a multicast network. The MIB contains the following tables:

- **IP Multicast Route Table:** Multicast route information including RPF neighbor and the name of the multicast routing protocol being used

- **IP Multicast Routing Next-Hop Table:** Information on the downstream interface list for particular source-group pairs
- **IP Multicast Routing Interface Table:** Interface information specific to multicast routing
- **IP Multicast Scope Boundary Table:** Boundary interfaces configured for administratively scoped multicast
- **IP Multicast Scope Name Table:** Names of the multicast scopes configured on the router

12.1.2 IGMP MIB (IGMPSTDMIB)

The IGMP MIB is defined in RFC 2933. It contains information about IGMP-enabled interfaces and current group membership of directly attached hosts. The OID is as follows:

```
.iso.org.dod.internet.mgmt.mib-2.igmpStdMIB = .1.3.6.1.2.1.85
```

The MIB contains the following two tables:

- **IGMP Interface Table:** Information about interfaces configured for IGMP
- **IGMP Cache Table:** Information about hosts that have joined multicast groups using IGMP

12.1.3 PIM MIB (PIMMIB)

The PIM MIB is specified in RFC 2934. The PIM MIB contains information about PIM interfaces, neighbors, RP group mappings, and multicast routing tables. The OID is as follows:

```
.iso.org.dod.internet.experimental.pimMIB = .1.3.6.1.3.61
```

The MIB contains the following tables:

- **PIM Interface Table:** Information about each of the router's PIM interfaces
- **PIM Neighbor Table:** Information about each of the router's PIM neighbors

- **PIM IP Multicast Route Table:** Information on PIM Join state from the perspective of the upstream interface
- **PIM Next-Hop Table:** Information on PIM Join state from the perspective of the downstream interface list
- **PIM RP Table (deprecated):** PIMv1 RP information
- **PIM RP-Set Table:** BSR RP-set information
- **PIM Candidate RP Table:** BSR candidate RP information
- **PIM Component Table:** Information on each of the PIM domains to which the router is connected

12.1.4 MSDP MIB (MSDPMIB)

The MSDP MIB is specified in an IETF draft maintained by the MSDP working group. The MIB contains information on MSDP peers and the Source-Active cache. The OID is as follows:

```
.iso.org.dod.internet.experimental.msdpMIB = .1.3.6.1.3.92
```

The MSDP MIB contains the following tables:

- **Requests Table:** The longest-match table used to determine the peer to which SA Requests are sent for a given group
- **Peer Table:** Information on each of the router's MSDP peers
- **Source-Active Cache Table:** Information about the SA cache

12.2 THE MTRACE FACILITY

Currently mtrace is specified in an IETF draft titled "A 'traceroute' facility for IP Multicast." On a UNIX host, you can use man mtrace to learn about the specific mtrace application installed on the system. The mtrace utility is intended to be used for assessing IP multicast connectivity problems. It provides a method for troubleshooting multicast problems similar to what standard IP traceroute does for unicast connectivity problems.

The mtrace utility uses the IGMP protocol number. A host initiates an mtrace query specifying a source hostname or IP address. The mtrace query is passed along hop-by-hop using each router's RPF route for the source address. Along the way, information is collected about hop addresses, packet counts, and routing error conditions.

The final hop (either a router directly connected to the source or a router that has no RPF route for the source) returns an mtrace response to the host that initiated the mtrace query. The standard mtrace query is sent to the ALL-ROUTERS link-local multicast group and has a TTL of 1.

Optionally, a receiver address and group address can be specified in the mtrace query. If no receiver address is specified, the address of the host that generated the query is used. If a receiver address is specified, mtrace finds the router connected directly to that receiver. It is able to locate the last-hop router by sending the mtrace query to the group address of interest.

This mechanism for finding the last-hop router requires that the intended receiver has joined the ASM group or subscribed to two SSM channels. These channels consist of one with the local host being the source of the SSM channel and the second with the specified source as the source of the SSM channel. Alternatively, the last-hop router can be specified in the mtrace command line.

If there is no response from the initial mtrace query, the application automatically switches to hop-by-hop mode. In hop-by-hop mode, tracing queries are started with a maximum hop count of 1 and are incremented until the last-hop router is reached or there is no response.

It is also possible to specify the number of hops an mtrace query can travel. When the maximum number of hops is specified, the mtrace query travels along the RPF patch from the receiver to the source incrementing the hop count at each router. Once the maximum number of hops has been reached, the router returns the mtrace response as if it were directly connected to the source.

Specifying the maximum hop count is useful because it enables a partial trace if the mtrace query is blackholed because a router along the path does not support mtrace or because an RPF route exists but some other problem (such as a firewall filter) is causing an outage.

Each router inserts the following information into the mtrace query:

- IP address of the hop
- TTL required to forward
- Flags to indicate routing errors
- Total number of packets on the incoming interface
- Total number of packets on the outgoing interfaces
- Total number of packets forwarded for the specified group

A good strategy is to run mtrace when multicast routing is working between common sources and receivers. Store the results for reference when there is a loss of connectivity. When problems occur, use the MIBs (discussed in section 12.1, earlier in this chapter) on the routers (or access the routers directly) along the path captured from the working mtrace to attempt to hunt down the problem.

The following is sample output from the mtrace man page. The mtrace man page can be viewed by installing mtrace on a UNIX host and typing **man mtrace**.

```
oak.isi.edu 80# mtrace -l caraway.lcs.mit.edu 224.2.0.3
Mtrace from 18.26.0.170 to 128.9.160.100 via group 224.2.0.3
Querying full reverse path...
  0  oak.isi.edu (128.9.160.100)
 -1  cub.isi.edu (128.9.160.153)  DVRMP  thresh^ 1   3 ms
 -2  la.dart.net (140.173.128.1)  DVRMP  thresh^ 1  14 ms
 -3  dc.dart.net (140.173.64.1)   DVRMP  thresh^ 1  50 ms
 -4  bbn.dart.net (140.173.32.1)  DVRMP  thresh^ 1  63 ms
 -5  mit.dart.net (140.173.48.2)  DVRMP  thresh^ 1  71 ms
 -6  caraway.lcs.mit.edu (18.26.0.170)
Round trip time 124 ms

Waiting to accumulate statistics... Results after 101 seconds:
```

```
        Source        Response Dest   Packet Statistics For   Only For Traffic
      18.26.0.170     128.9.160.100   All Multicast Traffic   From 18.26.0.170
          |        __/ rtt   125 ms   Lost/Sent = Pct  Rate      To 224.2.0.3
          v       /   hop    65 ms    --------------------    -------------------
      18.26.0.144
      140.173.48.2   mit.dart.net
          |     ^      ttl    1        0/6    = --%   0 pps   0/2  = --%  0 pps
          v     |      hop    8 ms     1/52   =  2%   0 pps   0/18 =  0%  0 pps
      140.173.48.1
      140.173.32.1   bbn.dart.net
          |     ^      ttl    2        0/6    = --%   0 pps   0/2  = --%  0 pps
          v     |      hop    12 ms    1/52   =  2%   0 pps   0/18 =  0%  0 pps
      140.173.32.2
      140.173.64.1   dc.dart.net
          |     ^      ttl    3        0/271  =  0%  27 pps   0/2  = --%  0 pps
          v     |      hop    34 ms   -1/2652 =  0%  26 pps   0/18 =  0%  0 pps
      140.173.64.2
      140.173.128.1  la.dart.net
          |     ^      ttl    4       -2/831  =  0%  83 pps   0/2  = --%  0 pps
          v     |      hop    11 ms   -3/8072 =  0%  79 pps   0/18 =  0%  0 pps
      140.173.128.2
      128.9.160.153  cub.isi.edu
          |      \__   ttl    5        833         83 pps     2           0 pps
          v        \  hop    -8 ms     8075        79 pps     18          0 pps
      128.9.160.100  128.9.160.100
        Receiver     Query Source
```

In Cisco Systems IOS software, the `mstat` command is the equivalent of the second half of the mtrace output.

12.3 THE MSDP TRACEROUTE FACILITY

The MSDP traceroute utility traces the control path for MSDP Source-Active messages from any MSDP-speaking router to the originating RP for the message. This is accomplished by each router along the path forwarding the MSDP traceroute packet to its RPF peer for the originating RP address.

The MSDP traceroute utility is currently described in an Internet-Draft (draft-ietf-msdp-traceroute-06.txt).

Other Related Topics

This chapter provides a brief overview of various protocols that are not core to current deployments of IMR but may be of interest in future deployments or as potential Trivial Pursuit questions. We provide a brief overview of where the protocol fits in the grand scheme, how it operates, and where to find the specs.

13.1 BORDER GATEWAY MULTICAST PROTOCOL (BGMP)

BGMP is the proverbial promised land for IMR. It is specified in an Internet-Draft titled "Border Gateway Multicast Protocol (BGMP): Protocol Specification" (draft-ietf-bgmp-spec.txt). BGMP requires that each multicast group be associated with a single root domain. BGMP-speaking routers require a mechanism that maps a group address to a next hop toward that group's root domain. **Multicast Address Set Claim Protocol (MASC)** is one mechanism that can be used to create such a mapping. MASC dynamically distributes information about the associations of group addresses to root domains. This information is stored in the G-RIB table. Using the information in the G-RIB, BGMP builds shared trees for active groups and then enables each domain to build source-based trees.

BGMP uses TCP (port 264) as its transport protocol. Like BGP, BGMP is an incremental protocol, meaning that routing updates are only sent once and are explicitly withdrawn (periodic refresh of state is not required).

One roadblock that has slowed the deployment of BGMP is the complexities involved with the G-RIB and a dynamic protocol (such as MASC) used to fill it with information. The root domain is encoded in IPv6 multicast groups, so BGMP deployment in an all IPv6 Internet will be a much easier task. A mechanism similar to the one described for IPv6 could be devised for IPv4 multicast addresses. An Internet-Draft, "Unicast-Prefix-Based IPv6 Multicast Addresses" (draft-ietf-ipngwg-uni-based-mcast-03.txt), describes the format of IPv6 multicast addresses with encoded root domains. The format is as follows:

```
|   8    | 4 | 4 |   8    |   8    |       64       |   32     |
+--------+----+----+--------+--------+----------------+----------+
|11111111|00PT|Scop|00000000|  Plen  | Network Prefix | Group ID |
+--------+----+----+--------+--------+----------------+----------+
```

P = 0 indicates a multicast address that is not assigned based on the network prefix. P = 1 indicates a multicast address that is assigned based on the network prefix. The setting of the T bit is defined in RFC 2373. When P = 1, the Plen field indicates the actual length of the network prefix portion of the address, and the Network Prefix field identifies the unicast subnet that owns the multicast group.

13.2 MULTICAST ADDRESS SET CLAIM PROTOCOL (MASC)

MASC, which is specified in RFC 2909, is used to declare a group prefix as being owned by a domain. The multicast groups that are associated with a domain are injected into MBGP with the AFI/SAFI set to 1/4 and are used to populate a G-RIB that can be used by BGMP to construct interdomain shared trees.

13.3 BI-DIRECTIONAL PIM (BI-DIR PIM)

Bi-Directional PIM (Bi-Dir PIM) is another mode of operation for PIM (in contrast to sparse mode and dense mode). When a group is forwarded based on

Bi-Dir rules, data packets are routed along a bidirectional shared tree to the RP for the group. Bi-Dir PIM is designed for multicast applications with many sources, where all sources and receivers are in the same PIM domain. It is not intended to be used for IMR.

Bi-Dir PIM does not keep (S,G) Join state, which reduces the overall amount of state that is kept on routers throughout the domain. Sources join the shared tree (even if they do not want to receive traffic for the group) and send traffic upstream. Bi-Dir PIM is specified in an Internet-Draft, "Bi-directional Protocol Independent Multicast (BIDIR-PIM)" (draft-ietf-pim-bidir-03.txt).

13.4   MULTICAST DATA PACKETS AND REAL-TIME TRANSPORT PROTOCOL (RTP)

Real-Time Transport Protocol (RTP), which is defined in RFC 1889, provides host-to-host transport over IP networks that is suitable for real-time applications such as video and audio streaming. The underlying IP forwarding mechanism can be either unicast or multicast. One of the common uses of IP multicast is to transport live and scheduled multimedia traffic, where RTP is often used as the transport layer protocol for multicast data packets. RTP is commonly run on top of UDP, with both protocols sharing part of the transport layer responsibilities. Using RTP over UDP instead of just UDP for transporting real-time data has several advantages, including the following:

- Payload type identification
- Sequence numbering
- Time stamping
- Delivery monitoring

RTP in itself does not provide any guarantee of timely delivery. It relies on network layer mechanisms to provide differentiated quality of service.

IGMP Packet Formats

This appendix includes the packet formats from the specifications of the three versions of IGMP.

A.1 IGMP Version 3 Packet Formats

IGMPv3 is the result of the collective work of Brad Cain, Steve Deering, Bill Fenner, Isidor Kouvelas, and Ajit Thyagarajan. The packet formats are described in section 4 of the current specification. Here is section 4 from the specification in its entirety (it has been reformatted for consistency).

4. Message Formats

IGMP messages are encapsulated in IPv4 datagrams, with an IP protocol number of 2. Every IGMP message described in this document is sent with an IP Time-to-Live of 1 and carries an IP Router Alert option [RFC-2113] in its IP header.

There are two IGMP message types of concern to the IGMPv3 protocol described in this document:

- **0x11:** Membership Query
- **0x22:** Version 3 Membership Report

An implementation of IGMPv3 MUST also support the following three message types, for interoperation with previous versions of IGMP:

- **0x12:** Version 1 Membership Report [RFC-1112]
- **0x16:** Version 2 Membership Report [RFC-2236]
- **0x17:** Version 2 Leave Group [RFC-2236]

Unrecognized message types MUST be silently ignored. Other message types may be used by newer versions or extensions of IGMP, by multicast routing protocols, or for other uses.

In this document, unless otherwise qualified, the capitalized words "Query" and "Report" refer to IGMP Membership Queries and IGMP Version 3 Membership Reports, respectively.

4.1. Membership Query Message

Membership Queries are sent by IP multicast routers to query the multicast reception state of neighboring interfaces. Queries have the following format:

```
 0                   1                   2                   3
 0 1 2 3 4 5 6 7 8 9 0 1 2 3 4 5 6 7 8 9 0 1 2 3 4 5 6 7 8 9 0 1
+-+-+-+-+-+-+-+-+-+-+-+-+-+-+-+-+-+-+-+-+-+-+-+-+-+-+-+-+-+-+-+-+
| Type = 0x11  | Max Resp Code |           Checksum            |
+-+-+-+-+-+-+-+-+-+-+-+-+-+-+-+-+-+-+-+-+-+-+-+-+-+-+-+-+-+-+-+-+
|                         Group Address                         |
+-+-+-+-+-+-+-+-+-+-+-+-+-+-+-+-+-+-+-+-+-+-+-+-+-+-+-+-+-+-+-+-+
| Resv  |S| QRV |     QQIC      |     Number of Sources (N)     |
+-+-+-+-+-+-+-+-+-+-+-+-+-+-+-+-+-+-+-+-+-+-+-+-+-+-+-+-+-+-+-+-+
|                       Source Address [1]                      |
+-                                                             -+
|                       Source Address [2]                      |
+-                             .                               -+
.                             .                               .
.                             .                               .
+-                             .                               -+
|                       Source Address [N]                      |
+-+-+-+-+-+-+-+-+-+-+-+-+-+-+-+-+-+-+-+-+-+-+-+-+-+-+-+-+-+-+-+-+
```

4.1.1. Max Resp Code The Max Resp Code field specifies the maximum time allowed before sending a responding report. The actual time allowed, called the Max Resp Time, is represented in units of 1/10 second and is derived from the Max Resp Code as follows:

If Max Resp Code < 128, Max Resp Time = Max Resp Code

If Max Resp Code >= 128, Max Resp Code represents a floating-point value as follows:

```
 0 1 2 3 4 5 6 7
+-+-+-+-+-+-+-+-+
|1| exp | mant  |
+-+-+-+-+-+-+-+-+
```

Max Resp Time = (mant | 0x10) << (exp + 3)

Small values of Max Resp Time allow IGMPv3 routers to tune the "leave latency" (the time between the moment the last host leaves a group and the moment the routing protocol is notified that there are no more members). Larger values, especially in the exponential range, allow tuning of the burstiness of IGMP traffic on a network.

4.1.2. Checksum The Checksum is the 16-bit one's complement of the one's complement sum of the whole IGMP message (the entire IP payload). For computing the checksum, the Checksum field is set to zero. When receiving packets, the checksum MUST be verified before processing a packet.

4.1.3. Group Address The Group Address field is set to zero when sending a General Query and set to the IP multicast address being queried when sending a Group-Specific Query or Group-and-Source-Specific Query (see section 4.1.9).

4.1.4. Resv (Reserved) The Resv field is set to zero on transmission and ignored on reception.

4.1.5. S Flag (Suppress Router-Side Processing) When set to one, the S Flag indicates to any receiving multicast routers that they are to suppress the normal timer updates they perform upon hearing a Query. It does not, however, suppress the querier election or the normal "host-side" processing of a Query that a router may be required to perform as a consequence of itself being a group member.

4.1.6. QRV (Querier's Robustness Variable) If non-zero, the QRV field contains the [Robustness Variable] value used by the querier, i.e., the sender of the Query. If the querier's [Robustness Variable] exceeds 7, the maximum value of the QRV field, the QRV is set to zero. Routers adopt the QRV value from the most recently received Query as their own [Robustness Variable] value, unless that most recently received QRV was zero, in which case the receivers use the default [Robustness Variable] value or a statically configured value.

4.1.7. QQIC (Querier's Query Interval Code) The Querier's Query Interval Code field specifies the [Query Interval] used by the querier. The actual interval, called the Querier's Query Interval (QQI), is represented in units of seconds and is derived from the Querier's Query Interval Code as follows:

If QQIC < 128, QQI = QQIC

If QQIC >= 128, QQIC represents a floating-point value as follows:

```
 0 1 2 3 4 5 6 7
+-+-+-+-+-+-+-+-+
|1| exp | mant  |
+-+-+-+-+-+-+-+-+
```

QQI = (mant | 0x10) << (exp + 3)

Multicast routers that are not the current querier adopt the QQI value from the most recently received Query as their own [Query Interval] value, unless that most recently received QQI was zero, in which case the receiving routers use the default [Query Interval] value.

4.1.8. Number of Sources (N) The Number of Sources (N) field specifies how many source addresses are present in the Query. This number is zero in a General Query or a Group-Specific Query and non-zero in a Group-and-Source-

Specific Query. This number is limited by the MTU of the network over which the Query is transmitted. For example, on an Ethernet with an MTU of 1500 octets, the IP header including the Router Alert option consumes 24 octets, and the IGMP fields up to and including the Number of Sources (N) field consume 12 octets, leaving 1464 octets for source addresses, which limits the number of source addresses to 366 (1464/4).

4.1.9. Source Address [i] The Source Address [i] fields are a vector of n IP unicast addresses, where n is the value in the Number of Sources (N) field.

4.1.10. Additional Data If the Packet Length field in the IP header of a received Query indicates that there are additional octets of data present, beyond the fields described here, IGMPv3 implementations MUST include those octets in the computation to verify the received IGMP Checksum but MUST otherwise ignore those additional octets. When sending a Query, an IGMPv3 implementation MUST NOT include additional octets beyond the fields described here.

4.1.11. Query Variants There are three variants of the Query message:

* A "General Query" is sent by a multicast router to learn the complete multicast reception state of the neighboring interfaces (that is, the interfaces attached to the network on which the Query is transmitted). In a General Query, both the Group Address field and the Number of Sources (N) field are zero.

* A "Group-Specific Query" is sent by a multicast router to learn the reception state, with respect to a *single* multicast address of the neighboring interfaces. In a Group-Specific Query, the Group Address field contains the multicast address of interest, and the Number of Sources (N) field contains zero.

* A "Group-and-Source-Specific Query" is sent by a multicast router to learn if any neighboring interface desires reception of packets sent to a specified multicast address from any of a specified list of sources. In a Group-and-Source-Specific Query, the Group Address field contains the multicast address of interest, and the Source Address [i] fields contain the source address(es) of interest.

4.1.12. IP Destination Addresses for Queries In IGMPv3, General Queries are sent with an IP destination address of 224.0.0.1, the all-systems multicast address. Group-Specific and Group-and-Source-Specific Queries are sent with an IP destination address equal to the multicast address of interest. *However*, a system MUST accept and process any Query whose IP Destination Address field contains *any* of the addresses (unicast or multicast) assigned to the interface on which the Query arrives.

4.2. *Version 3 Membership Report Message*

Version 3 Membership Reports are sent by IP systems to report (to neighboring routers) the current multicast reception state, or changes in the multicast reception state, of their interfaces. Reports have the following format:

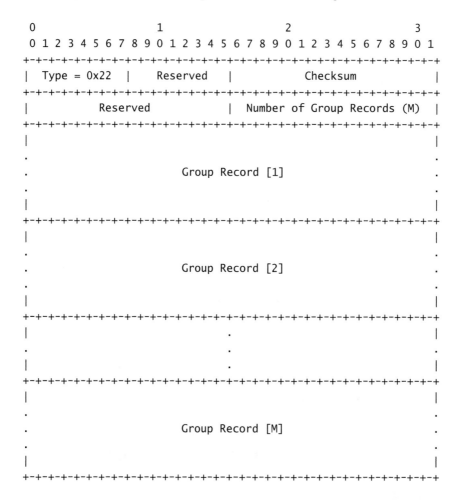

where each Group Record has the following internal format:

```
+-+-+-+-+-+-+-+-+-+-+-+-+-+-+-+-+-+-+-+-+-+-+-+-+-+-+-+-+-+-+-+-+
|  Record Type  | Aux Data Len  |     Number of Sources (N)     |
+-+-+-+-+-+-+-+-+-+-+-+-+-+-+-+-+-+-+-+-+-+-+-+-+-+-+-+-+-+-+-+-+
|                       Multicast Address                       |
+-+-+-+-+-+-+-+-+-+-+-+-+-+-+-+-+-+-+-+-+-+-+-+-+-+-+-+-+-+-+-+-+
|                     Source Address [1]                        |
+-                                                            -+
|                     Source Address [2]                        |
+-                                                            -+
.                             .                                .
.                             .                                .
.                             .                                .
+-                                                            -+
|                     Source Address [N]                        |
+-+-+-+-+-+-+-+-+-+-+-+-+-+-+-+-+-+-+-+-+-+-+-+-+-+-+-+-+-+-+-+-+
|                                                               |
.                                                               .
.                       Auxiliary Data                          .
.                                                               .
|                                                               |
+-+-+-+-+-+-+-+-+-+-+-+-+-+-+-+-+-+-+-+-+-+-+-+-+-+-+-+-+-+-+-+-+
```

4.2.1. Reserved The Reserved fields are set to zero on transmission and ig-nored on reception.

4.2.2. Checksum The Checksum is the 16-bit one's complement of the one's complement sum of the whole IGMP message (the entire IP payload). For com-puting the checksum, the Checksum field is set to zero. When receiving packets, the checksum MUST be verified before processing a message.

4.2.3. Number of Group Records (M) The Number of Group Records (M) field specifies how many Group Records are present in this Report.

4.2.4. Group Record Each Group Record is a block of fields containing infor-mation pertaining to the sender's membership in a single multicast group on the interface from which the Report is sent.

4.2.5. Record Type See section 4.2.12, later in this appendix.

4.2.6. Aux Data Len The Aux Data Len field contains the length of the Auxiliary Data field in this Group Record, in units of 32-bit words. It may contain zero, to indicate the absence of any auxiliary data.

4.2.7. Number of Sources (N) The Number of Sources (N) field specifies how many source addresses are present in this Group Record.

4.2.8. Multicast Address The Multicast Address field contains the IP multicast address to which this Group Record pertains.

4.2.9. Source Address [i] The Source Address [i] fields are a vector of n IP unicast addresses, where n is the value in this record's Number of Sources (N) field.

4.2.10. Auxiliary Data The Auxiliary Data field, if present, contains additional information pertaining to this Group Record. The protocol specified in this document, IGMPv3, does not define any auxiliary data. Therefore implementations of IGMPv3 MUST NOT include any auxiliary data (i.e., MUST set the Aux Data Len field to zero) in any transmitted Group Record and MUST ignore any auxiliary data present in any received Group Record. The semantics and internal encoding of the Auxiliary Data field are to be defined by any future version or extension of IGMP that uses this field.

4.2.11. Additional Data If the Packet Length field in the IP header of a received Report indicates that there are additional octets of data present, beyond the last Group Record, IGMPv3 implementations MUST include those octets in the computation to verify the received IGMP Checksum but MUST otherwise ignore those additional octets. When sending a Report, an IGMPv3 implementation MUST NOT include additional octets beyond the last Group Record.

4.2.12. Group Record Types There are a number of different types of Group Records that may be included in a Report message:

A "Current-State Record" is sent by a system in response to a Query received on an interface. It reports the current reception state of that interface, with respect to a single multicast address. The Record Type of a Current-State Record may be one of the following two values:

- **MODE_IS_INCLUDE:** Indicates that the interface has a filter mode of INCLUDE for the specified multicast address. The Source Address [i] fields in this Group Record contain the interface's source list for the specified multicast address, if it is nonempty.
- **MODE_IS_EXCLUDE:** Indicates that the interface has a filter mode of EXCLUDE for the specified multicast address. The Source Address [i] fields in this Group Record contain the interface's source list for the specified multicast address, if it is nonempty.

A "Filter-Mode-Change Record" is sent by a system whenever a local invocation of IPMulticastListen causes a change of the filter mode (e.g., a change from IN-CLUDE to EXCLUDE, or from EXCLUDE to INCLUDE) of the interface-level state entry for a particular multicast address.

The Record is included in a Report sent from the interface on which the change occurred. The Record Type of a Filter-Mode-Change Record may be one of the following two values:

- **CHANGE_TO_INCLUDE_MODE:** Indicates that the interface has changed to INCLUDE filter mode for the specified multicast address. The Source Address [i] fields in this Group Record contain the interface's new source list for the specified multicast address, if it is nonempty.
- **CHANGE_TO_EXCLUDE_MODE:** Indicates that the interface has changed to EXCLUDE filter mode for the specified multicast address. The Source Address [i] fields in this Group Record contain the interface's new source list for the specified multicast address, if it is nonempty.

A "Source-List-Change Record" is sent by a system whenever a local invocation of IPMulticastListen causes a change of source list that is *not* coincident with a change of filter mode of the interface-level state entry for a particular multicast address. The Record is included in a Report sent from the interface on which the change occurred. The Record Type of a Source-List-Change Record may be one of the following two values:

- **ALLOW_NEW_SOURCES:** Indicates that the Source Address [i] fields in this Group Record contain a list of the additional sources that the system wishes to hear from, for packets sent to the specified multicast address. If the change was to an INCLUDE source list, these are the addresses that were added to the list; if the change was to an EXCLUDE source list, these are the addresses that were deleted from the list.
- **BLOCK_OLD_SOURCES:** Indicates that the Source Address [i] fields in this Group Record contain a list of the sources that the system no longer wishes to hear from, for packets sent to the specified multicast address. If the change was to an INCLUDE source list, these are the addresses that were deleted from the list; if the change was to an EXCLUDE source list, these are the addresses that were added to the list.

If a change of source list results in both allowing new sources and blocking old sources, then two Group Records are sent for the same multicast address, one of type ALLOW_NEW_SOURCES and one of type BLOCK_OLD_SOURCES.

We use the term "State-Change Record" to refer to either a Filter-Mode-Change Record or a Source-List-Change Record.

Unrecognized Record Type values MUST be silently ignored.

4.2.13. IP Destination Addresses for Reports Version 3 Reports are sent with an IP destination address of 224.0.0.22, to which all IGMPv3-capable multicast routers listen. A system that is operating in version 1 or version 2 compatibility mode sends version 1 or version 2 Reports to the multicast group specified in the Group Address field of the Report. In addition, a system MUST accept and process any version 1 or version 2 Report whose IP Destination Address field contains *any* of the addresses (unicast or multicast) assigned to the interface on which the Report arrives.

4.2.14. Notation for Group Records   In the rest of this document, we use the following notations to describe the contents of a Group Record pertaining to a particular multicast address:

- **IS_IN (x):** Type MODE_IS_INCLUDE, source addresses x
- **IS_EX (x):** Type MODE_IS_EXCLUDE, source addresses x
- **TO_IN (x):** Type CHANGE_TO_INCLUDE_MODE, source addresses x
- **TO_EX (x):** Type CHANGE_TO_EXCLUDE_MODE, source addresses x
- **ALLOW (x):** Type ALLOW_NEW_SOURCES, source addresses x
- **BLOCK (x):** Type BLOCK_OLD_SOURCES, source addresses x

where x is either:

- A capital letter (e.g., "A") to represent the set of source addresses
- A set expression (e.g., "A+B"), where "A+B" means the union of sets A and B, "A*B" means the intersection of sets A and B, and "A√B" means the removal of all elements of set B from set A.

4.2.15. Membership Report Size   If the set of Group Records required in a Report does not fit within the size limit of a single Report message (as determined by the MTU of the network on which it will be sent), the Group Records are sent in as many Report messages as needed to report the entire set.

If a single Group Record contains so many source addresses that it does not fit within the size limit of a single Report message, if its Type is not MODE_IS_ EXCLUDE or CHANGE_TO_EXCLUDE_MODE, it is split into multiple Group Records, each containing a different subset of the source addresses and each sent in a separate Report message. If its Type is MODE_IS_EXCLUDE or CHANGE_ TO_EXCLUDE_MODE, a single Group Record is sent, containing as many source addresses as can fit, and the remaining source addresses are not reported. Although the choice of which sources to report is arbitrary, it is preferable to report the same set of sources in each subsequent report rather than reporting different sources each time.

A.2 IGMP VERSION 2 PACKET FORMATS

IGMPv2 is the result of work by Bill Fenner. The packet formats are described in section 2 of RFC 2236. Here is section 2 from the specification in its entirety (it has been reformatted for consistency).

2. INTRODUCTION

The Internet Group Management Protocol (IGMP) is used by IP hosts to report their multicast group memberships to any immediately neighboring multicast routers. This memo describes only the use of IGMP between hosts and routers to determine group membership.

Routers that are members of multicast groups are expected to behave as hosts as well as routers and may even respond to their own queries. IGMP may also be used between routers, but such use is not specified here.

Like **ICMP,** IGMP is a integral part of IP. It is required to be implemented by all hosts wishing to receive IP multicasts. IGMP messages are encapsulated in IP datagrams, with an IP protocol number of 2. All IGMP messages described in this document are sent with IP TTL 1 and contain the IP Router Alert option (RFC 2113) in their IP header. All IGMP messages of concern to hosts have the following format:

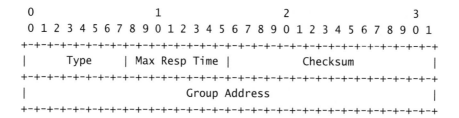

```
 0                   1                   2                   3
 0 1 2 3 4 5 6 7 8 9 0 1 2 3 4 5 6 7 8 9 0 1 2 3 4 5 6 7 8 9 0 1
+-+-+-+-+-+-+-+-+-+-+-+-+-+-+-+-+-+-+-+-+-+-+-+-+-+-+-+-+-+-+-+-+
|      Type     | Max Resp Time |           Checksum            |
+-+-+-+-+-+-+-+-+-+-+-+-+-+-+-+-+-+-+-+-+-+-+-+-+-+-+-+-+-+-+-+-+
|                         Group Address                         |
+-+-+-+-+-+-+-+-+-+-+-+-+-+-+-+-+-+-+-+-+-+-+-+-+-+-+-+-+-+-+-+-+
```

2.1. Type
There are three types of IGMP messages of concern to the host-router interaction:

- **0x11:** Membership Query

  There are two subtypes of Membership Query messages:

  - **General Query:** Used to learn which groups have members on an attached network
  - **Group-Specific Query:** Used to learn if a particular group has any members on an attached network

    These two messages are differentiated by the Group Address. Membership Query messages are referred to simply as "Query" messages.

- **0x16:** Version 2 Membership Report
- **0x17:** Leave Group

  There is an additional type of message, for backwards-compatibility with IGMPv1:

- **0x12:** Version 1 Membership Report

This document refers to Membership Reports simply as "Reports." When no version is specified, the statement applies equally to both versions.

Unrecognized message types should be silently ignored. New message types may be used by newer versions of IGMP, by multicast routing protocols, or other uses.

2.2. Max Response Time

The Max Response Time field is meaningful only in Membership Query messages and specifies the maximum allowed time before sending a responding report in units of 1/10 second. In all other messages, it is set to zero by the sender and ignored by receivers.

Varying this setting allows IGMPv2 routers to tune the "leave latency" (the time between the moment the last host leaves a group and the routing protocol is notified that there are no more members). It also allows tuning of the burstiness of IGMP traffic on a subnet.

2.3. Checksum

The checksum is the 16-bit one's complement of the one's complement sum of the whole IGMP message (the entire IP payload). For computing the checksum, the checksum field is set to zero. When transmitting packets, the checksum MUST be computed and inserted into this field.

When receiving packets, the checksum MUST be verified before processing a packet.

2.4. Group Address

In a Membership Query message, the Group Address field is set to zero when sending a General Query and set to the group address being queried when sending a Group-Specific Query.

In a Membership Report or Leave Group message, the Group Address field holds the IP multicast group address of the group being reported or left.

2.5. Other Fields

Note that IGMP messages may be longer than 8 octets, especially future backwards-compatible versions of IGMP. As long as the Type is one that is recognized, an IGMPv2 implementation MUST ignore anything past the first 8 octets while processing the packet. However, the IGMP checksum is always computed over the whole IP payload, not just over the first 8 octets.

A.3 IGMP VERSION 1 PACKET FORMATS

IGMPv1 is the result of work completed by Steve Deering. The packet formats are described in Appendix I of RFC 1112. Here is the part of Appendix I from the specification that describes packet formats (it has been reformatted for consistency).

APPENDIX I. INTERNET GROUP MANAGEMENT PROTOCOL (IGMP)

The Internet Group Management Protocol (IGMP) is used by IP hosts to report their host group memberships to any immediately-neighboring multicast routers. IGMP is an asymmetric protocol and is specified here from the point of view of a host rather than a multicast router. (IGMP may also be used, symmetrically or asymmetrically, between multicast routers. Such use is not specified here.)

Like ICMP, IGMP is a integral part of IP. It is required to be implemented by all hosts conforming to level 2 of the IP multicasting specification. IGMP messages are encapsulated in IP datagrams, with an IP protocol number of 2. All IGMP messages of concern to hosts have the following format:

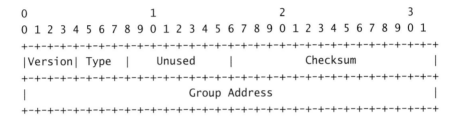

```
 0                   1                   2                   3
 0 1 2 3 4 5 6 7 8 9 0 1 2 3 4 5 6 7 8 9 0 1 2 3 4 5 6 7 8 9 0 1
+-+-+-+-+-+-+-+-+-+-+-+-+-+-+-+-+-+-+-+-+-+-+-+-+-+-+-+-+-+-+-+-+
|Version| Type  |     Unused    |            Checksum           |
+-+-+-+-+-+-+-+-+-+-+-+-+-+-+-+-+-+-+-+-+-+-+-+-+-+-+-+-+-+-+-+-+
|                         Group Address                         |
+-+-+-+-+-+-+-+-+-+-+-+-+-+-+-+-+-+-+-+-+-+-+-+-+-+-+-+-+-+-+-+-+
```

- Version

   This memo specifies version 1 of IGMP. Version 0 is specified in RFC-988 and is now obsolete.

- Type

   There are two types of IGMP message of concern to hosts:

   – Host Membership Query
   – Host Membership Report

- Unused

   Unused field, zeroed when sent, ignored when received.

- Checksum

   The checksum is the 16-bit one's complement of the one's complement sum of the 8-octet IGMP message. For computing the checksum, the checksum field is zeroed.

- Group Address

  In a Host Membership Query message, the Group Address field is zeroed when sent, ignored when received. In a Host Membership Report message, the Group Address field holds the IP host group address of the group being reported.

PIM Packet Formats

This appendix includes the packet formats from the specifications of the two versions of PIM.

B.1 PIM Version 2 Packet Formats

PIMv2 is the result of the collective work of Bill Fenner, Mark Handley, Hugh Holbrook, and Isidor Kouvelas. The packet formats are described in section 4.9 of the current specification, which is included here in its entirety (it has been reformatted for consistency).

4.9. PIM Packet Formats

This section describes the details of the packet formats for PIM control messages.

All PIM control messages have IP protocol number 103. PIM messages are either unicast (e.g., Registers and Register-Stop) or multicast with TTL 1 to the ALL-PIM-ROUTERS group (e.g., Join/Prune, Asserts, etc.). The source address used for unicast messages is a domainwide reachable address; the source address used for multicast messages is the link-local address of the interface on which the message is being sent.

The IPv4 ALL-PIM-ROUTERS group is 224.0.0.13. The IPv6 ALL-PIM-ROUTERS group is ff02::d.

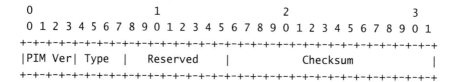

- PIM Ver

  PIM Version number is 2.

- Type

  Types for specific PIM messages. PIM Types are listed in the table that follows:

Message Type	Destination
0 = Hello	Multicast to ALL-PIM-ROUTERS
1 = Register	Unicast to RP
2 = Register-Stop	Unicast to source of Register packet
3 = Join/Prune	Multicast to ALL-PIM-ROUTERS
4 = Bootstrap	Multicast to ALL-PIM-ROUTERS
5 = Assert	Multicast to ALL-PIM-ROUTERS
6 = Graft (used in PIM-DM only)	Multicast to ALL-PIM-ROUTERS
7 = Graft-Ack (used in PIM-DM only)	Unicast to source of Graft packet
8 = Candidate-RP-Advertisement	Unicast to Domain's BSR

- Reserved

  Set to zero on transmission. Ignored upon receipt.

- Checksum

  The checksum is a standard IP checksum, i.e., the 16-bit one's complement of the one's complement sum of the entire PIM message, excluding the data portion in the Register message. For computing the checksum, the checksum field is zeroed.

For IPv6, the checksum also includes the IPv6 pseudo-header, as specified in RFC 2460, section 8.1 [9]. This pseudo-header is prepended to the PIM header for the purposes of calculating the checksum. The Upper-Layer Packet Length in the pseudo-header is set to the length of the PIM message. The Next Header value used in the pseudo-header is 103. If the packet's length is not an integral number of 16-bit words, the packet is padded with a byte of zero before performing the checksum.

4.9.1. Encoded Source and Group Address Formats

An Encoded-Unicast address takes the following format:

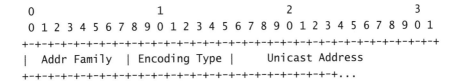

```
 0                   1                   2                   3
 0 1 2 3 4 5 6 7 8 9 0 1 2 3 4 5 6 7 8 9 0 1 2 3 4 5 6 7 8 9 0 1
+-+-+-+-+-+-+-+-+-+-+-+-+-+-+-+-+-+-+-+-+-+-+-+-+-+-+-+-+-+-+-+-+
|  Addr Family  | Encoding Type |      Unicast Address
+-+-+-+-+-+-+-+-+-+-+-+-+-+-+-+-+-+-+-+-+-+-+-+-+-+-+...
```

- Addr Family

  The PIM address family of the Unicast Address field of this address.

  Values of 0–127 are as assigned by the IANA for Internet Address Families in [5]. Values 128–250 are reserved to be assigned by the IANA for PIM-specific Address Families. Values 251–255 are designated for private use. As there is no assignment authority for this space, collisions should be expected.

- Encoding Type

  The type of encoding used within a specific Address Family. The value 0 is reserved for this field and represents the native encoding of the Address Family.

- Unicast Address

  The Unicast Address as represented by the given Address Family and Encoding Type.

Encoded-Group Addresses take the following format:

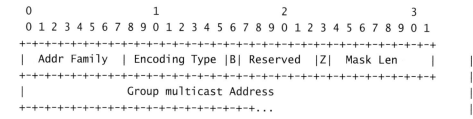

```
 0                   1                   2                   3
 0 1 2 3 4 5 6 7 8 9 0 1 2 3 4 5 6 7 8 9 0 1 2 3 4 5 6 7 8 9 0 1
+-+-+-+-+-+-+-+-+-+-+-+-+-+-+-+-+-+-+-+-+-+-+-+-+-+-+-+-+-+-+-+-+
|  Addr Family  | Encoding Type |B| Reserved  |Z|  Mask Len    |    |
+-+-+-+-+-+-+-+-+-+-+-+-+-+-+-+-+-+-+-+-+-+-+-+-+-+-+-+-+-+-+-+-+    |
|                   Group multicast Address                    |    |
+-+-+-+-+-+-+-+-+-+-+-+-+-+-+-+-+-+-+-+-+-+-+-+...                   |
```

- Addr Family

  Described above.

- Encoding Type

  Described above.

- [B]idirectional PIM

  Indicates the group range should use Bidirectional PIM [6]. For PIM-SM defined in this specification, this bit MUST be zero.

- Reserved

  Transmitted as zero. Ignored upon receipt.

- Admin Scope [Z]one

  Indicates the group range is an admin scope zone. This is used in the Bootstrap Router Mechanism [4] only. For all other purposes, this bit is set to zero and ignored on receipt.

- Mask Len

  The Mask length field is 8 bits. The value is the number of contiguous one bits left-justified used as a mask that, combined with the group address, describes a range of groups. It is less than or equal to the address length in bits for the given Address Family and Encoding Type. If the message is sent for a single group, then the Mask length must equal the address length in bits for the given Address Family and Encoding Type. (e.g., 32 for IPv4 native encoding and 128 for IPv6 native encoding).

- Group Multicast Address

  Contains the group address.

An Encoded-Source address takes the following format:

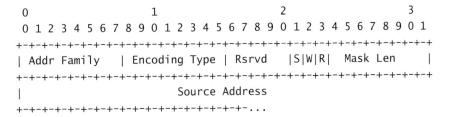

```
 0                   1                   2                   3
 0 1 2 3 4 5 6 7 8 9 0 1 2 3 4 5 6 7 8 9 0 1 2 3 4 5 6 7 8 9 0 1
+-+-+-+-+-+-+-+-+-+-+-+-+-+-+-+-+-+-+-+-+-+-+-+-+-+-+-+-+-+-+-+-+
| Addr Family   | Encoding Type | Rsrvd   |S|W|R|  Mask Len    |
+-+-+-+-+-+-+-+-+-+-+-+-+-+-+-+-+-+-+-+-+-+-+-+-+-+-+-+-+-+-+-+-+
|                        Source Address
+-+-+-+-+-+-+-+-+-+-+-+-+-+-+-+-+-+-+-+-+- ...
```

- Addr Family

  Described above.

- Encoding Type

  Described above.

- Reserved

  Transmitted as zero, ignored on receipt.

- S

  The Sparse bit is a 1-bit value, set to 1 for PIM-SM. It is used for PIM version 1 compatibility.

- W

  The WC (or WildCard) bit is a 1-bit value for use with PIM Join/Prune messages (see section 4.9.5.1).

- R

  The RPT (or Rendezvous Point Tree) bit is a 1-bit value for use with PIM Join/Prune messages (see section 4.9.5.1). If the WC bit is 1, the RPT bit MUST be 1.

- Mask Len

  The mask length field is 8 bits. The value is the number of contiguous one bits left-justified used as a mask that, combined with the Source Address, describes a source subnet. The mask length MUST be equal to the mask length in bits for the given Address Family and Encoding Type (32 for IPv4 native and 128 for IPv6 native). A router SHOULD ignore any messages received with any other mask length.

- Source Address

  The Source Address.

4.9.2. Hello Message Format
It is sent periodically by routers on all interfaces.

```
 0                   1                   2                   3
 0 1 2 3 4 5 6 7 8 9 0 1 2 3 4 5 6 7 8 9 0 1 2 3 4 5 6 7 8 9 0 1
+-+-+-+-+-+-+-+-+-+-+-+-+-+-+-+-+-+-+-+-+-+-+-+-+-+-+-+-+-+-+-+-+
|PIM Ver| Type  |   Reserved    |           Checksum            |
+-+-+-+-+-+-+-+-+-+-+-+-+-+-+-+-+-+-+-+-+-+-+-+-+-+-+-+-+-+-+-+-+
|          OptionType           |          OptionLength         |
+-+-+-+-+-+-+-+-+-+-+-+-+-+-+-+-+-+-+-+-+-+-+-+-+-+-+-+-+-+-+-+-+
|                         OptionValue                           |
|                            ...                                |
+-+-+-+-+-+-+-+-+-+-+-+-+-+-+-+-+-+-+-+-+-+-+-+-+-+-+-+-+-+-+-+-+
|                             .                                |
|                             .                                |
|                             .                                |
+-+-+-+-+-+-+-+-+-+-+-+-+-+-+-+-+-+-+-+-+-+-+-+-+-+-+-+-+-+-+-+-+
|          OptionType           |          OptionLength         |
+-+-+-+-+-+-+-+-+-+-+-+-+-+-+-+-+-+-+-+-+-+-+-+-+-+-+-+-+-+-+-+-+
|                         OptionValue                           |
|                            ...                                |
+-+-+-+-+-+-+-+-+-+-+-+-+-+-+-+-+-+-+-+-+-+-+-+-+-+-+-+-+-+-+-+-+
```

- PIM Version, Type, Reserved, Checksum

  Described above.

- OptionType

  The type of the option given in the following OptionValue field.

- OptionLength

  The length of the OptionValue field in bytes.

- OptionValue

  A variable-length field, carrying the value of the option.

  The Option fields may contain the following values:

  – OptionType 1: Hold Time

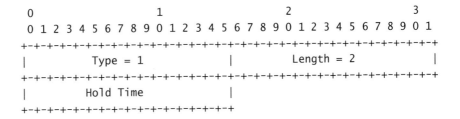

```
0                   1                   2                   3
0 1 2 3 4 5 6 7 8 9 0 1 2 3 4 5 6 7 8 9 0 1 2 3 4 5 6 7 8 9 0 1
+-+-+-+-+-+-+-+-+-+-+-+-+-+-+-+-+-+-+-+-+-+-+-+-+-+-+-+-+-+-+-+-+
|              Type = 1             |            Length = 2             |
+-+-+-+-+-+-+-+-+-+-+-+-+-+-+-+-+-+-+-+-+-+-+-+-+-+-+-+-+-+-+-+-+
|          Hold Time                |
+-+-+-+-+-+-+-+-+-+-+-+-+-+-+-+-+-+
```

  – Hold Time

    The amount of time a receiver must keep the neighbor reachable, in seconds. If the Holdtime is set to 0xffff, the receiver of this message never times out the neighbor. This may be used with dial-on-demand links, to avoid keeping the link up with periodic Hello messages.

    Hello messages with a Holdtime value set to 0 are also sent by a router on an interface about to go down or changing IP address. These are effectively good-bye messages, and the receiving routers should immediately time-out the neighbor information for the sender.

- OptionType 2: LAN Prune Delay

```
 0                   1                   2                   3      |
 0 1 2 3 4 5 6 7 8 9 0 1 2 3 4 5 6 7 8 9 0 1 2 3 4 5 6 7 8 9 0 1    |
+-+-+-+-+-+-+-+-+-+-+-+-+-+-+-+-+-+-+-+-+-+-+-+-+-+-+-+-+-+-+-+-+    |
|          Type = 2             |          Length = 4          | |
+-+-+-+-+-+-+-+-+-+-+-+-+-+-+-+-+-+-+-+-+-+-+-+-+-+-+-+-+-+-+-+-+    |
|T|        LAN Delay            |        Override Interval     | |
+-+-+-+-+-+-+-+-+-+-+-+-+-+-+-+-+-+-+-+-+-+-+-+-+-+-+-+-+-+-+-+-+    |
```

- The LAN_Prune_Delay option is used to tune the prune propagation delay on multiaccess LANs.

The T bit specifies the ability of the sending router to disable joins suppression.

LAN Delay and Override Interval are time intervals in units of milliseconds used to tune the value of the J/P Override Interval and its derived timer values.

- OptionType 3 to 16: reserved to be defined in future versions of this document.
- OptionType 18: Deprecated and should not be used.
- OptionType 19: DR Priority

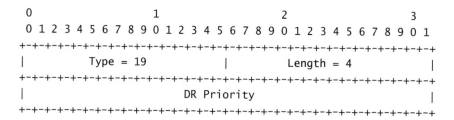

```
 0                   1                   2                   3
 0 1 2 3 4 5 6 7 8 9 0 1 2 3 4 5 6 7 8 9 0 1 2 3 4 5 6 7 8 9 0 1
+-+-+-+-+-+-+-+-+-+-+-+-+-+-+-+-+-+-+-+-+-+-+-+-+-+-+-+-+-+-+-+-+
|            Type = 19          |          Length = 4           |
+-+-+-+-+-+-+-+-+-+-+-+-+-+-+-+-+-+-+-+-+-+-+-+-+-+-+-+-+-+-+-+-+
|                         DR Priority                           |
+-+-+-+-+-+-+-+-+-+-+-+-+-+-+-+-+-+-+-+-+-+-+-+-+-+-+-+-+-+-+-+-+
```

DR Priority is a 32-bit unsigned number and should be considered in the DR election.

- OptionType 20: Generation ID

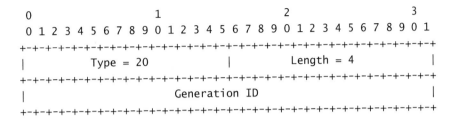

```
0                   1                   2                   3
0 1 2 3 4 5 6 7 8 9 0 1 2 3 4 5 6 7 8 9 0 1 2 3 4 5 6 7 8 9 0 1
+-+-+-+-+-+-+-+-+-+-+-+-+-+-+-+-+-+-+-+-+-+-+-+-+-+-+-+-+-+-+-+-+
|           Type = 20           |          Length = 4           |
+-+-+-+-+-+-+-+-+-+-+-+-+-+-+-+-+-+-+-+-+-+-+-+-+-+-+-+-+-+-+-+-+
|                         Generation ID                         |
+-+-+-+-+-+-+-+-+-+-+-+-+-+-+-+-+-+-+-+-+-+-+-+-+-+-+-+-+-+-+-+-+
```

Generation ID is a random 32-bit value for the interface on which the Hello message is sent. The Generation ID is regenerated whenever PIM forwarding is started or restarted on the interface.

OptionTypes 17–65000 are assigned by the IANA. OptionTypes 65001–65535 are reserved for Private Use, as defined in [7].

Unknown options may be ignored. The Hold Time option MUST be implemented; the DR Priority and Generation ID options SHOULD be implemented.

4.9.3. Register Message Format

A Register message is sent by the DR or a PMBR to the RP when a multicast packet needs to be transmitted on the RP-tree. The IP source address is set to the address of the DR, the destination address to the RP's address. The IP TTL of the PIM packet is the system's normal unicast TTL.

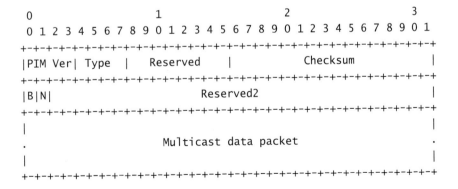

```
0                   1                   2                   3
0 1 2 3 4 5 6 7 8 9 0 1 2 3 4 5 6 7 8 9 0 1 2 3 4 5 6 7 8 9 0 1
+-+-+-+-+-+-+-+-+-+-+-+-+-+-+-+-+-+-+-+-+-+-+-+-+-+-+-+-+-+-+-+-+
|PIM Ver| Type  |   Reserved    |            Checksum           |
+-+-+-+-+-+-+-+-+-+-+-+-+-+-+-+-+-+-+-+-+-+-+-+-+-+-+-+-+-+-+-+-+
|B|N|                       Reserved2                           |
+-+-+-+-+-+-+-+-+-+-+-+-+-+-+-+-+-+-+-+-+-+-+-+-+-+-+-+-+-+-+-+-+
|                                                               |
.                     Multicast data packet                     .
|                                                               |
+-+-+-+-+-+-+-+-+-+-+-+-+-+-+-+-+-+-+-+-+-+-+-+-+-+-+-+-+-+-+-+-+
```

- PIM Version, Type, Reserved, Checksum

  Described earlier. Note that the checksum for Registers is done only on first 8 bytes of packet, including the PIM header and the next 4 bytes, excluding the data packet portion. For interoperability reasons, a message carrying a checksum calculated over the entire PIM register message should be accepted.

- B

  The Border bit. If the router is a DR for a source that it is directly connected to, it sets the B bit to 0. If the router is a PMBR for a source in a directly connected cloud, it sets the B bit to 1.

- N

  The Null-Register bit. Set to 1 by a DR that is probing the RP before expiring its local Register-Suppression timer. Set to 0 otherwise.

- Reserved2

  Transmitted as zero, ignored on receipt.

- Multicast data packet

  The original packet sent by the source. This packet must be the of the same address family as the encapsulating PIM packet, e.g., an IPv6 data packet must be encapsulated in an IPv6 PIM packet. Note that the TTL of the original packet is decremented before encapsulation, just like any other packet that is forwarded. In addition, the RP decrements the TTL after decapsulating, before forwarding the packet down the shared tree.

  For (S,G) null Registers, the Multicast data packet portion contains only a dummy header with S as the source address, G as the destination address, and a data length of zero.

4.9.4. Register-Stop Message Format

A Register-Stop is unicast from the RP to the sender of the Register message. The IP source address is the address to which the register was addressed. The IP destination address is the source address of the register message.

```
 0                   1                   2                   3
 0 1 2 3 4 5 6 7 8 9 0 1 2 3 4 5 6 7 8 9 0 1 2 3 4 5 6 7 8 9 0 1
+-+-+-+-+-+-+-+-+-+-+-+-+-+-+-+-+-+-+-+-+-+-+-+-+-+-+-+-+-+-+-+-+
|PIM Ver| Type |   Reserved    |            Checksum            |
+-+-+-+-+-+-+-+-+-+-+-+-+-+-+-+-+-+-+-+-+-+-+-+-+-+-+-+-+-+-+-+-+
|            Group Address (Encoded-Group format)              |
+-+-+-+-+-+-+-+-+-+-+-+-+-+-+-+-+-+-+-+-+-+-+-+-+-+-+-+-+-+-+-+-+
|          Source Address (Encoded-Unicast format)             |
+-+-+-+-+-+-+-+-+-+-+-+-+-+-+-+-+-+-+-+-+-+-+-+-+-+-+-+-+-+-+-+-+
```

- PIM Version, Type, Reserved, Checksum Described above.

- Group Address

  The group address from the multicast data packet in the Register. Format described in section 4.9.1. Note that for Register-Stops, the Mask Len field contains the full address length * 8 (e.g., 32 for IPv4 native encoding), if the message is sent for a single group.

- Source Address

  The host address of the source from the multicast data packet in the register. The format for this address is given in the Encoded-Unicast address in section 4.9.1. A special wildcard value consisting of an address field of all zeroes can be used to indicate any source.

4.9.5. Join/Prune Message Format

A Join/Prune message is sent by routers toward upstream sources and RPs. Joins are sent to build shared trees (RP trees) or source trees (SPT). Prunes are sent to prune source trees when members leave groups as well as sources that do not use the shared tree.

```
 0                   1                   2                   3
 0 1 2 3 4 5 6 7 8 9 0 1 2 3 4 5 6 7 8 9 0 1 2 3 4 5 6 7 8 9 0 1
+-+-+-+-+-+-+-+-+-+-+-+-+-+-+-+-+-+-+-+-+-+-+-+-+-+-+-+-+-+-+-+-+
|PIM Ver| Type |   Reserved    |            Checksum            |
+-+-+-+-+-+-+-+-+-+-+-+-+-+-+-+-+-+-+-+-+-+-+-+-+-+-+-+-+-+-+-+-+
|        Upstream Neighbor Address (Encoded-Unicast format)    |
+-+-+-+-+-+-+-+-+-+-+-+-+-+-+-+-+-+-+-+-+-+-+-+-+-+-+-+-+-+-+-+-+
```

```
| Reserved       | Num groups     |          Holdtime          |
+-+-+-+-+-+-+-+-+-+-+-+-+-+-+-+-+-+-+-+-+-+-+-+-+-+-+-+-+-+-+-+-+
|            Multicast Group Address 1 (Encoded-Group format)  |
+-+-+-+-+-+-+-+-+-+-+-+-+-+-+-+-+-+-+-+-+-+-+-+-+-+-+-+-+-+-+-+-+
|  Number of Joined Sources    |    Number of Pruned Sources   |
+-+-+-+-+-+-+-+-+-+-+-+-+-+-+-+-+-+-+-+-+-+-+-+-+-+-+-+-+-+-+-+-+
|           Joined Source Address 1 (Encoded-Source format)    |
+-+-+-+-+-+-+-+-+-+-+-+-+-+-+-+-+-+-+-+-+-+-+-+-+-+-+-+-+-+-+-+-+
|                              .                               |
|                              .                               |
+-+-+-+-+-+-+-+-+-+-+-+-+-+-+-+-+-+-+-+-+-+-+-+-+-+-+-+-+-+-+-+-+
|           Joined Source Address n (Encoded-Source format)    |
+-+-+-+-+-+-+-+-+-+-+-+-+-+-+-+-+-+-+-+-+-+-+-+-+-+-+-+-+-+-+-+-+
|           Pruned Source Address 1 (Encoded-Source format)    |
+-+-+-+-+-+-+-+-+-+-+-+-+-+-+-+-+-+-+-+-+-+-+-+-+-+-+-+-+-+-+-+-+
|                              .                               |
|                              .                               |
+-+-+-+-+-+-+-+-+-+-+-+-+-+-+-+-+-+-+-+-+-+-+-+-+-+-+-+-+-+-+-+-+
|           Pruned Source Address n (Encoded-Source format)    |
+-+-+-+-+-+-+-+-+-+-+-+-+-+-+-+-+-+-+-+-+-+-+-+-+-+-+-+-+-+-+-+-+
|                              .                               |
|                              .                               |
|                              .                               |
+-+-+-+-+-+-+-+-+-+-+-+-+-+-+-+-+-+-+-+-+-+-+-+-+-+-+-+-+-+-+-+-+
|            Multicast Group Address m (Encoded-Group format)  |
+-+-+-+-+-+-+-+-+-+-+-+-+-+-+-+-+-+-+-+-+-+-+-+-+-+-+-+-+-+-+-+-+
|  Number of Joined Sources    |    Number of Pruned Sources   |
+-+-+-+-+-+-+-+-+-+-+-+-+-+-+-+-+-+-+-+-+-+-+-+-+-+-+-+-+-+-+-+-+
|           Joined Source Address 1 (Encoded-Source format)    |
+-+-+-+-+-+-+-+-+-+-+-+-+-+-+-+-+-+-+-+-+-+-+-+-+-+-+-+-+-+-+-+-+
|                              .                               |
|                              .                               |
+-+-+-+-+-+-+-+-+-+-+-+-+-+-+-+-+-+-+-+-+-+-+-+-+-+-+-+-+-+-+-+-+
|           Joined Source Address n (Encoded-Source format)    |
+-+-+-+-+-+-+-+-+-+-+-+-+-+-+-+-+-+-+-+-+-+-+-+-+-+-+-+-+-+-+-+-+
|           Pruned Source Address 1 (Encoded-Source format)    |
+-+-+-+-+-+-+-+-+-+-+-+-+-+-+-+-+-+-+-+-+-+-+-+-+-+-+-+-+-+-+-+-+
|                              .                               |
|                              .                               |
+-+-+-+-+-+-+-+-+-+-+-+-+-+-+-+-+-+-+-+-+-+-+-+-+-+-+-+-+-+-+-+-+
|           Pruned Source Address n (Encoded-Source format)    |
+-+-+-+-+-+-+-+-+-+-+-+-+-+-+-+-+-+-+-+-+-+-+-+-+-+-+-+-+-+-+-+-+
```

- PIM Version, Type, Reserved, Checksum

  Described earlier.

- Unicast Upstream Neighbor Address

  The address of the RPF or upstream neighbor. The format for this address is given in the Encoded-Unicast address in section 4.9.1. This address should be the link-local address of the upstream neighbor, as obtained from the RPF lookup.

- Reserved

  Transmitted as zero, ignored on receipt.

- Holdtime

  The amount of time a receiver must keep the Join/Prune state alive, in seconds. If the Holdtime is set to 0xffff, the receiver of this message should hold the state until canceled by the appropriate canceling Join/Prune message or timed out according to local policy. This may be used with dial-on-demand links to avoid keeping the link up with periodic Join/Prune messages.

  Note that the HoldTime must be larger than the J/P_Override_Interval.

- Number of Groups

  The number of multicast group sets contained in the message.

- Multicast group address

  For format description see Section 4.9.1.

- Number of Joined Sources

  Number of join source addresses listed for a given group.

- Join Source Address 1 .. n

  This list contains the sources that the sending router will forward multicast datagrams for if received on the interface this message is sent on.

See Encoded-Source-Address format in section 4.9.1.

- Number of Pruned Sources

  Number of prune source addresses listed for a group.

- Prune Source Address 1 .. n

  This list contains the sources that the sending router does not want to forward multicast datagrams for when received on the interface this message is sent on.

4.9.5.1. Group Set Source List Rules As described earlier, Join/Prune messages are composed by one or more group sets. Each set contains two source lists, the Join Sources and the Prune Sources. This section describes the different types of group sets and source list entries that can exist in a Join/Prune message.

There are two valid group set types:

- Wildcard Group Set

  The wildcard group set is represented by the entire multicast range—the beginning of the multicast address range in the group address field and the prefix length of the multicast address range in the mask length field of the Multicast Group Address, e.g., 224.0.0.0/4 for IPv4. Each wildcard group set may contain one or more (*,*,RP) source list entries in either the Join or **Prune lists**.

  A (*,*,RP) source list entry may only exist in a wildcard group set. When added to a Join source list, this type of source entry expresses the routers' interest in receiving traffic for all groups mapping to the specified RP. When added to a Prune source list a (*,*,RP) entry expresses the routers' interest to stop receiving such traffic.

  (*,*,RP) source list entries have the Source-Address set to the address of the RP, the Source-Address Mask-Len set to the full length of the IP address and to both the WC and RPT bits of the Source-Address set to 1.

- Group Specific Set

  For IPv4, a Group Specific Set is represented by a valid IP multicast address in the group address field and the full length of the IP address in the mask length field of the Multicast Group Address. Each group specific set may contain (*,G), (S,G,rpt), and (S,G) source list entries in the Join or Prune lists.

  - (*,G)

    The (*,G) source list entry is used in Join/Prune messages sent toward the RP for the specified group. It expresses interest (or lack of) in receiving traffic sent to the group through the Rendezvous-Point shared tree. There may only be one such entry in both the Join and Prune lists of a group specific set.

    (*,G) source list entries have the Source-Address set to the address of the RP for group G, the Source-Address Mask-Len set to the full length of the IP address and have both the WC and RPT bits of the Encoded-Source-Address set.

  - (S,G,rpt)

    The (S,G,rpt) source list entry is used in Join/Prune messages sent toward the RP for the specified group. It expresses interest (or lack of) in receiving traffic through the shared tree sent by the specified source to this group. For each source address, the entry may exist in only one of the Join and Prune source lists of a group specific set but not both. (S,G,rpt) source list entries have the Source-Address set to the address of the source S, the Source-Address Mask-Len set to the full length of the IP address and have the WC bit clear and the RPT bit set in the Encoded-Source-Address.

  - (S,G)

    The (S,G) source list entry is used in Join/Prune messages sent toward the specified source. It expresses interest (or lack of) in receiving traffic through the shortest path tree sent by the source to the specified group. For each source address the entry may exist in only one of the Join and Prune source lists of a group specific set but not both. (S,G) source list entries have the Source-Address set to the address of the source S, the Source-Address Mask-Len set to the full length of the IP address and have both the WC and RPT bits of the Encoded-Source-Address cleared.

The rules described earlier are sufficient to prevent invalid combinations of source list entries in group-specific sets. There are however a number of combinations that have a valid interpretation but are not generated by the protocol as described in this specification:

- Combining a (*,G) Join and a (S,G,rpt) Join entry in the same message is redundant as the (*,G) entry covers the information provided by the (S,G,rpt) entry.
- The same applies for (*,G) Prunes and (S,G,rpt) Prunes.
- The combination of an (*,G) Prune and a (S,G,rpt) Join is also not generated. (S,G,rpt) Joins are only sent when the router is receiving all traffic for a group on the shared tree and it wishes to indicate a change for the particular source. As a (*,G) prune indicates that the router no longer wishes to receive shared tree traffic, the (S,G,rpt) Join is meaningless.
- As Join/Prune messages are targeted to a single PIM neighbor, including both an (S,G) Join and an (S,G,rpt) Prune in the same message is redundant. The (S,G) Join informs the neighbor that the sender wishes to receive the particular source on the shortest path tree. It is therefore unnecessary for the router to say that it no longer wishes to receive it on the shared tree.
- The combination of an (S,G) Prune and an (S,G,rpt) Join could possibly be used by a router to switch from receiving a particular source on the shortest-path tree back to receiving it on the shared tree (provided that the RPF neighbor for the shortest-path and shared trees is common). However Sparse-Mode PIM does not provide a mechanism for switching back to the shared tree.

The rules are summarized in the table on the next page.

```
+-----------++-------+---------+------------+------------+--------+--------+
|           ||(*,G)J | (*,G)P  | (S,G,rpt)J | (S,G,rpt)P | (S,G)J | (S,G)P |
+-----------++-------+---------+------------+------------+--------+--------+
|(*,G)J     ||-      | no      | ?          | yes        | yes    | yes    |
+-----------++-------+---------+------------+------------+--------+--------+
|(*,G)P     ||       | -       | ?          | ?          | yes    | yes    |
+-----------++-------+---------+------------+------------+--------+--------+
|(S,G,rpt)J ||       |         | -          | no         | yes    | yes    |
+-----------++-------+---------+------------+------------+--------+--------+
|(S,G,rpt)P ||       |         |            | -          | ?      | ?      |
+-----------++-------+---------+------------+------------+--------+--------+
|(S,G)J     ||       |         |            |            | -      | no     |
+-----------++-------+---------+------------+------------+--------+--------+
|(S,G)P     ||       |         |            |            |        | -      |
+-----------++-------+---------+------------+------------+--------+--------+
```

- yes

  Allowed and expected.

- no

  Combination is not allowed by the protocol and MUST not be generated by a router.

- ?

  Combination not expected by the protocol but well defined. A router MAY accept it but SHOULD not generate it.

The order of source list entries in a group set source list is not important. As a result, the table above is symmetric, and only entries on the upper-right half have been specified because entries on the lower left are just a mirror.

4.9.5.2. Group Set Fragmentation When building a Join/Prune for a particular neighbor, a router should try and include in the message as much of the information it needs to convey to the neighbor as possible. This implies adding one group set for each multicast group that has information pending transmission and within each set including all relevant source list entries.

On a router with a large amount of multicast state, the number of entries that must be included may result in packets that are larger in the maximum IP packet size. In most such cases, the information may be split into multiple messages.

There is an exception with group sets that contain a (*,G) Join source list entry. The group set expresses the routers' interest in receiving all traffic for the specified group on the shared tree, and it MUST include an (S,G,rpt) Prune source list entry for every source that the router does not wish to receive. This list of (S,G,rpt) Prune source-list entries MUST not be split in multiple messages.

If only N (S,G,rpt) Prune entries fit into a maximum-sized Join/Prune message, but the router has more than N (S,G,rpt) Prunes to add, then the router MUST choose to include the first N (numerically smallest) IP addresses.

4.9.6. Assert Message Format

The Assert message is used to resolve forwarder conflicts between routers on a link. It is sent when a multicast data packet is received on an interface that the router would normally forward that packet. Assert messages may also be sent in response to an Assert message from another router.

```
 0                   1                   2                   3
 0 1 2 3 4 5 6 7 8 9 0 1 2 3 4 5 6 7 8 9 0 1 2 3 4 5 6 7 8 9 0 1
+-+-+-+-+-+-+-+-+-+-+-+-+-+-+-+-+-+-+-+-+-+-+-+-+-+-+-+-+-+-+-+-+
|PIM Ver| Type |   Reserved    |            Checksum            |
+-+-+-+-+-+-+-+-+-+-+-+-+-+-+-+-+-+-+-+-+-+-+-+-+-+-+-+-+-+-+-+-+
|            Group Address (Encoded-Group format)              |
+-+-+-+-+-+-+-+-+-+-+-+-+-+-+-+-+-+-+-+-+-+-+-+-+-+-+-+-+-+-+-+-+
|           Source Address (Encoded-Unicast format)           |
+-+-+-+-+-+-+-+-+-+-+-+-+-+-+-+-+-+-+-+-+-+-+-+-+-+-+-+-+-+-+-+-+
|R|                  Metric Preference                         |
+-+-+-+-+-+-+-+-+-+-+-+-+-+-+-+-+-+-+-+-+-+-+-+-+-+-+-+-+-+-+-+-+
|                         Metric                              |
+-+-+-+-+-+-+-+-+-+-+-+-+-+-+-+-+-+-+-+-+-+-+-+-+-+-+-+-+-+-+-+-+
```

- PIM Version, Type, Reserved, Checksum

  Described earlier.

- Group Address

  The group address for which the router wishes to resolve the forwarding conflict. This is an Encoded-Group address, as specified in 4.9.1.

- Source Address

  Source address for which the router wishes to resolve the forwarding conflict. The source address MAY be set to INADDR_ANY for (*,G) asserts (see below). The format for this address is given in Encoded-Unicast-Address in section 4.9.1.

- R

  RPT-bit is a 1 bit value. The RPT-bit is set to 1 for (*,G) Assert messages and 0 for (S,G) assert messages.

- Metric Preference

  Preference value assigned to the unicast routing protocol that provided the route to the multicast source or Rendezvous-Point.

- Metric

  The unicast routing table metric associated with the route used to reach the multicast source or Rendezvous-Point. The metric is in units applicable to the unicast routing protocol used.

Assert message can be sent to resolve a forwarding conflict for all traffic to a given group or for a specific source and group.

- (S,G) Asserts

  Source-specific asserts are sent by routers forwarding a specific source on the shortest-path tree (SPT bit is TRUE). (S,G) Asserts have the Group-Address field set to the group G and the Source-Address field set to the source S. The RPT-bit is set to 0, the Metric-Preference is set to MRIB.pref(S), and the Metric is set to MRIB.metric(S).

- (*,G) Asserts

Group-specific asserts are sent by routers forwarding data for the group and source(s) under contention on the shared tree. (*,G) asserts have the Group-Address field set to the group G. For data-triggered Asserts, the Source-Address field MAY be set to the IP source address of the data packet that triggered the Assert and is set to INADDR_ANY otherwise. The RPT-bit is set to 1, the Metric-Preference is set to MRIB.pref(RP(G)), and the Metric is set to MRIB.metric(RP(G)).

B.2 PIM VERSION I PACKET FORMATS

PIMv1 is the result of the collective work of Steve Deering, Deborah Estrin, Dino Farinacci, and Van Jacobsen. The packet formats are described in section 4 in the specification, which is included here in its entirety (it has been reformatted for consistency).

4. PACKET TYPES

RFC-1112 specifies two types of IGMP packets for hosts and routers to convey multicast group membership and reachability information. An IGMP-Host-Query packet is transmitted periodically by routers to ask hosts to report which multicast groups they are members of. An IGMP-Host-Report packet is transmitted by hosts in response to received queries advertising group membership.

This document introduces new types of IGMP packets that are used by PIM routers. The packet format is shown in Figure 1.

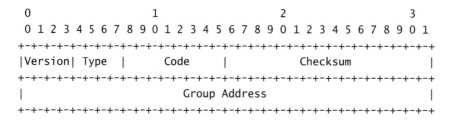

Figure 1: (Figure 8 in orig.) IGMP packet format

- Version: This memo specifies version 1 of IGMP. Version 0 is specified in RFC-988 and is now obsolete.

- Type: There are five types of IGMP messages:
  - 1 = Host Membership Query
  - 2 = Host Membership Report
  - 3 = Router DVMRP Messages
  - 4 = Router PIM Messages
  - 5 = Trace Messages

- Code: Codes for specific message types. Used only by DVMRP and PIM. PIM codes are:
  - 0 = Router-Query
  - 1 = Register
  - 2 = Register-Stop
  - 3 = Join/Prune
  - 4 = RP-Reachability
  - 5 = Assert
  - 6 = Graft (dense-mode PIM only)
  - 7 = Graft-Ack (dense-mode PIM only)
  - 8 = Mode

- Checksum: The checksum is the 16-bit one's complement of the one's complement sum of the entire IGMP message. For computing the checksum, the checksum field is zeroed.

- Group Address: In a IGMP-Host-Query message, the group address field is zeroed when sent, ignored when received. In an IGMP-Host-Report message, the group address field holds the IP host group address of the group being reported. PIM-Join/Prune, PIM-Assert, and PIM-Mode messages have the group address field zeroed when sent to a point-to-point link and have the next-hop router address in it when sent to a multiaccess LAN. PIM-Register and Register-Stop messages have the group address field zeroed when sent. (See section 4.2 for RP-Reachability format.) PIM-Query message has the first 30 bits in the group address zeroed. The thirtieth bit carries the sparse mode reset flag, if 1, the modes of entries in the downstream routers are reset to periodic join mode. The thirty-first bit carries the mode of the interface where the PIM-Query is sent, if 1, the mode on the interface is configured as sparse mode only; if 0, the mode on the interface is configured as dense mode acceptable.

4.1. PIM-Join/Prune, PIM-Assert and PIM-Mode Messages

PIM-Join/Prune, PIM-Assert, and PIM-Mode messages have the following additional information appended to the fixed header (RP-Reachability message type will be described in section 4.2). The format of the additional information is shown in Figure 2.

- Reserved: Unused field, zeroed when sent, ignored when received.
- Addr Length: The length in bytes of the encoded source addresses in the Join and Prune lists.
- Maddr Length: The length in bytes of the encoded multicast addresses.
- Number of Groups: The number of multicast group sets contained in the message.
- Multicast group address: For IP, it is a 4-byte Class D address.
- Multicast group address mask: A bit mask used against the multicast group address. This is the method to describe a range of multicast addresses. If the multicast group address field describes a single group address, the value must be 255.255.255.255.
- Number of Join Sources: Number of join source addresses listed for a given group. For PIM-Assert message, this is the number of assert source addresses listed for a group. For PIM-Mode message, this is the number of source addresses listed for a group whose modes are changed.
- Join Source Address-1 .. n: This list contains the sources that the sending router will forward multicast datagrams for if received on the interface this message is sent on. The address 0.0.0.0 indicates a Join for all sources.
- Number of Prune Sources: Number of prune source addresses listed for a given group. PIM-Assert and PIM-Mode messages only use the **join list**, so the number of prune sources should always be 0.

```
 0                   1                   2                   3
 0 1 2 3 4 5 6 7 8 9 0 1 2 3 4 5 6 7 8 9 0 1 2 3 4 5 6 7 8 9 0 1
+-+-+-+-+-+-+-+-+-+-+-+-+-+-+-+-+-+-+-+-+-+-+-+-+-+-+-+-+-+-+-+-+
|   Reserved    | Maddr Length  |  Addr Length  |  Num groups   |
+-+-+-+-+-+-+-+-+-+-+-+-+-+-+-+-+-+-+-+-+-+-+-+-+-+-+-+-+-+-+-+-+
|                   Multicast Group Address-1                   |
+-+-+-+-+-+-+-+-+-+-+-+-+-+-+-+-+-+-+-+-+-+-+-+-+-+-+-+-+-+-+-+-+
|                 Multicast Group Address-1 Mask                |
+-+-+-+-+-+-+-+-+-+-+-+-+-+-+-+-+-+-+-+-+-+-+-+-+-+-+-+-+-+-+-+-+
|    Number of Join Sources     |    Number of Prune Sources    |
+-+-+-+-+-+-+-+-+-+-+-+-+-+-+-+-+-+-+-+-+-+-+-+-+-+-+-+-+-+-+-+-+
|                     Join Source Address-1                     |
+-+-+-+-+-+-+-+-+-+-+-+-+-+-+-+-+-+-+-+-+-+-+-+-+-+-+-+-+-+-+-+-+
|                               .                               |
|                               .                               |
+-+-+-+-+-+-+-+-+-+-+-+-+-+-+-+-+-+-+-+-+-+-+-+-+-+-+-+-+-+-+-+-+
|                     Join Source Address-n                     |
+-+-+-+-+-+-+-+-+-+-+-+-+-+-+-+-+-+-+-+-+-+-+-+-+-+-+-+-+-+-+-+-+
|                    Prune Source Address-1                     |
+-+-+-+-+-+-+-+-+-+-+-+-+-+-+-+-+-+-+-+-+-+-+-+-+-+-+-+-+-+-+-+-+
|                               .                               |
|                               .                               |
+-+-+-+-+-+-+-+-+-+-+-+-+-+-+-+-+-+-+-+-+-+-+-+-+-+-+-+-+-+-+-+-+
|                    Prune Source Address-n                     |
+-+-+-+-+-+-+-+-+-+-+-+-+-+-+-+-+-+-+-+-+-+-+-+-+-+-+-+-+-+-+-+-+
|                               .                               |
|                               .                               |
|                               .                               |
+-+-+-+-+-+-+-+-+-+-+-+-+-+-+-+-+-+-+-+-+-+-+-+-+-+-+-+-+-+-+-+-+
|                   Multicast Group Address-n                   |
+-+-+-+-+-+-+-+-+-+-+-+-+-+-+-+-+-+-+-+-+-+-+-+-+-+-+-+-+-+-+-+-+
|                 Multicast Group Address-n Mask                |
+-+-+-+-+-+-+-+-+-+-+-+-+-+-+-+-+-+-+-+-+-+-+-+-+-+-+-+-+-+-+-+-+
|    Number of Join Sources     |    Number of Prune Sources    |
+-+-+-+-+-+-+-+-+-+-+-+-+-+-+-+-+-+-+-+-+-+-+-+-+-+-+-+-+-+-+-+-+
|                     Join Source Address-1                     |
+-+-+-+-+-+-+-+-+-+-+-+-+-+-+-+-+-+-+-+-+-+-+-+-+-+-+-+-+-+-+-+-+
|                               .                               |
|                               .                               |
```

Figure 2: (Figure 9 in orig.) Additional packet format for PIM-Join/Prune

```
+-+-+-+-+-+-+-+-+-+-+-+-+-+-+-+-+-+-+-+-+-+-+-+-+-+-+-+-+-+-+-+-+
|                     Join Source Address-n                     |
+-+-+-+-+-+-+-+-+-+-+-+-+-+-+-+-+-+-+-+-+-+-+-+-+-+-+-+-+-+-+-+-+
|                     Prune Source Address-1                    |
+-+-+-+-+-+-+-+-+-+-+-+-+-+-+-+-+-+-+-+-+-+-+-+-+-+-+-+-+-+-+-+-+
|                              .                                |
|                              .                                |
+-+-+-+-+-+-+-+-+-+-+-+-+-+-+-+-+-+-+-+-+-+-+-+-+-+-+-+-+-+-+-+-+
|                     Prune Source Address-n                    |
+-+-+-+-+-+-+-+-+-+-+-+-+-+-+-+-+-+-+-+-+-+-+-+-+-+-+-+-+-+-+-+-+
```

Figure 2: *Continued*

- Prune Source Address-1 .. n: This list contains the sources that the sending router does not want to forward multicast datagrams for when received on the interface this message is sent on. The address 0.0.0.0 indicates a prune for all sources.

4.1.1 Source Address Format In PIM messages, all source addresses have the format shown in Figure 3.

- Reserved: Unused field, zeroed when sent, ignored when received.
- MD: Used when sending Mode messages. An upstream router indicates to downstream neighbor(s) if the specific group should operate in periodic join mode. If the bit is clear, the routers should operate in implicit join mode, which means they do not send periodic join messages to the upstream router. The Source Address should be set to 0.0.0.0 in Mode messages with the WC bit and RP bit set to 0 if wildcarding is used.

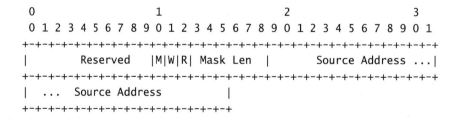

```
 0                   1                   2                   3
 0 1 2 3 4 5 6 7 8 9 0 1 2 3 4 5 6 7 8 9 0 1 2 3 4 5 6 7 8 9 0 1
+-+-+-+-+-+-+-+-+-+-+-+-+-+-+-+-+-+-+-+-+-+-+-+-+-+-+-+-+-+-+-+-+
|       Reserved      |M|W|R| Mask Len |    Source Address ...|
+-+-+-+-+-+-+-+-+-+-+-+-+-+-+-+-+-+-+-+-+-+-+-+-+-+-+-+-+-+-+-+-+
| ...   Source Address           |
+-+-+-+-+-+-+-+-+-+-+-+-+-+-+-+-+-+
```

Figure 3: (Figure 10 in orig.) Source address format

- WC: The WC bit is a 1 bit value. If 1, the Join or Prune applies to the (*,G) entry. If 0, the Join or Prune applies to the (S,G) entry where S is Source Address. Joins and Prunes sent toward the RP should have this bit set.
- RP: The RP bit is a 1 bit value. If 1, the information about (S,G) is sent toward the RP. If 0, the information should be sent about (S,G) toward S, where S is Source Address.
- Mask Length: Mask length is 6 bits. The value is the number of contiguous bits left-justified used as a mask which describes the address. The mask length must be less than or equal to Addr Length * 8.
- Source Address: The address length is indicated from the Addr Length field at the beginning of the header. For IP, the value is 4 octets. This address is either an RP address (WCbit = 1) or a source address (WCbit = 0). When it is a source address, it is coupled with the group address to make (S,G).

Represented in the form of <WCbit><RPbit><Mask length><Source address>:

A source address could be a host IP address :

< 0 >< 0 >< 32 >< 192.1.1.17 >

A source address could be the RP's IP address :

< 1 >< 1 >< 32 >< 131.108.13.111 >

A source address could be a subnet address to prune from the RP-tree :

< 0 >< 1 >< 28 >< 192.1.1.16 >

A source address could be a general aggregate :

< 0 >< 0 >< 16 >< 192.1.0.0 >

4.2. RP-Reachability Message

RP-Reachability messages have the packet format shown in Figure 4.

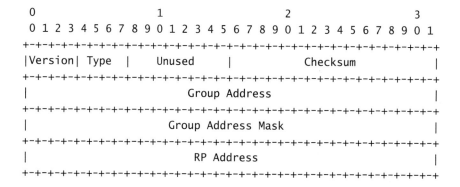

```
 0                   1                   2                   3
 0 1 2 3 4 5 6 7 8 9 0 1 2 3 4 5 6 7 8 9 0 1 2 3 4 5 6 7 8 9 0 1
+-+-+-+-+-+-+-+-+-+-+-+-+-+-+-+-+-+-+-+-+-+-+-+-+-+-+-+-+-+-+-+-+
|Version| Type  |    Unused     |           Checksum            |
+-+-+-+-+-+-+-+-+-+-+-+-+-+-+-+-+-+-+-+-+-+-+-+-+-+-+-+-+-+-+-+-+
|                        Group Address                          |
+-+-+-+-+-+-+-+-+-+-+-+-+-+-+-+-+-+-+-+-+-+-+-+-+-+-+-+-+-+-+-+-+
|                     Group Address Mask                        |
+-+-+-+-+-+-+-+-+-+-+-+-+-+-+-+-+-+-+-+-+-+-+-+-+-+-+-+-+-+-+-+-+
|                         RP Address                            |
+-+-+-+-+-+-+-+-+-+-+-+-+-+-+-+-+-+-+-+-+-+-+-+-+-+-+-+-+-+-+-+-+
```

Figure 4: (Figure 11 in orig.) RP-Reachability message packet format

Each RP will send RP-Reachability messages to all routers on its distribution tree for a particular group. These messages are sent so routers can detect that an RP is reachable. Routers that have attached host members for a group will process the message.

The RPs will address the RP-Reachability messages to 224.0.0.2.

Routers that have state for the group with respect to the RP distribution tree will propagate the message. Otherwise, the message is discarded. If an RP address timer expires, the router should attempt to send an PIM Join message toward an alternate RP provided for that group if one is available.

- Group Address: Group address associated with RP.
- Group Address Mask: A bit mask that allows the description of group ranges. Must be set to 255.255.255.255 when Group Address describes a single group address.
- RP Address: The rendezvous point IP address of the sender.

Finally, in a future version of this document we will specify a new IGMP message type that allows hosts to advertise a list of 1 to n RP addresses associated with a particular group address.

MSDP Packet Formats

This appendix includes the packet formats from the latest specification of versions of MSDP.

C.1 MSDP Packet Formats

MSDP is the result of the collective work of many individuals. David Meyer and Bill Fenner serve as editors of the specification. The packet formats are described in section 16 of the current specification, which is included here in its entirety (it has been reformatted for consistency).

16. Packet Formats

MSDP messages will be encoded in TLV format. If an implementation receives a TLV that has length that is longer than expected, the TLV SHOULD be accepted. Any additional data SHOULD be ignored.

16.1. MSDP TLV format

```
 0                   1                   2                   3
 0 1 2 3 4 5 6 7 8 9 0 1 2 3 4 5 6 7 8 9 0 1 2 3 4 5 6 7 8 9 0 1
+-+-+-+-+-+-+-+-+-+-+-+-+-+-+-+-+-+-+-+-+-+-+-+-+-+-+-+-+-+-+-+-+
|     Type      |           Length          | Value ....    |
+-+-+-+-+-+-+-+-+-+-+-+-+-+-+-+-+-+-+-+-+-+-+-+-+-+-+-+-+-+-+-+-+
```

- Type (8 bits)

  Describes the format of the Value field.

- Length (16 bits)

  Length of Type, Length, and Value fields in octets. The minimum length required is 4 octets, except for Keepalive messages. The maximum TLV length is 1400.

- Value (variable length)

  Format is based on the Type value. See below. The length of the Value field is Length field minus 3. All reserved fields in the Value field MUST be transmitted as zeros and ignored on receipt.

16.2. Defined TLVs

The following TLV Types are defined:

Code	Type
1	IPv4 Source-Active
2	IPv4 Source-Active Request
3	IPv4 Source-Active Response
4	KeepAlive
5	Notification

Each TLV is described below.

In addition, the following TLV Types are assigned but not described in this memo:

Code	Type
6	MSDP traceroute in progress
7	MSDP traceroute reply

16.2.1. IPv4 Source-Active TLV The maximum size SA message that can be sent is 9192 octets. The 9192 octet size does not include the TCP, IP, layer-2 headers.

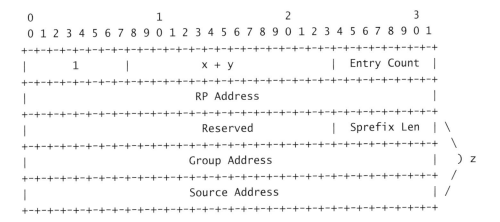

```
 0                   1                   2                   3
 0 1 2 3 4 5 6 7 8 9 0 1 2 3 4 5 6 7 8 9 0 1 2 3 4 5 6 7 8 9 0 1
+-+-+-+-+-+-+-+-+-+-+-+-+-+-+-+-+-+-+-+-+-+-+-+-+-+-+-+-+-+-+-+-+
|       1       |            x + y              | Entry Count   |
+-+-+-+-+-+-+-+-+-+-+-+-+-+-+-+-+-+-+-+-+-+-+-+-+-+-+-+-+-+-+-+-+
|                         RP Address                            |
+-+-+-+-+-+-+-+-+-+-+-+-+-+-+-+-+-+-+-+-+-+-+-+-+-+-+-+-+-+-+-+-+
|                  Reserved               | Sprefix Len | \
+-+-+-+-+-+-+-+-+-+-+-+-+-+-+-+-+-+-+-+-+-+-+-+-+-+-+-+-+-+-+ \
|                      Group Address                      |  ) z
+-+-+-+-+-+-+-+-+-+-+-+-+-+-+-+-+-+-+-+-+-+-+-+-+-+-+-+-+-+-+ /
|                      Source Address                     | /
+-+-+-+-+-+-+-+-+-+-+-+-+-+-+-+-+-+-+-+-+-+-+-+-+-+-+-+-+-+-+
```

- Type

  IPv4 Source-Active TLV is type 1.

- Length x

  Is the length of the control information in the message. x is 8 octets (for the first two 32-bit quantities) plus 12 times Entry Count octets.

- Length y

  If 0, no data is encapsulated. Otherwise, an IPv4 packet follows, and y is the length of the total length field of the IPv4 header encapsulated. If there are multiple SA TLVs in a message, and data is also included, y must be 0 in all SA TLVs except the last one, and the last SA TLV must reflect the source and destination addresses in the IP header of the encapsulated data.

- Entry Count

  Is the count of z entries (note above) that follow the RP address field. This is so multiple (S,G)s from the same domain can be encoded efficiently for the same RP address.

- RP Address

  The address of the RP in the domain the source has become active in.

- Reserved

  The Reserved field MUST be transmitted as zeros and MUST be ignored by a receiver.

- Sprefix Len

  The route prefix length associated with source address. This field MUST be transmitted as 32 (/32). An Invalid Sprefix Len Notification SHOULD be sent upon receipt of any other value.

- Group Address

  The group address the active source has sent data to.

- Source Address

  The IP address of the active source.

Multiple SA TLVs MAY appear in the same message and can be batched for efficiency at the expense of data latency. This would typically occur on intermediate forwarding of SA messages.

16.2.2. IPv4 Source-Active Request TLV The Source-Active Request is used to request SA-state from an MSDP peer. If an RP in a domain receives a PIM

Join message for a group, creates (*,G) state, and wants to know all active sources for group G, it may send an SA-Request message for the group.

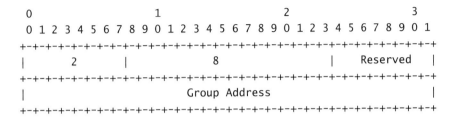

* Type

  IPv4 Source-Active Request TLV is type 2.

* Reserved

  Must be transmitted as zero and ignored on receipt.

* Group Address

  The group address the MSDP peer is requesting.

16.2.3. IPv4 Source-Active Response TLV The Source-Active Response is sent in response to a Source-Active Request message. The Source-Active Response message has the same format as a Source-Active message but does not allow encapsulation of multicast data.

* Type

  IPv4 Source-Active Response TLV is type 3.

- Length x

  Is the length of the control information in the message. x is 8 octets (for the first two 32-bit quantities) plus 12 times Entry Count octets.

16.2.4. KeepAlive TLV A KeepAlive TLV is sent to an MSDP peer if and only if there were no MSDP messages sent to the peer within [KeepAlive-Period] seconds.

This message is necessary to keep the MSDP connection alive:

```
 0                   1                   2                   3
 0 1 2 3 4 5 6 7 8 9 0 1 2 3 4 5 6 7 8 9 0 1 2 3 4 5 6 7 8 9 0 1
+-+-+-+-+-+-+-+-+-+-+-+-+-+-+-+-+-+-+-+-+-+-+-+-+-+-+-+-+-+-+-+-+
|       4       |               3               |
+-+-+-+-+-+-+-+-+-+-+-+-+-+-+-+-+-+-+-+-+-+-+-+-+
```

The length of the message is 3 octets, which encompasses the one-octet Type field and the two-octet Length field.

16.2.5. Notification TLV A Notification message, which has the following form, is sent when an error condition is detected:

```
 0                   1                   2                   3
 0 1 2 3 4 5 6 7 8 9 0 1 2 3 4 5 6 7 8 9 0 1 2 3 4 5 6 7 8 9 0 1
+-+-+-+-+-+-+-+-+-+-+-+-+-+-+-+-+-+-+-+-+-+-+-+-+-+-+-+-+-+-+-+-+
|       5       |             x + 5             |0| Error Code  |
+-+-+-+-+-+-+-+-+-+-+-+-+-+-+-+-+-+-+-+-+-+-+-+-+-+-+-+-+-+-+-+-+
| Error subcode |              ...                              |
+-+-+-+-+-+-+-+-+                                               |
|                             Data                             |
|                              ...                              |
+-+-+-+-+-+-+-+-+-+-+-+-+-+-+-+-+-+-+-+-+-+-+-+-+-+-+-+-+-+-+-+-+
```

- Type

  The Notification TLV is type 5.

- Length

  Length is a two-octet field with value x + 5, where x is the length of the notification data field.

- O-bit

  Open bit. If clear, the connection will be closed.

- Error code

  This 7-bit unsigned integer indicates the type of Notification.

The following Error Codes have been defined:

Error Code	Symbolic Name
1	Message Header Error
2	SA-Request Error
3	SA-Message/SA-Response Error
4	Hold Timer Expired
5	Finite State Machine Error
6	Notification
7	Cease

- Error subcode:

  This one-octet unsigned integer provides more specific information about the reported error. Each Error Code may have one or more Error Subcodes associated with it. If no appropriate Error Subcode is defined, then a zero (Unspecific) value is used for the Error Subcode field, and the O-bit must be cleared (i.e., the connection will be closed). The used notation in the error description below is: MC = Must Close connection = O-bit clear; CC = Can Close connection = O-bit MAY be cleared.

- Message Header Error subcodes:
  - 0: Unspecific (MC)
  - 2: Bad Message Length (MC)
  - 3: Bad Message Type (CC)

- SA-Request Error subcodes (the O-bit is always clear):
  - 0: Unspecific (MC)
  - 1: Invalid Group (MC)

- SA-Message/SA-Response Error subcodes
  - 0: Unspecific (MC)
  - 1: Invalid Entry Count (CC)
  - 2: Invalid RP Address (MC)
  - 3: Invalid Group Address (MC)
  - 4: Invalid Source Address (MC)
  - 5: Invalid Sprefix Length (MC)
  - 6: Looping SA (Self is RP) (MC)
  - 7: Unknown Encapsulation (MC)
  - 8: Administrative Scope Boundary Violated (MC)

- Hold Timer Expired subcodes (the O-bit is always clear):
  - 0: Unspecific (MC)

- Finite State Machine Error subcodes (the O-bit is always clear):
  - 0: Unspecific (MC)
  - 1: Unexpected Message Type FSM Error (MC)

- Notification subcodes (the O-bit is always clear):
  - 0: Unspecific (MC)

- Cease subcodes (the O-bit is always clear):
  - 0: Unspecific (MC)

Glossary

This glossary lists key terms, abbreviations, and acronyms with their definitions and indicates whether the term is applicable to a particular protocol, routing environment, or "context."

Term	Context	Description
(*,G) route entry	PIM-SM	Group members join the RP tree for a particular group. This tree is represented by (*,G) multicast route entries along the shared tree branches between the RP and the group members.
ABR	OSPF	area border router—Routers within a nonbackbone area that connect to area 0.
AFI	MBGP	address family identifier—A number referencing network protocols.
AFI	IS-IS	authority and format indicator—A byte in NSAP format used to describe the organization that assigned the address and the meaning of the fields that follow.
anycast	Packet delivery	A method of delivering packets to exactly one member of the anycast group. The specific host to which the packet is delivered cannot be determined by the sender.

Term	Context	Description
anycast RP	PIM-SM	A method in which multiple routers are configured with the same IP address, typically on their loopback interface. This shared address is used in the RP-to-group mapping, which enables multicast groups to have multiple active RPs in a PIM-SM domain for the same group range.
AS	BGP	autonomous system—A collection of routers, typically operated by a single administrative function, coordinated to implement the same routing policy.
ASM	IP multicast	Any-Source Multicast—One-to-many and many-to-many communications model outlined in RFC 1112. ASM is the original vision of multicast.
ASP	Networking	application service provider—An organization that provides content-hosting services.
ASSERT message	PIM	Provides a mechanism for avoiding a condition where multiple routers exist for a LAN and more than one router forwards the same multicast data packets to the LAN.
ATM	Link layer	Asynchronous Transfer Mode—A circuit-switched, link-layer protocol.
auto-RP	PIM-SM	A method for dynamically learning of the RP. Originally proprietary to Cisco Systems, it is now fully supported by Juniper Networks.
BGMP	Multicast routing protocols	Border Gateway Multicast Protocol—Interdomain multicast routing protocol that is expected to be implemented in IPv6.
BGP	Routing protocols	Border Gateway Protocol—The interdomain unicast routing protocol used in the Internet. BGP is an EGP.
BGP4	Routing protocols	Border Gateway Protocol version 4—The current version of BGP.
BGP peer	BGP	A router with which a BGP session is established.
BGP session	BGP	An instance of BGP running between two routers.
BGP speaker	BGP	A router configured to send and receive route information via BGP. BGP speakers form adjacencies with peer routers to exchange route information.
Bi-Dir PIM	Multicast routing protocols	Bi-Directional PIM—A distinct mode of operation for PIM, in contrast to sparse mode and dense mode. When a group is forwarded based on Bi-Dir rules, data packets are routed along a bidirectional shared tree to the RP for the group.

Term	Context	Description
blackhole	Geek slang	When used as a noun, "blackhole" is a router that advertises reachability to a network but discards any packets it receives destined for that network. When used as a verb, it means to act like such a router.
Bootstrap message	PIM-SM	A method for a router to dynamically learn of the RP. Each candidate BSR sends these messages out all of its interfaces. When neighboring routers receive the message, they process the packet and forward a copy of the packet out all interfaces except the interface on which the Bootstrap message was received.
broadcast	Packet delivery	A method of data delivery in which data is delivered to all hosts, regardless of an expression of interest, also referred to as *one-to-all delivery*.
BSR	PIM-SM	bootstrap router—A dynamically elected router within a PIM-SM domain. A bootstrap router is responsible for constructing the RP-set and originating Bootstrap messages.
capabilities negotiation	BGP	A process of BGP in which routers determine the capabilities—such as whether MBGP is supported, multiprotocol capabilities, which address families are supported—that exist with each other when a session is established.
CGMP	IP multicast	Cisco Group Management Protocol—A proprietary mechanism implemented on Cisco Systems routers and switches that determines which hosts are actually interested in receiving multicast traffic, preventing multicast traffic from being flooded to all hosts connected to the switch. CGMP provides functionality similar to IGMP snooping.
CIDR	IP	classless interdomain routing—A manner of referring to IP prefixes that requires an explicit prefix length be specified. CIDR is in contrast to classful routing, which assumes a natural prefix length based on the first octet of the address.
classful	IP	A way of referring to IP prefixes. The class is implicit based on the value of the leftmost octet. All multicast addresses fall in the class D range of the IPv4 address space.
CLNP	ISO	Connectionless Network Protocol—An ISO protocol that realizes the CLNS model.
CLNS	ISO	Connectionless Network Service—An ISO service model for best effort packet delivery.

Term	Context	Description
COMMUNITY	BGP	An attribute of a BGP route that contains a list of 32-bit values used to classify or tag a route.
control packet	Networking	A type of packet sent for the purpose of exchanging information between networked devices. For example, routing protocol packets are considered control packets. Control packets are used to set up the facilities needed to transmit data packets.
core router	Network design	A router, operated by an ISP, that has two primary purposes: to serve as a node in the wide area backbone, terminating relatively high-bandwidth circuits to other core routers, and to connect to local access routers.
CSNP	IS-IS	Complete Sequence Number PDU—An IS-IS PDU that contains a summary of all of the LSPs a router has in its database.
data packet	Networking	Data packets contain the actual data transmitted within a network, as distinct from information in a message meant for control of delivery of the message.
dense protocol	Multicast routing protocol	A category of multicast routing protocols that use a flood-and-prune model of distribution; they assume a dense distribution of receivers throughout a domain, where each subnet probably has at least one interested receiver for every active group. Dense protocols are not well suited to interdomain deployment on the Internet.
DIS	IS-IS	designated intermediate system—An IS-IS router that acts as a spokesperson for a LAN.
distribution tree	IP multicast	A path for delivering data to interested listeners created by joining and pruning branches of delivery, also referred to as a *multicast data path*.
DNS	IP	Domain Name System—A system used on the Internet that enables nodes to be referenced as alphanumeric names (that is, mnemonics) that are resolvable into numeric IP addresses and vice versa.
domain	PIM-SM	A group of PIM-SM speakers interconnected with physical links and/or tunnels that agree on the same RP-to-group mapping matrix for all or a subset of the 224/4 address range.
DoS	Network security	denial of service—A denial-of-service type of network attack is usually caused by individuals or groups of individuals intentionally disrupting communications.

Term	Context	Description
downstream	IP multicast	In the direction toward multicast receivers; also referred to as the *outgoing* or *outbound interface.*
DR	OSPF	designated router—An OSPF router that acts as a spokes-person for a LAN.
DR	PIM-SM	designated router—A router directly connected to hosts that are multicast sources or receivers. A PIM-SM DR sets up multicast route entries and sends corresponding Join/Prune and Register messages on behalf of directly connected receivers and sources, respectively. The DR may or may not be the same router as the IGMP querier. The DR may or may not be the long-term, last-hop router for the group; a router on the LAN that has a lower metric route to the data source, or to the group's RP, may take over the role of sending Join/Prune messages.
DVMRP	Multicast routing protocols	Distance Vector Multicast Routing Protocol—A flood-and-prune multicast routing protocol that uses a RIP-like distance-vector unicast routing protocol to populate a routing table used for RPF checks.
distance-vector protocol	Routing protocols	A broad type of routing protocol in which periodic updates of entire routing tables are sent.
EBGP	BGP	External Border Gateway Protocol—A use of BGP between routers within different ASs. EBGP is used to distribute routes between different ASs.
EGP	Routing protocols	exterior gateway protocol—A generic term for the inter-domain unicast routing protocol. BGP is the primary example of an EGP.
EMSDP	MSDP	External Multicast Source Discovery Protocol—Peering between MSDP peers in different domains.
exclude mode	IGMP	Enables a host to request multicast packets for a group from all sources except those specified in the exclude list.
explicit join	Multicast routing protocols	A type of multicast routing protocol (for example, PIM-SM) where routers receive multicast data only when they have explicitly requested it.
explicit leave	IGMP	This message enables hosts to report they are no longer interested in a group.
fanout	IP multicast	Refers to the maximum number of outgoing interfaces for which a router can replicate traffic for a single group.

Term	Context	Description
FIX	Networking	Federal Internet Exchange—A network access point where government agencies exchange IP traffic, as in NASA Ames Research Center FIX-West in Mountain View, California.
flood-and-prune	Multicast routing protocols	A model used by dense protocols for informing routers of active multicast sources.
forwarding	Networking	The process of receiving a packet of an input interface, performing a lookup on the packet's destination address, and copying the packet to the appropriate output interface.
forwarding table	Router software	The database used to identify the outgoing interfaces for IP prefixes.
FPC	Juniper Networks	Flexible PIC Concentrator—Hardware modules that carry PICs in Juniper Networks routers.
FTP	IP	File Transfer Protocol—A protocol used on the Internet to transfer files between hosts.
fxp0	Juniper Networks	External management Ethernet interface for Juniper Networks RE.
fxp1	Juniper Networks	Internal management Ethernet interface for Juniper Networks RE.
General Query message	IGMP	A message used to check whether interested listeners still exist for both ASM and SSM groups but does not include any source or group information.
GLOP	IP multicast	A mechanism that enables organizations with an ASN to derive a /24 of multicast addresses for static assignment.
GMI	IGMP	group membership interval—A value to which a timer is reset when a router receives a Membership Report for a group on an IGMP-enabled interface.
GRE	IP	generic routing encapsulation—A tunneling protocol used to encapsulate one packet inside another.
group address	IP multicast	A multicast IP address in the class D range (224/4).
group cache	IGMP	A table that tracks the following information: • All groups that have interested hosts • The IP address of the host that last reported interest for each group • The timeout value for each entry in the table

Term	Context	Description
Hello message	Routing protocols	Sent periodically by routers on each protocol-enabled interface, these messages announce their router's existence on the subnet so all routers can form adjacencies.
hold timer	Routing protocols	A timer that controls the amount of time a protocol-speaker should wait before considering its neighbor down.
host	Networking	A node in a network that is an end station.
HTTP	IP	Hypertext Transfer Protocol—The protocol used to support the exchange of information that renders a Web page (usually a file formatted according to the Hypertext Markup Language standard).
IANA	Networking	Internet Assigned Numbers Authority—The agency that controls the assignment of Internet address ranges and subranges.
IBGP	BGP	Internal Border Gateway Protocol—A use of BGP between routers within the same AS. IBGP is used to distribute routes within the AS that were learned from some other source (for example, EBGP and static routes).
ICD	ISO	international code designator—A field in some formats of NSAP addresses that is intended to identify an international organization. The registration authority for the international code designator is maintained by the British Standards Institute. The length of this field is two octets.
ICMP	IP	Internet Control Message Protocol—The diagnostic part of the network layer used in the IP protocol for reporting status information, checking connectivity, and so on.
IETF	Networking	Internet Engineering Task Force—The organization that develops standards for TCP/IP protocols.
IGMP	IP multicast	Internet Group Management Protocol—The protocol used to communicate group membership information between hosts and routers on a LAN. A host must support IGMP to receive multicast packets.
IGMP proxying	IGMP	A method for supporting multicast transmissions for last-hop routers that do not support multicast routing protocols; a nonsupporting router that hears an IGMP report from a host simply relays that IGMP message to an upstream router that does support a multicast routing protocol.

Term	Context	Description
IGMP snooping	IGMP	The examination of IGMP messages by an Ethernet switch to determine which hosts are actually interested in receiving a multicast transmission. Multicast packets are only forwarded out of ports that connect to a host that is an interested listener of a specified group, preventing multicast traffic from being flooded to all hosts connected to the switch.
IGP	Routing protocols	interior gateway protocol—A generic type of routing protocol used among routers in the same AS.
IIF	IP multicast	incoming interface—The IIF of a multicast route entry indicates the interface from which multicast data packets are accepted for forwarding. The IIF is initialized when the entry is created. IIF always is the RPF interface.
IMSDP	MSDP	Internal Multicast Source Discovery Protocol—Peering between MSDP peers in the same domain.
include mode	IGMP	Enables a host to request multicast packets for a group from only the sources specified in the include list. Include mode enables hosts to participate in SSM.
Internet-Draft	IETF	Internet-Drafts are working documents of the IETF, its areas, and its working groups.
IOS	Cisco Systems	Internetwork Operating System—The operating system for routers of Cisco Systems.
IP	IP	Internet Protocol—The network layer protocol used on the Internet. The current version of IP is 4, designated IPv4.
IP/TV	Multicast applications	Cisco Systems application for delivering multicast multimedia content, supporting multicast content only.
IP-IP tunneling	IP	A tunneling protocol used to encapsulate one packet inside of another.
IPv4	IP	Internet Protocol version 4—The current version of IP.
IPX	Networking	Internetwork Packet Exchange—Another type of network layer protocol other than IP.
IS-IS	ISO/IP routing protocols	Intermediate System to Intermediate System—A link-state routing protocol developed by ISO and later integrated to support routing for IP prefixes. IS-IS is an IGP.
ISP	Networking	Internet service provider—An organization that provides connections to the Internet.

Term	Context	Description
Join list	PIM	One of two lists of addresses that is included in a Join/Prune message; each address refers to a source or RP. The join list indicates those sources or RPs which downstream receiver(s) wish to join.
Join message	PIM	A Join/Prune message containing at least one Join field.
Join/Prune message	PIM	A message that holds information for joining and/or pruning a distribution tree.
JUNOS software	Juniper Networks	The operating system for routers of Juniper Networks.
Keepalive message	Routing protocols	*See* Hello message.
LAN	networking	local area network—A network, such as an Ethernet, that connects computers in a limited geographic area (such as within one building).
last-hop router	PIM	The last-hop router is the last router to receive multicast data packets before they are delivered to directly connected member hosts. In general, the last-hop router is the DR for the LAN. However, under various conditions described in this document, a parallel router connected to the same LAN may take over as the last-hop router in place of the DR.
link-state protocols	Routing protocols	A category of routing protocols in which the routing information advertised into the network contains an identifier for the node along with all the other nodes to which it connects. Each router stores this information in a database for use in shortest path calculations.
listener	Multicast	A multicast group member.
load balancing	Networking	The process of distributing load (could be state or processing, not just traffic) between two or more parallel paths to a destination so that the split is relatively even.
Loc-RIB	BGP	The place where routes accepted and selected by a BGP speaker are stored. The specification uses this term as a conceptual explanation; implementers are not required to implement an actual Loc-RIB.
longest match	Routing	The process of finding an entry in a forwarding or routing table associated with a particular address so the entry matches more bits in the destination address than any other entry.

Term	Context	Description
loopback interface	Router software	Also known as a *virtual interface*, a loopback interface is in a node that is not associated with any physical circuit or piece of hardware but is considered active as long as the node itself is up.
LSA	OSPF	link-state advertisement—A unit of OSPF data describing the local state of a router or network. For a router, the LSA includes the state of the router's interfaces and adjacencies. Each LSA is flooded throughout the routing domain. The collected LSAs of all routers and networks form the protocol's link-state database.
LSDB	OSPF, IS-IS	link-state database—The collection of the LSAs/LSPs about which a router currently knows.
LSP	IS-IS	link-state protocol data unit—The message that holds the information a router advertises into the network. The IS-IS equivalent of an OSPF LSA.
MAC address	Ethernet	Media Access Control address—A 48-bit address for devices on an Ethernet LAN.
MASC	IP multicast	Multicast Address Set Claim—Specified in RFC 2909, used to declare a group prefix as being owned by a domain.
mask	IP	A string of bits used along with an address to indicate the number of leading bits in the address that correspond with the network part.
MBGP	BGP	Multiprotocol Border Gateway Protocol—Extensions to the BGP protocol that enable the exchange of reachability information for routed protocols other than IPv4. MBGP can also be used to exchange IPv4 reachability information for multiple virtual topologies.
MBone	IP multicast	Multicast Backbone—The multicast-enabled portion of the Internet. *MBone* often refers to the original multicast network of DVMRP routers connected by tunnels.
MED	BGP	multiple exit discriminator—A BGP path attribute.
Membership Report message	IGMP	A report that enables a host to specify interest in a multicast group or channel.
mesh group	MSDP, IS-IS	A group of peers within which each router has a peering session with every other router in the group.

Term	Context	Description
metrics	Routing	Values applied to routes and/or links in a routing protocol used to select the best route or path—that is, the one having the least cost. The *metric* is also referred to as the *cost*.
MIB	SNMP	Management Information Base—The means for establishing consistent language among all SNMP-speaking devices, a MIB is written in human-readable language and saved as a text file.
M-ISIS	IS-IS	Multitopology Routing in IS-IS—Extends the capabilities of the unicast IS-IS routing protocol in a way that enables multiple routing topologies for, say, IPv6 and multicast.
MIX	Networking	Multicast Internet Exchange—Public peering point for exchanging multicast traffic between ISPs. Mixs usually are found in NAPs.
MOSPF	Multicast routing protocols	Multicast Extensions to OSPF—Multicast routing protocol based on extensions to OSPF.
MSDP	IP multicast	Multicast Source Discovery Protocol—A protocol that enables multiple PIM-SM domains to interconnect.
MTs	M-ISIS	Multitopologies—A numbered virtual topology in an M-ISIS network. Certain MT ID values are assigned to serve predetermined purposes. For example, MT ID #3 is reserved for multicast RPF topology.
multicast	Packet delivery	A method of data delivery in which data is delivered to all hosts that have expressed interest; also referred to as *one-to-many delivery*.
multicast address	IP multicast	A special type of address used to deliver a packet to all members of a multicast group.
multicast scoping	IP multicast	A method for enabling a network operator to configure interfaces not to receive or transmit packets for specific multicast groups defined in RFC 2365, "Administratively Scoped IP Multicast."
multihoming	Networking	Having multiple connections to a network or networks.
NAP	Networking	network access point—Public peering point where ISPs exchange traffic.

Term	Context	Description
NET	IS-IS	network entity title—An ISO network address with an n-selector byte of 0x00. Most end systems have one NET. Intermediate systems that participate in multiple areas can have multiple NETs.
NLRI field	BGP	network layer reachability information field—A field within the BGP Update message that contains a list of destination prefixes that share the same path attributes. The NLRI field is used to convey IP address prefix and subnet mask information.
NLSP	IPX	NetWare Link Services Protocol—A link-state routing protocol for IPX.
NMS	SNMP	network management systems—A host that runs SNMP client software.
nontransitive	BGP	A characteristic of a BGP attribute that results in the attribute not being passed along if it is not understood by the local router.
NSAP	IS-IS	network service access point—The address format in IS-IS.
Null-Register message	PIM-SM	A Register message without encapsulated data. The primary purpose of a Null-Register message is to tell the RP that the source is still active, thus, refreshing state without having to encapsulate any data.
OIL	IP multicast	outgoing interface list—Each multicast route entry has a list (also known as an *olist*) containing the outgoing interfaces to which multicast packets should be forwarded.
olist	IP multicast	*See* OIL.
OSI	Networking	Open Systems Interconnection—The seven-layer model of network protocols of the International Organization for Standardization. From layer 7 down to layer 1, the layers are application, presentation, session, transport, network, data link, and physical.
OSPF	Routing protocols	Open Shortest Path First—A link-state routing protocol developed by the IETF. OSPF is an IGP.
PDU	ISO	protocol data unit—An ISO packet.
peer-RPF flooding	MSDP	The process of sending SA messages to all other MSDP peers if an SA message is received from the appropriate peer.

Term	Context	Description
PFE	Juniper Networks	Packet Forwarding Engine—A hardware component that handles the packet-forwarding function for Juniper Networks routers.
PIC	Juniper Networks	Physical Interface Card—Hardware modules on Juniper Networks routers.
PIM-DM	Multicast routing protocols	PIM dense mode—A flood-and-prune multicast routing protocol that can use any underlying unicast routing protocol to populate a routing table used for RPF checks.
PIM-SM	Multicast routing protocols	PIM sparse mode—Explicit join multicast routing protocol that can use any underlying unicast routing protocol to populate a routing table used for RPF checks.
PMBR	PIM-SM	PIM Multicast Border Router—Connects a PIM domain to other multicast routing domain(s).
port number	TCP, UDP	The value in a transport protocol header that indicates the application process to which a packet is destined.
prefix	CIDR	A group of contiguous bits, from 0 to 32 bits in length, that defines a set of addresses. For example, what used to be referred to as a *class C network* would use a 24-bit prefix.
Prune list	PIM	The second list of addresses included in a Join/Prune message. It indicates those sources or RPs from which downstream receiver(s) wish to prune.
Prune message	PIM	A Join/Prune message containing at least one Prune field.
PSNP	IS-IS	Partial Sequence Number PDU— An IS-IS PDU used to request a retransmit of link state information.
PSTN	Networking	public switched telephone network—The residential and commercial network of telephones and related hardware connected principally through physical lines and cables and switching centers, formerly operated as a public utility by AT&T.
querier	IGMP	IGMP-speaking router responsible for sending IGMP query messages.
query interval	IGMP	The interval between general queries sent by a querier; default value = 125 seconds.
query response interval	IGMP	The amount of time hosts have to respond to an IGMP query.

Term	Context	Description
RAS	Networking	remote access servers—Dialup access devices.
RE	Juniper Networks	Routing Engine—Handles the route control function for Juniper Networks routers.
receiver	IP multicast	A host that expresses interest in receiving packets sent to a specific group address. A *receiver* also is referred to as a *group member* or *listener*.
recursive lookup	routing	If a route lookup results in a next hop that is not directly reachable, a recursive lookup is used to decide how to reach the indirect next hop.
Register message	PIM-SM	The message a PIM-SM designated router connected to a source sends to an RP when the router begins receiving a multicast packet from the source. Register messages inform the RP of active sources within a domain.
RFCs	IETF	Request for Comments—If an IETF working group decides to advance an Internet-Draft for standardization, the draft is submitted to the IETF's Internet Engineering Steering Group (IESG) to become an RFC. You can find more information at *http://www.ietf.org/ID.html*.
RIB	Router software	routing information base—A routing table.
RIP	Routing protocols	Routing Information Protocol—A distance-vector routing protocol most often used as a simple IGP within small networks.
robustness variable	IGMP	Defines the number of queries that can be sent without receiving a response before the cache entry times out; the default value is 2.
route reflection	IBGP	An approach to IBGP scaling. Rather than require a full mesh of IBGP connections, one or more clusters of route reflectors and route reflector clients are used; the route reflectors reflect the routes between their clients and the rest of the AS.
route reflector	IBGP	A BGP speaker that readvertises to other IBGP neighbors routes learned from its route reflector clients and vice versa.
router	Networking	A network layer device that typically has two or more interfaces on different networks and enables forwarding of packets between those networks.

Term	Context	Description
routing	Networking	The process by which a router calculates a forwarding table by using its knowledge of the network taken from local configuration and dynamic routing protocols.
routing policy	Router software	The ability of a router (and an AS) to control the routes it accepts from and advertises to other routers (and ASs) as well as the ability to modify the attributes associated with the routes accepted and advertised.
routing table	Router software	Also known as RIB, a routing table is a conceptual data structure used to hold routing information populated by routing protocols.
RP	PIM-SM	rendezvous point—A meeting point for multicast sources and receivers in a PIM-SM domain.
RPF	IP multicast	reverse path forwarding—Used to select the appropriate incoming interface for a multicast route entry. The RPF neighbor for an address X is the next-hop router used to forward packets toward X. The RPF interface is the interface connecting to that RPF neighbor. In the common case, the RPF neighbor is the next hop used by the unicast routing protocol for sending unicast packets toward X. In cases where unicast and multicast routes are not congruent, the RPF interface can be different from the interface used to forward unicast packets to the multicast source.
RP-set	PIM-SM	The RP-to-group mapping of a PIM-SM domain.
RPT	PIM-SM	rendezvous point tree—Within PIM-SM, a shared tree. The first-hop router of a receiver tells the upstream router it is interested in receiving multicast packets for the group via the RPT. An RPT is a distribution tree rooted at the RP, while an SPT is a distribution tree rooted at the source.
RTP	IP	real-time transport protocol—Defined in RFC 1889, RTP provides host-to-host transport over IP networks that is suitable for real-time applications such as video and audio streaming.
SA message	MSDP	Source-Active message—Originated by the RP of a source, the SA message contains the source address, the group address, and the address of the RP and is exchanged between MSDP speakers via peer-RPF flooding.
SAP	IP multicast	Session Announcement Protocol—A protocol used to advertise multicast sessions.

Term	Context	Description
SDP	IP multicast	Session Description Protocol—General-purpose formatting protocol used to describe multicast sessions.
SDR	Multicast applications	Session Directory Tool—A multicast application that uses the SAP/SDP protocols to provide a directory service for multicast sessions. SDR launches other applications, such as VIC and VAT, that enable multicast content, which is typically multimedia, to be accessed.
service model	IP multicast	A method or practice for data delivery. IP multicast has two service models, ASM and SSM. ASM supports one-to-many and many-to-many data delivery, while SSM supports only one-to-many delivery.
(S,G) route entry	PIM, DVMRP	(S,G) is a source-specific route entry. It may be created in response to data packets, Join/Prune messages, or Assert messages. The (S,G) state in routers creates a source-rooted SPT. (S,G) RPT bit entries are source-specific entries on the shared RP tree; these entries are used to prune particular sources from the shared tree.
shared tree	IP multicast	A distribution tree in which the root is a core node in the network.
SNMP	IP	Simple Network Management Protocol—An application-level protocol in IP used for managing devices.
sparse protocol	Multicast routing protocol	A multicast routing protocol that uses a mechanism other than flood-and-prune to distribute multicast packets.
SPF algorithm	Link-state protocols	shortest path first algorithm—The process of calculating the shortest path to all destinations by using an LSDB, which includes all the nodes and links in a network along with the metrics associated with those links. Also known as *Dijkstra's algorithm.*
SPT	IP multicast	shortest path tree—A distribution tree in which the root of the tree is the source.
SSM	IP multicast	Source-Specific Multicast—The one-to-many communications service model that guarantees multicast delivery from only one specified source to its receivers.
state	Routing software	Information maintained in a router for the purposes of forwarding unicast or multicast packets.
subscribe	SSM	To join an SSM channel.

Term	Context	Description
TCP	IP	Transmission Control Protocol—Reliable transport protocol used in the IP protocol.
throughput	Networking	Refers to the maximum amount of traffic a router can forward (in packets per second or bits per second).
TLV	IS-IS, MSDP	type length value—The message structure used in IS-IS and MSDP that indicates the type and length of the message and the actual information in the message.
TNP	Juniper Networks	Trivial Network Protocol—An internal communications protocol for Juniper Networks RE.
transitive	BGP	A characteristic of a BGP attribute that results in the attribute being passed on even if it is not understood.
TTL	IP	time-to-live—A field in the IP header that determines the maximum number of routers the packet can traverse.
tunnel	Networking	A virtual link between routers formed by encapsulating packets into other packets.
UDP	IP	User Datagram Protocol—An unreliable transport protocol used in IP.
unicast	Packet delivery	A method of data delivery in which data is delivered to one specific recipient from one specific source, also referred to as *one-to-one delivery.*
unicast routing protocol	Networking	A protocol that provides dynamic information used to route unicast packets.
unsubscribe	SSM	To leave an SSM channel.
Update message	BGP	The BGP message that defines routes and path attributes.
upstream	IP multicast	In the direction toward the multicast source, also referred to as the *incoming* or *inbound* interface.
VAT	Multicast applications	visual audio tool—An application typically launched by SDR for playing multicast audio content.
VIC	Multicast applications	video conferencing tool—Application typically launched by SDR for playing multicast video content.
virtual interface	Router software	A logical interface that does not correspond to a physical interface on the router—for example, loopback interfaces and tunnel interfaces.

Term	Context	Description
VLAN	Networking	virtual LAN—A network of computers that behave as if they are connected to the same wire even though they may actually be physically located on different segments of a LAN. VLANs are configured through software rather than hardware, which makes them extremely flexible. One of the major advantages of VLANs is that when a computer is physically moved to another location, it can stay on the same VLAN without any hardware reconfiguration.
well-known attribute	BGP	A BGP attribute required to be known by all BGP implementations.
WMP	Multicast applications	Windows Media Player—A popular application for accessing unicast and multicast audio and video content.
worm	Network security	Self-replicating code that does not attach itself to other files or programs but adversely affects networks by propagating unwanted message traffic.

Bibliography

Albanna, Z., K. Almeroth, D. Meyer, M. Schipper. "IANA Guidelines for IPv4 Multicast Address Assignments," RFC 3171, August 2001.

Bates, T., Y. Rekhter, R. Chandra, D. Katz. "Multiprotocol Extensions for BGP-4," RFC 2858, June 2000.

Bhattacharyya, Supratik, Christophe Diot, Leonard Giuliano, Rob Rockell, John Meylor, David Meyer, Greg Shepherd, Brian Haberman. "An Overview of Source-Specific Multicast (SSM) Deployment," Work in progress.

Cain, Brad, Steve Deering, Bill Fenner, Isidor Kouvelas, and Ajit Thyagarajan. "Internet Group Management Protocol, Version 3," work in progress.

Callon, R. "Use of OSI IS-IS for Routing in TCP/IP and Dual Environments," RFC 1195, December 1990.

Cisco Product Documentation. *http://www.cisco.com/univercd/home/home.htm.*

Deering, S. "Host Extensions for IP Multicasting," RFC 1112, August 1989.

Deering, S., Deborah Estrin, Dino Farinacci, Van Jacobson, Ahmed Helmy, David Meyer, Liming Wei. "Protocol Independent Multicast Version 2 Dense Mode Specification," work in progress.

Doyle, Jeff. *Routing TCP/IP, Volume I: A Detailed Examination of Interior Routing Protocols,* Cisco Press, 1998.

Estrin, D., D. Farinacci, A. Helmy, D. Thaler, S. Deering, M. Handley, V. Jacobson, C. Liu, P. Sharma, and L. Wei. "Protocol Independent Multicast Sparse Mode (PIM-SM): Protocol Specification," RFC 2362, June 1998.

Fenner, Bill, and Dave Thaler. "Multicast Source Discovery protocol MIB," work in progress.

Fenner, Bill, Mark Handley, Hugh Holbrook, and Isidor Kouvelas. "Protocol Independent Multicast—Sparse Mode (PIM-SM): Protocol Specification (Revised)," work in progress.

Fenner, Bill, Mark Handley, Roger Kermode, and David Thaler. "Bootstrap Router (BSR) Mechanism for PIM Sparse Mode," work in progress.

Fenner, W. "Internet Group Management Protocol, Version 2," RFC 2236, November 1997.

Giuliano, Leonard. "Deploying Native Multicast across the Internet," whitepaper.

Halabi, Bassam. *Internet Routing Architectures: The Definitive Resource for Internetworking Design Alternatives and Solutions.* Cisco Press, 1997.

Handley, M., and V. Jacobson. "SDP: Session Description Protocol," RFC 2327, April 1998.

Handley, M., C. Perkins, and E. Whelan. "Session Announcement Protocol," RFC 2974, October 2000.

Handley, Mark, Van Jacobson, and Colin Perkins. "SDP: Session Description Protocol," work in progress.

Holbrook, H. and B. Cain. "Source-Specific Multicast for IP," work in progress.

Holbrook, H. and B. Cain. "Using IGMPv3 For Source-Specific Multicast," work in progress.

JUNOS Internet Software Documentation. *http://www.juniper.net/techpubs/software.html.*

Katz, Dave. "OSPF and IS-IS: A Comparative Anatomy," In Proceedings of NANOG, June 2000.

Kim, Dorian, David Meyer, Henry Kilmer, and Dino Farinacci. "Anycast RP Mechanism using PIM and MSDP," work in progress.

Li, T., T. Przygienda, H. Smit. "Domain-wide Prefix Distribution with Two-Level IS-IS," RFC 2966, October 2000.

Li, T., Henk Smit. "IS-IS Extensions for Traffic Engineering," work in progress.

McCloghrie, K., D. Farinacci, and D. Thaler. "Internet Group Management Protocol (IGMP) MIB," RFC 2933, October 2000.

McCloghrie, K., D. Farinacci, and D. Thaler. "IPv4 Multicast Routing MIB," RFC 2932, October 2000.

McCloghrie, K., D. Farinacci, D. Thaler, and B. Fenner. "Protocol Independent Multicast MIB for IPv4," RFC 2934, October 2000.

Meyer, D. "Administratively Scoped IP Multicast," RFC 2365, July 1998.

Meyer, D. "Extended Assignments in 233/8," work in progress.

Meyer D., P. Lothberg. "GLOP Addressing in 233/8," RFC 3180, September 2001.

Meyer, David , editor and Bill Fenner, editor. "Multicast Source Discovery Protocol (MSDP)," work in progress.

Moy, J. "OSPF Version 2," RFC 2328, April 1998.

Nickless, B. "IPv4 Multicast Best Current Practice," work in progress.

Perlman, Radia. *Interconnections, Second Edition: Bridges, Routers, Switches, and Protocols.* Addison Wesley, 2000.

Postel, J. "Internet Protocol," STD 5, RFC 791, September 1981.

Przygienda, Tony, Naiming Shen, and Nischal Sheth. "M-ISIS: Multi Topology Routing in IS-IS," work in progress.

Przygienda, T., "Reserved TLV Codepoints in ISIS," work in progress.

Pusateri, T. "Distance Vector Multicast Routing Protocol," work in progress.

Rekhter, Y., and T. Li. "A Border Gateway Protocol 4 (BGP-4)," RFC 1771, March 1995.

Shepherd, Greg, E. Luczycki, and Rob Rockell. "Source-Specific Protocol Independent Multicast in 232/8," work in progress.

Wegner, J.D., Robert Rockell, Marc Blanchet. *IP Addressing and Subnetting, Including IPv6*. Syngress Media, 1999

Williamson, Beau. *Developing IP Multicast Networks: The Definitive Guide to Designing and Deploying Cisco IP Multicast Networks, Volume I*. Cisco Press, 2000.

About the Authors

BRIAN M. EDWARDS

Brian is the customer support engineer for premium accounts in Juniper Networks Technical Assistance Center (JTAC). On a daily basis, he troubleshoots problems affecting the largest ISP networks in the world. He is the designated subject matter expert for multicast routing at Juniper Networks and has completed the highest levels of Cisco Systems and Juniper Networks certification programs (CCIE #6187 and JNCIE #9). He earned a B.S. in computer engineering from the University of Florida in 1997.

LEONARD A. GIULIANO

Leonard is a systems engineer for Juniper Networks, supporting large ISPs in the architecture, design, and operation of backbone networks. He specializes in IP multicast, IP core routing, and traffic engineering. Leonard previously worked as a multicast architect for SprintLink, the world's first native multicast-enabled Internet backbone. He has coauthored many published documents on multicast networking including the IETF's SSM Framework specification. He is also a member of the IETF's MSDP Protocol Design Team and is a Juniper Networks

Certified Internet Specialist (JNCIS). He earned his B.S.E. in electrical engineering from Duke University in 1997.

BRIAN R. WRIGHT

Brian is a technical documentation specialist currently developing the system documentation set for the MasterCard Debit System (MDS) application. He wrote the operations guide for the Tandem computer-based point-of-sale (POS) system of Bank One and the system document for the Exxon retail store POS system. He also helped compose the documentation set for MPACT EDI systems messaging and EDI translation software, and was senior writer/editor for EDS corporate communications, automotive product engineer for American Motors, senior design engineer for gas turbine engine accessories at Williams International, and project engineer at the Wayne State University Biomechanics Department. He has worked as a freelance journalist and writer and is a member of the Society for Technical Communication. Brian earned his BSME at Wayne State University in 1975.

Index

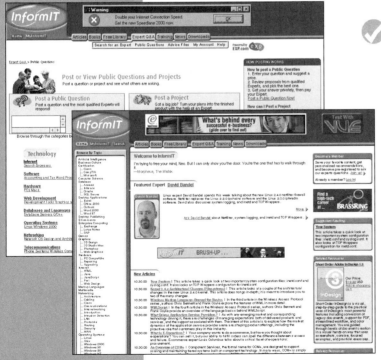
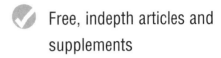

Register
Your Book

at www.aw.com/cseng/register

You may be eligible to receive:

- Advance notice of forthcoming editions of the book
- Related book recommendations
- Chapter excerpts and supplements of forthcoming titles
- Information about special contests and promotions throughout the year
- Notices and reminders about author appearances, tradeshows, and online chats with special guests

Contact us

If you are interested in writing a book or reviewing manuscripts prior to publication, please write to us at:

Editorial Department
Addison-Wesley Professional
75 Arlington Street, Suite 300
Boston, MA 02116 USA
Email: AWPro@aw.com

Visit us on the Web: http://www.aw.com/cseng